P9-DNG-477

What Others Are Saying About This Book

"You'd be nuts to run a call center without devouring *Fast Forward*. This well-written and eminently usable guide addresses every arcane aspect of call center management...in a readable way! From Erlang C to CTI and all the other topics you'd like to think you understand, Mayben and Cleveland gracefully demystify the gibberish. After reading it, you can actually put the proven principles and techniques to work!...You immediately know this volume will stay on your reference shelf and get plenty of use."

- George R. Walther, author of Phone Power, Power Talking,
and Upside-Down Marketing

"If you run a call center, you need this book! Don't let anything stop you from getting it. First read it, then do it."

- Harry Green, President of Pacific Netcom, Inc. and author of the
Irwin Handbooks of Telecommunications and Telecom Management

"Brad Cleveland and Julia Mayben have put together the building blocks that are needed to effectively run a call center. *Call Center Management on Fast Forward* takes you from a brief look at the past to the identification of many new opportunities as we approach the 21st century. They combine theory with sound, practical methods to help you succeed in the art of call center management."

- Tony Romanus, Support Center Manager, United Parcel Service

"This is THE "how-to" book for establishing an incoming call center and taking it to excellence. It covers the things you need to know in detail, and is also a great book on how to provide outstanding customer service."

- Günter Greff, author of Telefonverkauf Mit Noch Mehr Power and head of
Günter Greff Power Seminars

"Call centre history and new technology combined in such a way you just keep reading, and flipping the pages to learn more. A must if you are involved in a modern call centre."

- Magda M. Krayenbrink, Customer Support Manager,
Mainland Europe, Gateway2000

"If you want to turn your call center into the profit and customer-satisfaction center of your business, read every page of this book. Nowhere else will you get this kind of timely, practical, and strategy-oriented guidance."

- Gil Gordon, Principal, Gil Gordon Associates

"No one knows call centers better than Brad Cleveland. This book is an absolute must for every call center professional."

- Ian and Lis Angus, co-editors, Telemanagment magazine

"Bullseye! Brad Cleveland and Julia Mayben are right on target with *Call Center Management on Fast Forward*. This book covers the basics as well as the issues call center managers are facing today. More importantly, it provides insights into the challenges ahead."

- John Collins, Change Manager, TIAA-CREF

"...The authors' ability to demystify the mathematics of call centre forecasting and planning is head and shoulders above any other book I have read. This book will provide you with an invaluable 'aide-memoir,' especially in those times all call centre managers know: When the whole world has decided to phone your call centre, just after the latest flu virus has hit half your staff. I can honestly say, this book is a must for any aspiring call centre professional."

- Alan Vaughan, Managing Director, Call Centre Consultants

"This book will become the call centre bible for managers of call centres. The authors explain why we experience the issues we do, what we can do to be more cost-effective, achieve service levels, coach and provide quality, and run an efficient operation. The book is full of examples and wisdom to create compelling reading for any person who works in a call centre."

- Cindy Loudfoot, Strategic Initiative Manager, TELUS

"Just when you felt confident that you could answer any question, solve multitude of problems and champion your call centre(s) to senior management, *Call Center Management on Fast Forward* delivers a timely reminder of the dynamics and basics of our 'business' as call centre managers today and the future...Without question, this book is the most comprehensive insight into call centre management for today and tomorrow, a MUST READ (all my managers will be instructed to, although we will need to overlook the spelling of 'centre'!)."

- Phil Ashley, Manager, Reservations Sales Australia,
Qantas Airways Limited

"*Call Center Management on Fast Forward* is an outstanding treasure-trove, loaded with information critical to call center managers' successes. I keep my copy under lock and key."

- Ross M. Scovotti, Publisher, TeleProfessional Magazine

"At last, a book that depicts the call center as a strategic management asset. *Call Center Management on Fast Forward* is a must read for anyone wanting to succeed in the dynamic global inbound environment of the 21st century."

- H. Skip Weitzen, author of Hypergrowth, Infopreneurs & Telephone Magic

"Finally, an easy-to-follow educational book dealing with call center management. This is what Niagara College has been waiting for. This book is not only a must for call centre managers, but it will help TSRs to understand the significant role they play in the overall operation of an efficient call centre...We intend to incorporate this book in both our Call Centre Management Program as well as our Call Centre Service Representative Program."

- Danielle Brown, CPS, Coordinator of Call Centre Programs, Niagara College

"With the increase in call centres globally, *Call Center Management on Fast Forward* focuses on providing the theory and framework for management to understand the cause and effect to the business they are managing."

- Peter Cheong, Director of Operations, SITEL, Japan

"You will be able to re-read this book several times as your call centre evolves, each time learning new methods and tips...The call centre environment continues to change, the challenges over the next few years will stretch all call centre managers, those that succeed will be those that understand these changes, and the dynamics that cause them. *Call Center Management on Fast Forward* will guide you and your call centre to face these challenges and exploit them."

- Dean Yardley, Strategic Innovations Manager, British Airways

"*Call Center Management on Fast Forward* provides the essential framework and knowledge-base to enable call center managers to create truly world-class organizations. Call center neophytes and seasoned professionals will benefit from this work. Cleveland and Mayben cut through the intricacies of queuing theory and random call arrival to provide relevant information that is immediately applicable."

- Mark Debelack, Planning and Systems Managers, Nintendo of America

"A reliable and money-saving blueprint for a call center management plan."

- Larry J. Stuker, FCC National Call Center

"Those of us in the industry need all the assistance, expertise and knowledge we can get. *Call Center Management on Fast Forward* will ensure that this knowledge is further built upon."

- Jim Milligan, Managing Director, Callscan Australia

Call Center Management

On Fast Forward

Succeeding In Today's Dynamic Inbound Environment

Call Center

Management

On Fast Forward

Succeeding In Today's Dynamic Inbound Environment

Brad Cleveland
& Julia Mayben

First Edition

Call Center Press™

A Division of ICMI, Inc.

Annapolis, Maryland

Published by:
Call Center Press
A Division of ICMI, Inc.
P.O. Box 6177
Annapolis, Maryland 21401

Design by Michael Blair

Notice of Liability
This book is designed to provide information in regard to the subject matter covered. The purpose of this book is to educate and entertain. While every precaution has been taken in the preparation of this book, neither the authors nor Call Center Press (a division of ICMI, Inc.) shall have any liability or responsibility to any person or entity with respect to any loss or damage caused, or alleged to be caused, directly or indirectly by the information contained in this book. If you do not wish to be bound by this, you may return this book to the publisher for a full refund.

Copyright 1997 by Brad Cleveland and Julia Mayben
First printing 1997
Second printing 1998
Third printing 1998
Printed in the United States of America

Library of Congress Catalog Card Number: 97-68740

ISBN 0-9659093-0-1

To Kirsten, my spouse, confidant and best friend.

-Brad

To Patrick, the best friend a writer could have.

-Julia

Contents

Acknowledgments   xiii

Foreword   xv

Part One   The Vibrant Inbound Environment   1

Chapter 1   Familiar Challenges, New Opportunities   3

Chapter 2   Three Driving Forces in Incoming Call Centers   11

Part Two   A Planning and Management Framework   23

Chapter 3   Service Level, The Core Value   25

Chapter 4   Acquiring Necessary Data   45

Chapter 5   Forecasting Call Load...Etc.   53

Chapter 6   Determining Base Staff and Trunks Required   79

Chapter 7   Scheduling Efficiently and Sufficiently   107

Part Three Understanding Inbound Dynamics   127

Chapter 8   How Incoming Call Centers Behave   129

Chapter 9   Conveying Call Center Activity to Senior Management   145

Chapter 10   Managing Service Level in Real-Time   159

Part Four   Rethinking Quality and Productivity   177

Chapter 11   Service Level With Quality   179

Chapter 12   Assessing Performance in a New Era   201

Part Five   Leadership in the Digital Age   217

Chapter 13   New Technologies, New Possibilities   219

Chapter 14   Characteristics of the Best Managed Call Centers   235

Appendix   Sample Job Description for Incoming Call Center
            Managers   249

Notes   253

Glossary   259

Index   277

Acknowledgments

Our goal in writing this book is to provide you with practical, accurate information on how to manage an incoming call center. We don't mention reengineering, use the term "world-class" sparingly and never discuss core-competencies. We didn't even use a Dilbert cartoon (but, for the record, we do like some of them)! Our hope is that you find the material refreshing and highly usable.

There are many people who deserve thanks for making this project possible. My co-author, Julia Mayben, took chapters e-mailed from hither and yon and pieced them together. She researched facts, clarified passages, and was honest when sections needed to go "back to the shop." She also served as project manager and kept us on track (thank goodness). She is a true professional.

I also want to thank Michael Blair for his work in designing the book. Producing the scores of charts and graphs alone was a monumental task. He, too, is a real pro.

Many thanks to Linda Harden and her team at ICMI - Terrie Frazier, Jessica Pragada, Jamie Spriggs and Cara Visconti. They handled their workload and mine during this project. This book would never have happened without their help and support. I also want to thank Greg Levin, editor of *Service Level Newsletter*, for taking the time to read an advance copy of the book and forward invaluable suggestions.

My appreciation also extends to Nicolaas Aalhuizen, Henry Dortmans, Kathleen Peterson, Martin Prunty, Ann Smith, and Laurie Solomon - all Certified Associates of Incoming Calls Management Institute and top-notch independent consultants. They provided "sanity checks" and a great deal of valuable input.

I owe much gratitude to Gordon F. MacPherson, Jr., founder of ICMI and my business partner for over five years. When Julia and I asked Gordon to write the foreword, he initially resisted, suggesting that he was "too much of an insider." But we persisted for a simple reason: No one else has had more impact on the profession of incoming call center management. He presented the world's first comprehensive seminar on the subject just over a decade ago. He popularized the term "call center" in the mid 80s, and was then among the first to suggest the term no longer accurately describes the current environment. He created many of the tools and methodologies that today are used world-wide. He is a thinker and a visionary, and much of his original work is reflected in these pages.

A great deal of the material in this book comes from the work of both *Service Level Newsletter* and Incoming Calls Management Institute. I am grateful for the special permission to use it for this project.

There are a number of people who directly encouraged me to write a book, including Lauren Basham, Lis and Ian Angus, Alan Vaughan, and Günter Greff. Sorry it took so long...and thanks for your encouragement!

I am grateful to those who took the time to review sections of this book before publication: Ian and Lis Angus, Phil Ashley, Danielle Brown, Peter Cheong, John Collins, Mark Debelack, Gil Gordon, Harry Green, Günter Greff, Magda Krayenbrink, Cindy Loudfoot, Jim Milligan, Mary Murcott, Tony Murphy, Steve Pollack, Tony Romanus, Ross Scovotti, Larry Stuker, Alan Vaughan, George Walther, H. Skip Weitzen and Dean Yardley. Thanks again for your valuable suggestions and comments.

I also want to thank a few others who have influenced my thinking about call centers and the industry over the years: Philip Cohen, Paul Daubitz, Jim Gordon, Harry Green, Mike Hills, Al Hukle, Fred Knight, Janette Menday, Dale Mullen, Gerry Munro, Harry Newton, Pat Schaffer, Laura Sikorski and Todd Tanner. There are so many others who have provided assistance and encouragement that it would be impossible to mention everyone. If you fall in that category - my sincerest thanks.

I'd like to extend a special thanks to my parents, Doug and Annie Cleveland, who have encouraged and prayed for me since day one. My father was instrumental in developing my interest in telecommunications (I remember when we built a telephone for a third grade project, right down to the carbon and wiring!). Most of all, I want to thank Kirsten, who has more than put up with my projects and deadlines. She has helped and encouraged me every step of the way.

Brad Cleveland
Annapolis, Maryland
July, 1997

bradc@incoming.com

Foreword

Call Center Management on Fast Forward: Succeeding in Today's Dynamic Inbound Environment is a clear voice with an unconfusing message: To successfully manage an incoming call center you need a good understanding of the unique inbound environment and an effective planning and management framework.

This message was true when telephone operators used cord switchboards and when inbound telemarketing reps at catalog companies used pen and pencil to capture order information. It is just as true at the end of the 20th Century, as call center managers deal with skill-based call routing, Web site interaction, virtual call centers and call centers that follow the sun to offer cost-effective 24 hour a day service. And it will continue to be true in the future as call centers increasingly heed the demands of customers to allow them a continuously improving and expanding array of choices for how they will be served.

This book outlines principles that you can use and trust. They are not passing fads. For example, service level and queuing theory are not abstract concepts; they are material facts that can be learned. The behavior of humans relating to queuing is sometimes fickle and difficult to predict, but the resources it will take to consistently achieve a specific level of service is a matter of mathematics. A comprehension of service level and queuing makes it easy to understand incoming call center processes in any industry and rationalizes key decisions and crucially important budgets.

The truly wise understand that rapid and lasting learning comes from choosing well your instructors and texts. The best will not waste your time or go off on tangents. They will present their information in a way that makes it easy to learn and retain.

So...you must be truly wise because you have this book in your hands. Brad Cleveland has made a career of learning everything vital to incoming call center management and presenting it with a sparkle that reflects his enthusiasm and relative youth. He is the acknowledged leader in this field. Julia Mayben, his co-author, has written for *Service Level Newsletter* for many years and knows the incoming call center beat well.

Between them, these authors have put together a book that belongs on the shelf of every incoming call center manager. Turn the page now for the good stuff. You'll see what I mean!

Gordon F. MacPherson, Jr.

Call Center

Management

On Fast Forward

Succeeding In Today's Dynamic Inbound Environment

Part One:

The Vibrant Inbound Environment

To succeed in today's inbound call center, you must understand the new environment: More transactions, increasing complexity and heightened caller expectations. But to those who pay the price to learn the craft, call center management offers almost limitless opportunities.

Chapter 1:   Familiar Challenges, New Opportunities

Chapter 2:   Three Driving Forces in Incoming Call Centers

[Chapter 1:

→Familiar Challenges, New Opportunities

The future ain't what it used to be.

-Yogi Berra

It was the turn of the century and the dawn of a new age in communication. The telephone had been invented a few decades earlier, in 1876, and telephone service was proliferating rapidly. The public was beginning to depend on, and even expect, reliable service.

As the subscriber base grew, telephone companies were contending with new resource planning problems. Automated central offices hadn't been invented yet, so human operators were required to establish connections for callers.

One big question was, how many telephone operators are necessary? Too few, and service levels would be unacceptable to callers. But too many would be inefficient for telephone companies and would drive up costs for subscribers. Further complicating the issue: calls arrived randomly, driven by the myriad of motivations individual callers had for placing the calls.

In the years that followed, many bright people would grapple with these resource management challenges. One of the first was A.K. Erlang, an engineer with the Copenhagen Telephone Company, who in 1917, developed the queuing formula Erlang C. The formula is still widely used today in incoming call centers for calculating staffing requirements. Others who followed Erlang focused on developing disciplined forecasting techniques, scheduling methodologies and system reporting parameters. The advances continued.

Ring of Familiarity?

Things have come a long way since the early 1900s. Today, there is no need for operators to connect calls since the process has been automated. But if you manage a modern call center, there is at least a ring of familiarity to the challenges the early telephone pioneers faced. Forecasting calls accurately, staffing appropriately and getting the right people and other resources in the right places at the right times continue to be key objectives.

A Definition for Incoming Call Center Management

Incoming Calls Management Institute has developed a working definition of incoming call center management that, over recent years, has been published numerous times: "Incoming call center management is the art of having the right number of skilled people and supporting resources in place at the right times to handle an accurately forecasted workload, at

> Incoming call center management is the art of having the right number of skilled people and supporting resources in place at the right times to handle an accurately forecasted workload, at service level and with quality.

service level and with quality."

This definition can be boiled down to two major objectives: 1) get the right resources in the right places at the right times and 2) do the right things. Or more succinctly, provide service level with quality.

The ability for call centers to accomplish these objectives didn't happen overnight. The call center industry has evolved through three major stages:

1. Seat-of-the-pants management - very little consideration of service level in planning.

2. Service level awareness - an effort to maintain service level as calls arrive, but only a vague correlation to service level in planning.

3. Correlating service level to the organization's mission - choose an appropriate service level and tie resources to achieving it.

Many individual organizations have evolved through the same general stages, and most now have linked service level to quality and their overall mission. But to do so, a systematic planning and management process is required, which can be summarized in nine steps:

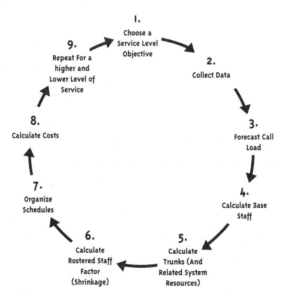

1. Choose a Service Level Objective. Service level, which takes the form of "X percent of calls answered in Y seconds," should be understood, taken seriously and adequately funded. It should be appropriate for the services being provided and the expectations of the callers using those services. Service level is the critical link between resources and results, as we will discuss in Chapter 3.

2. Collect Data. The ACD and computer systems are important sources of planning data, telling you how many calls you're getting, how long they last, what the patterns are, and how the call mix is changing. But you also need information on what marketing and other departments are doing, changes in legislation, competitor activities, and changes in customer needs and perceptions. We'll cover this process in Chapter 4.

3. Forecast Call Load. Call load includes three components: average talk time, average after-call work (wrap-up) and volume. A good forecast predicts all three components accurately for future time periods, usually down to a half-hour. But forecasting in today's call center must go beyond inbound calls. It must also reflect the other choices customers have for interacting with the organization, such as e-mail, faxes, video transactions and Web-integrated transactions. We'll discuss forecasting in Chapter 5.

4. Calculate Base Staff. Most call center managers use Erlang C to calculate staffing requirements. Erlang C is the formula used in virtually all workforce management software systems. But new capabilities, such as skill-based routing and complex network environments, are presenting new challenges. And computer simulation programs are holding promise for providing answers. We will address these issues in Chapter 6.

5. Calculate Trunks (and Related System Resources). Staffing and trunking issues are inextricably associated and must be calculated together. We will discuss this step in Chapter 6.

6. Calculate Rostered Staff Factor. Rostered staff factor, also referred to as shrink factor or shrinkage, adds realism to staffing requirements by accounting for breaks, absenteeism, training and non-phone work. We will review this important step in Chapter 7.

7. Organize Schedules. Schedules are essentially forecasts of who needs to be where and when. They should lead to getting the right people in the right places at the right times. We will discuss this process in Chapter 7.

8. Calculate Costs. This step projects costs for the resources required to meet service and quality objectives. We will cover cost issues throughout Parts 2 and 3.

9. Repeat for a Higher and a Lower Level of Service. Preparing three budgets around three different service levels provides an understanding of cost trade-offs, which is invaluable in budgeting decisions. We will discuss this step in Chapter 9.

The best managed call centers do a good job of resource planning and management. They have a process that is systematic, collaborative and accurate. But the call center world is changing...

New Opportunities, New Challenges

Today, we are creating enormous opportunities for interacting with customers. New services built around the World Wide Web, video capabilities and other multimedia technologies are notable examples. Many call center managers are justifiably wondering, where are the changes taking us?

In fact, the term *incoming call center* is being doggedly challenged by many just as it is becoming a household term. What is it? A center that handles calls? Hardly. *Calls* are just one type of transaction. (We will use the terms "call" and "transaction" interchangeably, throughout the book.) Further, the word *center* doesn't accurately depict the many multi-site environments, nor the growing number of organizations that have telecommuting programs. Call center has evolved into an umbrella term that can refer to reservations centers, help desks, information lines or customer service centers, regardless of how they are organized or what types of transactions they handle.

So, what about call center planning and management? Have the rules changed? Should the planning process change?

Our perspective is...yes and no. Consider integrated Web services. Assume that customers and potential customers browsing a Web site can click a button, be connected to the call center and receive immediate live assistance. To plan for and manage this environment, you first choose an appropriate service level for these transactions (Step 1). You then establish processes for collecting data related to these transactions (Step 2). Next, you forecast the load (Step 3), and calculate on-phone staff and system resources required (Steps 4 and 5). After that, you utilize rostered staff factor to add realism to scheduling requirements (Step 6), and organize schedules for the agents who will handle these transactions (Step 7). Finally, you analyze costs and compare them to other service levels

(Steps 8 and 9).

How about video calls? Again, you begin by choosing an appropriate service level objective. You then collect data, forecast the

> All told, effective, step-by-step planning and management will be as important as ever in the next generation of call centers.

video call load, calculate the base level of agents required, plan for system resources, etc. Your objectives would be to get the right number of video-equipped agents and necessary technology resources in the right places at the right times, doing the right things.

All told, effective, step-by-step planning and management will be as important as ever in the next generation of call centers. The fundamental resource planning challenge faced by young telephone companies almost a century ago continues to be important: Get the right people and

supporting resources in the right places at the right times. That will be true into the foreseeable future.

So, how will call center management be different than in the past? Perhaps most notably, there will be more types of transactions to manage. And those transactions will be increasingly complex, as tech-

nology automates simple and routine tasks leaving reps to manage inter-actions that require the human touch. Customer expectations will continue to climb, and callers will be unforgiving of organizations that do not provide the choices and services they demand. Reps will need good writing and customer service skills just as they did in pre-call center days. And finding the right mix of technology and human capital will be an ongoing effort.

Widely published business consultant Charles Handy says, "The past is important. We need a sense of history." But he also warns, "You can't walk into the future looking over your shoulder. You can't stumble backwards into the future."

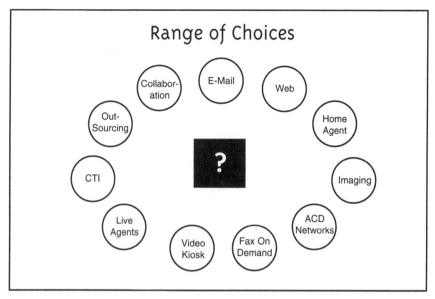

We're at an interesting point in call center history. We can learn from the past, but we are at the cusp of a new era and have the chance to shape it. Strategist Michael Porter predicts that "true leaders will be those that don't just optimize within an industry, but that actually reshape and redefine their industry."

The stakes are high. The challenges are real. And the opportunities are invigorating. Call it "call center management on fast forward!"

From the Back Room to the Boardroom

Recent studies are clear. In many sectors of the economy, call centers have become a major factor in customer retention, competitiveness and agility to adapt to changing markets. Senior executives are increasingly aware of that and are supporting initiatives to attract the

Professional Skills

- Leadership and management
- Communication - writing, speaking and interpersonal
- Project Management
- Performance Assessments
- Quantitative Analysis

best people possible to their call centers. As call centers play an ever-increasing role in regional, national and international economies, governments are rolling

> To call center managers who successfully meet the challenges, the opportunities for advancement are significant.

out the red carpet to attract new call center businesses and capable people to run them.

To call center managers who successfully meet the challenges, the opportunities for advancement are significant. The call center management profession - once in the category of "mystical arts" or a back room function - is at long last getting the attention it deserves.

An important step to meeting the challenges ahead is to recognize that you are in a legitimate, bona-fide profession. Treat it as such. That means staying in tune with the growing body of industry knowledge. It means continual personal growth and development. It means keeping abreast of evolving technologies and developing a network of other professionals and resources you can count on. In

Knowledge Requirements

- Customer service
- Random call arrival
- Queuing theory
- Caller behavior
- Forecasting
- Staffing and scheduling
- Systems and software
- Organizational behavior
- Ergonomics and workplace environment
- Industry vocabulary

short, it means that you have to pay the price in time and effort.

Whatever your background or level of experience, we hope that this book helps you in that effort. Thanks for coming along!

[Chapter 2:

Three Driving Forces

in Incoming Call Centers

Calls bunch up!
-Gordon F. MacPherson, 1987

Newcomers to the industry are often surprised at how *different* inbound call centers are compared with other types of customer service and support environments.

"The workload is volatile."

"Timing is so critical."

"I think callers sometimes picture us sitting around in the break room!"

Indeed, inbound call centers operate in a unique environment. The workload *does* change from moment to moment. And when callers can't see the queue, they often become impatient much quicker than they do in settings where they can "see" the line and the progress they are making.

In any inbound call center, three major forces are at work: random or peaked call arrival; callers' perception of the queue, be it visible or invisible to them; and caller tolerance. These "driving forces" help explain why the inbound environment is so unique. Understanding them is a prerequisite to making sense of the staffing and scheduling steps that will be covered in later chapters.

Call Arrival - Random or Peaked?

If you've spent more than about four minutes in an incoming call center, you've discovered a dominant fact of life: Calls arrive as they darn well please. They certainly do not arrive in anything resembling an even, orderly flow.

> ### Three Driving Forces
>
> • Call Arrival - Random or Peaked?
> • The Queue - Visible or Invisible?
> • The Seven Factors or Caller Tolerance

Random Arrival

Calls arrive *randomly* in most inbound call centers most of the time. Take a look at a monitor or the readerboard on the wall. Watch the dynamics. In comes a call. Then one, two more...there's another. And, two, three, four more...Exactly when calls arrive from moment to moment is the result of decisions made by callers who are motivated by a myriad of individual needs and conditions. Put another way, *calls bunch up!*

This figure illustrates two possible scenarios of random call arrival. The input for the chart came from a statistical table of random numbers.

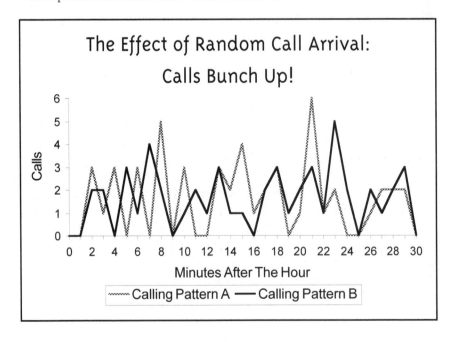

The Effect of Random Call Arrival: Calls Bunch Up!

However, there is an important distinction between random call arrival and predictable call arrival patterns. Virtually all inbound call centers - even those of the more volatile type, such as emergency services centers - have distinctive calling patterns, which are usually detectable down to at least a half-hour. You can predict that you will get around 240 calls next Tuesday between 11:00 and 11:30 a.m. What you can't predict with any precision is how many of those calls are going to arrive in the first minute, the second minute and so forth.

Consider another example. If you manage an ice cream stand, you can, with some analysis and practice, predict the number of customers and sales based on day of week, time of day, promotions, etc. Saturday afternoons during the summer months will be busy, but traffic will be light on mid-week mornings. You could also predict the traffic before and after promotions you run, and events in the community such as football games. But you wouldn't be able to predict the moment by moment arrival of customers.

There are several important implications to random call arrival. First, staffing must be calculated by using either a queuing formula that takes random call arrival into account or a computer simulation program that accurately models this phenomenon. Other approaches almost always lead to inaccurate staffing calculations. And unfortunately, it's not just staffing that will be off. Because staffing impacts the load the network and systems must carry, miscalculated staff inherently leads to miscalculated system and network resources.

Second, inbound call centers operate in a "demand-chasing" environment. At any given time, there are either more calls than staff to handle them or more staff than calls. That means call centers must augment good forecasting and staff-planning with real-time management. A solid understanding of random arrival is necessary to avoid overreacting to normal variation in traffic arrival and under-reacting to bona fide trends.

Third, performance objectives and standards must take random call arrival into account. For example, a standard of "N widgets per day" may make sense in a traditional assembly line setting, but it doesn't work in an environment where the workload arrives randomly. Unless the queue is always backed up and service is lousy, your reps will spend a portion of their day just waiting for calls to arrive.

Smooth and Peaked Traffic

In addition to random or "normal" traffic, there are two other general types of traffic in the telecommunications world: "smooth" and "peaked." Telecommunications traffic engineers have assigned statistical "variance-to-mean" ratios to designate each type of traffic, but essentially the patterns for each look like this:

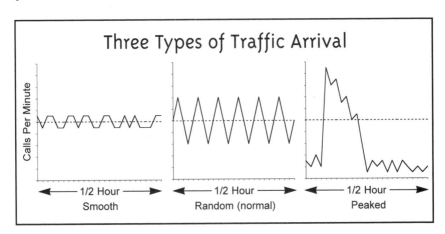

Smooth traffic is virtually non-existent in incoming call centers, but can apply in outbound environments. For example, a group of people may be assigned to make outbound calls, one after another after another for the duration of their shift. In that case, the number of circuits required is equal to the number of reps placing the calls.

Another type of call arrival, peaked traffic, is a reality in some incoming call centers. Many of us use the term "peak" in a general sense when referring to call traffic: What's your peak time of year? Peak day of the week? Peak time of day? But the term "peaked traffic" specifically refers to a surge of traffic beyond random variation. It is a *spike* within a short period of time.

Television and radio ads will often generate peaked traffic. For example, QVC gets a surge of calls when new products are advertised on its home shopping channel. Service bureaus that handle everything from exercise equipment to ginzu knives get peaked traffic when those television ads are aired. The large centers that handle these calls can go from zero to hundreds of calls a minute, almost instantly.

It is important to correctly distinguish between random and peaked traffic. When a catalog company such as L.L. Bean or Lands' End sends out thousands of new catalogs, they begin getting hit with calls within a day or two after the mail drop. But that's *not* peaked call arrival. It's random arrival, but at a much higher level than recent history. Similarly, a utility that has a power outage will get a lot of calls until the problem is fixed. But other than the few minutes following the outage, calls will arrive randomly, albeit at a much higher level than usual.

The key question is this: Is there a surge of calls that come and go within less than a half-hour? If the surge lasts longer than a half-hour, it's probably random call arrival.

Randomly Arriving Peaked Traffic?

Some call centers experience call arrival that is a hybrid between random and peaked traffic. Emergency services centers will get calls immediately following a traffic accident. In the past, call volume for a single event would amount to a handful of calls. Now, with the proliferation of mobile telephones, they often get flooded with calls, all reporting the same accident. We suppose that can be referred to as "randomly arriving peaked traffic!"

The distinction between random and peaked traffic is important. To correctly calculate staffing needs, you need to know what type of traffic you're going to get, as discussed in Chapter 6. Traffic arrival type also helps dictate what type of real-time management strategies you deploy, as covered in Chapter 10.

The Queue: Visible or Invisible?

Queue comes from the French word *cue*, which means "line of waiting people." Queues are a fact of life in many incoming call centers. Answering every call immediately would be about as practical for many call centers as it would be for airlines to check in every passenger immediately.

But the difference between an incoming call center and the lines at an airline counter, grocery store or Disneyland is that callers usually can't see how long the queue is and the progress they are making in it.

The top row of faces in the figure "Visible or Invisible Queue," reflect a queue that the customers can see. Few would choose to wait in line, so as they enter the queue they are represented by the first face. As they

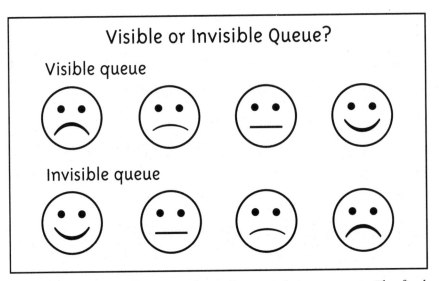

move forward, the subsequent faces illustrate their progress. The final face reflects the fact that they "made it." They are at the counter, hearing the sweet words "How may I help you?"

The second row of faces represents a setting where customers (callers) are ignorant of the queue they are entering. "Ignorance is bliss," and expectations are initially high. But after some amount of waiting, say 15 seconds of ringing, they begin to doubt that they are going to get right through (second face). The third face illustrates the transition from doubt to mild frustration. By now, they have probably heard the first delay announcement and it confirms that they are in a queue.

The fourth face represents the caller who, from their perspective, has waited *too darn long*. Often, the first thing they do when they reach a rep is tell them about the miserable experience they just had. And that's a bad situation because that will lengthen call handling time, which will back up the queue even more...which will cause even more callers to unload on your agents once their calls are answered.

There's another phenomenon that kicks in here. Callers who have waited a long time in queue tend to "dig in their heels" as they attempt to squeeze all the value out of the call that they can. Callers to help desks are the classic example: "Geesh, I waited this long to get through, I better go over a few more things while I have you."

FRANK & ERNEST ® by Bob Thaves

" ...PLEASE CONTINUE TO HOLD. YOUR CALL IS IMPORTANT TO US. ... BUT YOUR TIME ISN'T. "

With permission of Bob Thaves

Visible Queue

Software company Word Perfect (now owned by Corel) pioneered the "visible queue" in the mid 1980s. They set their system up to enable "queue jockeys" to make announcements of expected hold times to incoming callers. They could also play music and deliver announcements to keep callers entertained and informed while they waited in queue:

Thank you for calling Word Perfect. If you're calling for assistance with Version 2, there are nine of you in queue, and if you just joined us, it looks like the wait is just over three minutes. If you are calling for Version 3, there are 18 callers in queue. But we've got more staff there this morning, and it looks like your wait will be about two minutes. Now, here's Kenny G, from his latest album...

Word Perfect discovered that callers who abandon a visible queue do so at the beginning. Callers who decide to wait generally do so until they reach a rep.

Many call center managers keep a diligent eye on *how many* callers abandon. But *when* callers abandon is an important consideration as well. If they are abandoning early on because they are making an informed choice, that's a different story than waiting for what seems like forever in an invisible queue, then hanging up in frustration.

What the queue jockey never said, but what was implicit in the message, was something like:

Thanks for calling. If you're going to abandon, would you kindly do so now, before you get frustrated, drive up our costs and clog up the queue only to abandon before we get to you anyway...

Other software companies, such as Microsoft and Delrina, followed Word Perfect's lead. The feedback from callers was overwhelmingly positive. But having real-time, live queue jockeys is impractical for most organizations. Accordingly, in 1991, Rockwell introduced an ACD feature they called IQueue that enabled the ACD to "tell time." With this feature, the ACD is programmed to analyze real-time variables, make predictions and announce expected wait times to callers as they arrive. Most other major ACD vendors now offer this capability.

These systems provide fairly accurate predictions in reasonably straight-forward environments, especially in large agent groups. But if you are utilizing some form of complex, contingency-based routing, the ACD can outsmart itself. Some callers have found themselves actually moving backwards in queue as arriving priority callers are moved to the front of the line! By all means, if the feature isn't accurate in your environment, disable it! This is a challenge the manufacturers have yet to conquer.

There's currently quite a bit of debate and study around the question of how callers react to visible versus invisible queues. But we think that the debate misses the real point: *Given the choice, callers want to know what's happening!* You would. And so would we.

Someday, we'll look back on these pioneering '70's, '80's and '90's, and smile at our tolerance of queues that we as callers knew nothing about. With promising new multimedia technologies, the queue will most likely be represented graphically on the caller's computer or video screen. It's a trend you can count on. More and more inbound call centers will make their queues visible.

Seven Factors Affecting Caller Tolerance

Another important driving force is "caller tolerance." There are seven factors that affect caller tolerance. They influence everything from how long callers will wait in queue to how many will abandon, how many will retry when they get busy signals, and how they will react to automation, such as a voice response unit (VRU). They also affect how callers perceive the service the call center is providing.

1. Degree of motivation. How motivated are your callers? Callers experiencing a power outage will usually wait longer to reach their utility than those with billing questions.

2. Availability of substitutes. Are there substitutes the caller can use if they can't get through to the initial number they are trying? If they are highly motivated and have no substitutes, they will retry many times if they get busies and will generally wait a long time in queue if necessary. But if they

The Seven Factors of Caller Tolerance
1. Degree of Motivation
2. Availability of Substitutes
3. Competition's Service Level
4. Level of Expectations
5. Time Available
6. Who's Paying for the Call
7. Human Behavior

know of an alternative number to try, or if there are other selections in your automated attendant ("press one for this, two for that"), they may try those alternatives. Or they may try fax, Web or VRU-based services. They may even walk down the street if you have a retail outlet.

3. Competition's service level. If it's easier for callers to use competitive services or if they have a tough time reaching you, they may go elsewhere.

4. Level of expectations. An organization or industry's reputation for service - or the level of service being promoted - has a bearing on caller tolerance.

5. Time available. For example, a caller's occupation can affect caller tolerance. Doctors who call insurance providers are infamous for being intolerant of even modest queues. Retirees, on the other hand, may have more time to wait.

6. Who's paying for the call? In general, callers are more tolerant of a queue when toll-free service is available. They are intolerant of even short waits when they are paying for premium priced numbers (e.g., 900 service).

7. Human behavior. The weather, the caller's mood and the time of day all have a bearing on caller tolerance.

The seven factors are not static. They are constantly changing. Even so, it is important to have a general understanding of the factors affecting your callers' tolerance. Important questions to consider include:

• How motivated are your callers?
• What type of caller is least motivated? Why?
• What type of caller is most motivated? Why?

- What substitutes to calling you do they have?
- Which substitutes would you want them to use?
- Which substitutes would you not want them to use?
- What are their expectations?
- What level of service are others in the industry providing?
- Who pays for the calls?
- How might your callers' lifestyles influence their tolerance?
- All things considered, how high is their tolerance level?

Putting Abandonment in Perspective

In quite a few call centers, abandonment rate is viewed as a key measure of how adequately the call center is staffed. We often get questions like, what is an acceptable rate of abandonment? What is abandonment in such and such an industry? Are there any studies on how long callers will wait? What should our service level be to keep abandonment under X percent?

The usual assumptions are A) that there must be industry "standards" for abandonment and B) that abandonment is a good indicator of call center performance. But neither is true.

For one thing, abandonment is tough to forecast, at least with any consistent level of accuracy. That would mean you would be able to accurately predict the seven factors that affect caller tolerance. Good luck. Conditions are constantly changing, and there are an almost unlimited number of variables that can impact abandonment.

Further, abandonment can be a misleading measure of call center performance. The conventional wisdom is that longer queues translate into higher abandonment. But the seven factors can help explain apparent paradoxes:

- When the stock market swings significantly, mutual funds and others in the financial industry get a flood of calls. Even though service level may drop, abandonment also goes down because callers have a higher degree of motivation - and are willing to wait longer, if necessary.

- When airlines run "super-saver" specials, callers are generally willing to wait longer. Service level may drop because of heavy response to the promotions, but abandonment will likely be minimal.

- If callers encounter busy signals before they get into the queue, they will almost always wait longer if necessary. The psychology is, "At least I've made it into their system. I better hang in there."

British Airways Provides Concorde Tickets – And a Case Study in Caller Tolerance

To celebrate its 10th anniversary since privatization, British Airways launched an international phone promotion in February 1997 that drew millions of callers. The promotion offered callers the chance to win virtually free tickets to fly roundtrip on the Concorde, British Airway's legendary supersonic jet, if they were one of the first 100 callers to reach the center once the promotion officially began. With a great deal of pomp and circumstance, the promotion was kicked off at 10:00 p.m. Tuesday, February 11.

Just 25 minutes - and an amazing *20 million call attempts* - later, the promotion was over. The call center was prepared for the onslaught. The airline designated its New Castle, England call center to handle all calls during the promotion and doubled its staff. "On the dot of 10:00 p.m., we diverted all calls to the New Castle center," says David Wilson, of British Airways. "That time of night is not one of our busy periods, so we weren't worried about the promotion interfering with our regular service."

To minimize the use of annoying busy signals for callers during the promotion, British Airways used a recorded message that gave callers information about the promotion and thanked them for calling. As expected, callers who got the announcement kept on trying to get through. And those who reached the queue waited as long as it took to get connected to a rep. ■

While these may be obvious examples, what about the more subtle day-to-day shifts in caller tolerance? It can be baffling. Sometimes, when people have to wait a long time, they wait. Other times, when service level is really good, abandonment is higher than expected. If you don't believe it, graph out service level versus abandonment by half-hour for a few typical days. You are not likely to see an exact correlation.

In the final analysis, you can't control how callers will react to the myriad of circumstances that influence their behavior. You *can* control how accessible you are - how many reps are plugged in and taking calls, and how many trunks you have. Service level is a key measure of accessibility. That is the subject we'll take up in the next chapter.

We can control
Trunks available Skilled reps available
We cannot control
Caller behavior

Points to Remember

• Inbound call centers will either have random or peaked traffic arrival. The type of call arrival you get will dictate the staffing calculations you use.

• Callers behave differently, depending on whether the queue is visible or invisible. Most inbound call centers will have visible queues in the future.

• There are seven factors that affect caller tolerance, and these factors are constantly changing.

• You cannot directly control abandonment, but you can control your accessibility, or service level.

Part Two:

A Planning and

Management Framework

To effectively manage an inbound call center, you need a solid planning and management framework. Forecasting, staffing, scheduling and budgeting activities should be collaborative, focused on customer needs and expectations, and built on appropriate service level objectives.

Chapter 3:   Service Level, The Core Value

Chapter 4:   Acquiring Necessary Data

Chapter 5:   Forecasting Call Load...Etc.

Chapter 6:   Determining Base Staff and Trunks
              Required

Chapter 7:   Scheduling Efficiently and
              Sufficiently

[Chapter 3:

Service Level, The Core Value

Give me ambiguity or give me something else.

-Author Unknown

The principle of service level is at the heart of effective incoming call center management. Without a service level objective, the answers to many important questions would be left to chance. How accessible is the call center? How many staff do you need? How do you compare to the competition? Are you prepared to handle the response to marketing campaigns? How busy are your reps going to be? What are your costs going to be?

Service level ties the resources you need to the results you want to achieve. It measures the degree to which you're getting the transactions "in the front door" and to an agent. It is a stable target for planning and budgeting. It is a unifying concept. It is concrete.

Service level is tried and true in call centers worldwide for transactions that must be handled when they arrive. Inbound phone calls are today the most common example. New multimedia services such as video calls and calls integrated with the World Wide Web that must be handled when they arrive also fit into this category. Consequently, service level will remain an important objective in the next generation of call centers.

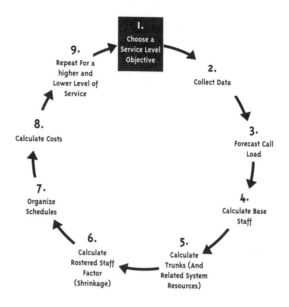

However, most incoming call centers are also increasingly responsible for transactions that belong in a second category, those that don't have to be handled at the time they arrive. Examples include postal correspondence, e-mail, faxes, voice mail and video mail. These transactions allow a larger window of time in which the call center can respond. But it is vital - and unfortunately far less common - for call centers to

Two Major Categories of Inbound Transactions

-Those that must be handled when they arrive (e.g., inbound calls).
Performance objective: Service Level.

-Those that can be handled at a later time (e.g., correspondence).
Performance objective: Response Time.

establish concrete "response time" objectives for these interactions and to ensure that the objectives are met, through disciplined resource planning and management.

There are various terms for service level in use. It is sometimes referred to as telephone service factor, or TSF. Some call it grade of service (GOS), although we don't prefer that term because it can be confused with the same term to denote the degree of blocking on a group of trunks. It can also be called accessibility and service standard. We will use the term service level, specifically as it applies to transactions that must be handled when they arrive.

Similarly, response time can be called speed of reply or even "service level" (not to be confused with how we will use the term here). We will use response time in a specific sense to describe the level of service assigned to transactions that can be handled at a later time.

Service Level, Defined

Service level is defined as "X percent of calls answered in Y seconds," such as 90 percent answered in 20 seconds. Unfortunately, service level is often misunderstood or mismanaged. For example, some managers define it as a percentage only, and it's often unclear what that percentage really means. For one manager, it means that X percent of all calls are answered. Period. That is the inverse of abandonment: 97 percent answer rate would inherently mean a 3 percent abandonment rate.

To other managers, service level means that X percent of the time the service level objective is met, whatever that objective may be. Others define service level as average speed of answer. Or, longest delayed call.

But service level should take the form "X percent of all calls answered in Y seconds." Planning should be based on achieving the target. Choosing an appropriate service level objective is the first step in effective planning and management.

Why Service Level?

Why service level and not percent answered, percent abandoned, average speed of answer or other alternatives? The answer is, "X percent answered in Y seconds" gives the clearest indication of what callers experience when they attempt to reach the call center. You know exactly what

Service Level:

- Impacts customer goodwill
- Impacts levels of lost calls
- Impacts agent burnout and errors
- Provides a link between resources and results
- Focuses all planning

happens to the percentage of callers you define. As we'll see in later chapters, service level is the most stable measurement of the queue.

Average speed of answer is a close cousin of service level and is derived from the same set of data. But a big problem with ASA is that it is often misinterpreted. Most of us assume that the average lies somewhere in the middle of a set of data, or that average represents a "typical experience." Not so with ASA! It is mathematically correct, but does not represent what happens to individual callers.

As we will see in Chapter 6, most callers get connected to a rep much quicker than the average, but some wait *far beyond* the average. For example, with an average speed of answer at 15 seconds, about 70 percent of callers get answered immediately, but a small percent of callers will wait three or four minutes in queue. Many people forget that reality when they look at ASA. ASA has its uses (e.g., in calculating trunk load), so don't throw it out the window. But service level is a more reliable and more telling measure of what callers experience.

What about abandoned calls? As discussed in Chapter 2, looking solely at abandonment rates as a measure of whether staffing levels were appropriate can be highly misleading. We aren't suggesting that you ignore abandonment. A high abandonment is probably a symptom of staffing problems. But a low abandonment doesn't necessarily mean everything is fine.

Further, if abandonment is beyond acceptable, what are you going to do? You are going to look at when it's out of whack, and why. You will likely run smack into a low service level. When service level is appropriate, abandonment tends to take care of itself.

A good question to ask for any service level is, "What happens to the calls that don't get answered in Y seconds?" Most Erlang C and computer simulation software programs will calculate the answers to that and other questions. For a service level of 80 percent answered in 20 seconds, you will discover that about 30 percent of your callers end up in queue, that the longest wait will be around three minutes, and that average speed of answer will be around 10 to 15 seconds.

All of this brings up an important point: Different callers have different experiences with your call center, even if they are part of the same set of data measured by service level, ASA and other reports. Why? Random call arrival! Because of this reality, you will need an understanding of what happens to different callers. At a high level, service level

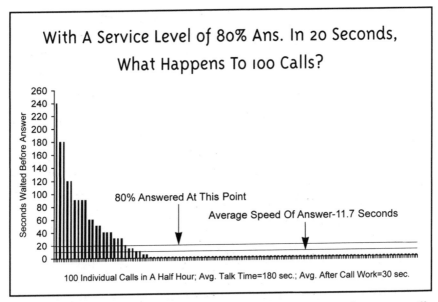

With A Service Level of 80% Ans. In 20 Seconds, What Happens To 100 Calls?

80% Answered At This Point

Average Speed Of Answer-11.7 Seconds

100 Individual Calls in A Half Hour; Avg. Talk Time=180 sec.; Avg. After Call Work=30 sec.

is the single best measure of these experiences. In later chapters, we'll identify other measures that will fill the gaps.

Giving Service Level Teeth

For service level to have meaning, it must be interpreted in light of blockage, or calls that aren't getting through. Any time a portion of callers are getting busies, whether the busies are generated by the system or are a result of a limited number of staff and trunks during a busy time of day, the reports only tell you what is happening to the calls that get through. In fact, you can make reports, such as service level and average speed of answer, look as good as you want them to by limiting the number of calls that get through.

You must also view service level over an appropriate time frame. Daily service level reports often conceal important information. Service level can take a big hit in the morning, but if you have staff handling every call immediately much of the afternoon, the daily report will look okay. On the other hand, the level of service from callers' perspective is a different story.

Further, managers who are held accountable for daily reports may have an incentive to manage inappropriately. If the morning was rough, they may keep people on the phones through the afternoon when the call load drops, just to make the reports look better. That's a waste of valuable time and resources, and it doesn't help callers who ran into poor service earlier in the day.

If daily reports are potentially misleading, monthly averages for service level are virtually meaningless. They simply don't reflect the day by day, half-hour by half-hour realities. Even so, monthly reports are a popular way to summarize activity to senior management, and we will suggest some better reporting alternatives in Chapter 9.

How ACDs Calculate Service Level

There are a number of alternative methods your ACD may use to calculate service level. With some systems, you can specify the calculation you prefer. Here are the most common:

1. Calls answered + calls abandoned in Y seconds/calls answered + calls abandoned: For most situations, we prefer this alternative because the calculation includes all of the traffic received by the ACD. It provides a

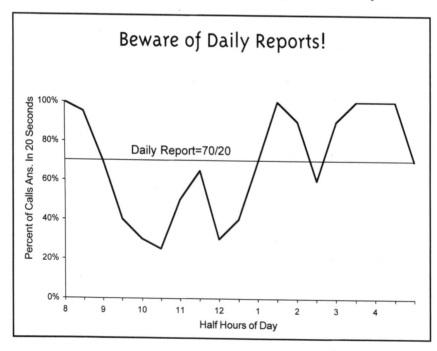

complete picture of what is happening.

2. Calls answered in Y seconds/calls answered: This alternative only considers answered calls, and therefore is not a good reflection of all activity. Abandonment is entirely ignored. We do not recommend this calculation.

3. Calls answered in Y seconds/calls answered + calls abandoned: This alternative tends to be the least popular among call center managers because calls that enter the queue but then abandon drive service level down. Canada-based consultant Cheryl Odee Helm, who has made call center reporting a focus of her practice, recommends that this measure is appropriate in situations where calls enter a queue *after* they hear a delay announcement. She does not recommend this calculation in settings where callers enter a queue before they hear the announcement.

4. Calls answered before Y seconds/calls answered + calls abandoned after Y seconds: With this calculation, abandoned calls only impact service level if they happen after the Y seconds specified. Consequently, this is a way to avoid getting "penalized" by callers who abandon quickly without ignoring abandoned calls altogether. This is an acceptable approach.

What About Quality?

When you talk a lot about service level, someone is bound to bring up an important point: You can achieve your service level objective regularly, and at the same time, be creating waste, extra work and low quality. It's true, an overly narrow focus on service level does not account for quality. You can have an excellent service level, but your reps can still:

- Misunderstand callers' requests
- Put down the wrong information
- Relay wrong information to callers
- Make callers mad
- Fail to accomplish your purpose (sell or service)
- Unnecessarily cause repeat calls
- Miss opportunities to capture valuable feedback

After all, service level simply states that not too many callers had to wait longer than a certain number of seconds before reaching a rep. The

ACD alone cannot measure whether the callers and your organization achieved the real purposes of the call. So, you can fall into a modern management trap - putting a lot of emphasis on what can be measured in numbers and missing the point of what you're really supposed to be doing.

However, the whole "service level versus quality" argument can be a cop-out. Can there be too much emphasis on service level? Yes, if that's all you are looking at and managing to. Of course, there are other important objectives, but a good service level is an enabler - it means that calls are getting in and answered, so that you and your callers can get on with what you're trying to do.

A poor service level will rob you of productivity. As service deteriorates, more and more callers are likely to verbalize their criticisms when their calls are finally answered. Your reps will spend valuable time apologizing to callers. This means they will not be able to answer as many calls as they would if service was better. Your costs will go up.

But that is just the beginning. Calls also get longer because reps will eventually pace themselves differently. If they can't get a "breather" between calls because the "in-between" time no longer exists, they may start taking their breathers while they're on calls, as a survival mechanism. When service level initially starts to slip, reps often try to clear up the queue. If this proves to be a futile effort, they even-

© Randy Glasbergen

GLASBERGEN

"At this time, we'd like to remind you to eat and drink at regular intervals. Thank you for continuing to hold."

Used with permission.

tually settle in for the long term. Call handling time goes up. If this condition continues, employee morale will sink. Turnover and burnout will go up. So will recruitment and training costs.

Somewhere along the way, quality begins to suffer, which has a further negative impact on service level. When your reps are overworked due to constant congestion in the queue, they become less accurate and can become less "customer friendly." Callers are telling them in no uncertain terms about the rotten time they had getting through. And reps make more mistakes. These mistakes contribute to repeat calls, unnecessary service calls, escalation of calls and complaints to higher management, callbacks, etc. - all of which drive service level down further. Poor service level tends to be a vicious cycle.

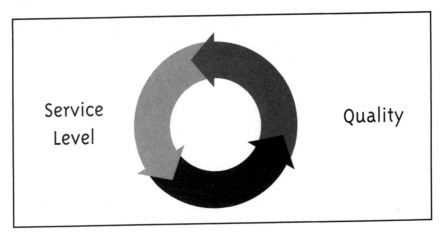

Service Level — Quality

In short, there is no such thing as quality *versus* service level - at least not in the longer term. Service level and quality must go hand in hand.

Choosing a Service Level Objective

The number of staff you need to handle transactions and the schedules you produce should flow from your service level objective. Imagine you are going to receive 50 calls that last an average of three minutes, in a half-hour period. If you have only two people to answer the calls, the delay time for most callers will be long, and you'll probably have high abandonment. As you add people, delay times will drop.

How many people should you add? Enough to reduce the queue to an acceptable level for you and your callers. In other words, the answer to that question becomes your service level target, and you won't be able to achieve your target without the correct level of resources.

There is generally no "industry standard" service level you can hang your hat on. (There are some exceptions. For example, service levels for cable TV companies in the U.S. are regulated.) The optimum service level is affected by a myriad of factors, including the value of the call, fully loaded labor costs, trunk costs and caller tolerances. An industry standard would have to be based on all call centers having the same values for these things.

Why There Is No "Industry Standard" Service Level

The optimum service level is affected by...
• The value of a call
• Labor costs
• Trunk costs
• The seven factors of caller tolerance
• The organization's desire to differentiate products or services by the level of service provided in the call center

---

The correct service level for you is the one which:

• Meets callers' needs and expectations
• Keeps abandonment at an acceptable level
• Minimizes agent burnout and errors
• Minimizes expenses
• Maximizes revenue
• Is agreed upon and supported by senior management

From a practical sense, no one service level would fit all situations affecting how long callers will wait. Consider the factors affecting caller tolerance. How motivated are callers to reach you? What is the availability of substitutes for calling you? What is your competition's service level? What are your callers' expectations based on their past experiences? How much time do they have? What are the conditions at the locations where they are calling from? Who is paying for the call?

There are essentially four approaches you can use to determine your service level objective, though all require some subjectivity and judgment.

One is to chose a "middle of the road" service level, such as 80 percent answer in 20 seconds. The 80/20 objective was once published in ACD manuals as an "industry standard." In reality, it never was, but many early call centers used this target. 80/20 is still fairly common because for many call centers it is a reasonable balance between callers' expectations and the practicality of having enough staff to meet the objective. But it may or may not be right for you.

Another popular method for choosing a service level is to benchmark competitors or organizations similar to yours, and use that input as a starting point.

Alternatives For Choosing A Service Level
1. Follow the crowd
2. Relate to competition
3. Minimize abandonment
4. Conduct a customer survey

Determining what others are doing can be as informal as simply asking for it or as involved as undertaking a full-blown benchmarking study. Whatever the approach, keep in mind that the results reported by others and what they are actually achieving may be two very different things. We recall working with three insurance companies with the same service level objective - 80 percent answer in 30 seconds. But the results they were achieving were very different.

A third approach is to choose a service level objective by essentially asking, how low can you go without losing callers? This assumes that a higher level of service means lower abandonment and vice versa. One big flaw with this approach is that it assumes that as long as callers don't abandon, service is acceptable. But that is not always the case. Further, as discussed in Chapter 2, abandonment is not static. It will fluctuate as the seven factors of caller tolerance change. As a result, abandonment is difficult to forecast, and choosing a service level around abandonment is building on the proverbial foundation of "shifting sand."

Incremental revenue analysis is a variation of this approach and is a more formal methodology to determine the potential impact of abandonment on overall costs. This approach has been traditionally applied in revenue-generating environments (such as reservation centers and catalog companies) where calls have a measurable value. It's much tougher to use in call centers where the value of calls are difficult to measure, such as customer service centers and help desks.

To use this approach, you attach a cost to abandoned calls and make assumptions around how many calls you would lose for various service levels. The theory is, you should continue to add reps and trunks as long as they produce positive incremental (marginal, additional) revenue (value) after paying for their own costs.

This approach can be a valuable exercise, when used in conjunction

Incremental Revenue Analysis
(Example Only)

Talk Time-180 sec.
After Call Work-30 sec.
Half Hour's Calls=200
Rostered Staff Factor=1.3

Agents On Phone	Rostered Staff (Agents x 1.3)	Calls Ans In 20 Sec	% Lost Calls (Assumed)	% Calls Lost Forever (Assumed)	Trunk Hours	Answered Calls	Gross Revenue Avg. Call $22.25	Labor Cost	Toll-free Trunk Cost: Per Min. 15	Net Revenue	$ Increm. Revenue
25	33	45%	26.0%	7.80%	14.6	184	$4,103	244	218	3641	0
26	34	62%	12.5%	3.75%	12.2	193	$4,293	254	182	3847	206
27	35	74%	6.5%	1.95%	11.2	196	$4,363	263	167	3933	85
28	36	83%	3.5%	1.05%	10.7	198	$4,403	273	160	3971	38
29	38	89%	2.0%	0.60%	10.4	199	$4,423	283	156	3985	14
30	39	93%	1.5%	0.45%	10.3	199	$4,430	293	154	3984	(1)
31	40	96%	1.0%	0.30%	10.2	199	$4,437	302	152	3982	(2)
32	42	97%	0.5%	0.15%	10.1	200	$4,443	312	152	3980	(2)

Optimum (↑ row 29)

with other approaches, as long as the assumptions are understood and communicated to others in the budgeting process. Nevertheless, don't let the scientific look of this approach fool you - it requires some pretty serious guesswork.

A fourth method for choosing service level is to conduct a customer survey. This involves analyzing the seven factors of caller tolerance.

While it's always a good idea to know what your callers expect, random call arrival means that different callers have different experiences with your call center. Even for a modest service level such as 80 percent answer in 60 seconds, over half the callers will get an immediate answer. Some, though, will wait in queue for three to five minutes (assuming no overflow or other contingency). As a result, many in that set of callers would say that your service level is great, while a handful would tell you that it is pretty crummy.

Some managers use a variation of a typical customer survey. They have taken samples of individual callers and then compared the responses to actual wait times of those calls. The results are interesting. In many customer service environments, waits of up to 60 and 90 seconds are generally okay with callers, and they have a fairly accurate idea of what

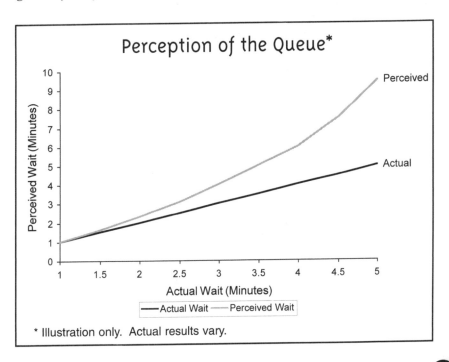

* Illustration only. Actual results vary.

actually happened. But beyond about 90 seconds, caller responses start looking a lot different than reality. Those who wait three minutes in queue may say they waited four or five. Those who wait five minutes will tell you they waited something like eight or ten minutes. Of course, answers will vary based on the type of organization and the seven factors affecting caller tolerance. But the issue remains: at some point, perception deteriorates beyond reality.

The overall best approach to choosing service level is an iterative process that combines the best of these methods. See where you are, run some calculations, look at what others are doing, assess what callers are saying, etc. In that sense, choosing a service level happens further down-line in the planning process. You need a forecast in order to calculate staff, schedules, etc. So, this step initially has to happen in parallel with others.

The Quick Version of Choosing a Service Level Objective

Sometimes we hear, "Okay, the analysis is fine, but let's get to the point. What should our service level objective be?"

Fair enough. If you're in a competitive industry (e.g., shipping, catalog and mutual funds) and want to be on the high end of the scale, 90/20 is fairly common. Others go for 85/15 or 90/15. Engineer for no more than 1 percent blockage on the trunks. If you hit these targets reasonably well, your abandonment rate will probably be around 1 percent or 2 percent.

Going for the middle of the road? 80/20 is common. That's what a lot of banks, insurance companies and travel reservation centers shoot for. 80/30 and 90/60 are other popular mid-range service levels. Don't allow more than 1 percent to 5 percent blockage on the trunks. Hit these objectives, and you'll probably see abandonment at 3 percent or 4 percent.

Want a service level that is more modest? 80/60, or 90/120, or even 80/300, with 5 percent to 15 percent blockage are targets common with software support centers and some government organizations. Abandonment can range up to 10 percent, 15 percent or higher. Hold your judgment - some of these organizations do a darn good job of hitting these objectives *consistently*, a lesson many with more lofty goals could use.

Of course, just throwing out numbers like this can be dangerous. There are exceptions to the norm in any industry. Also, interpret these numbers with common sense. If you are an emergency services center, you will target 100/0. On the other end of the scale, there are centers for which 80/300 is a dream. We worked with one center that is blocking over 70 percent of their calls, but still losing a large portion of those that get through.

Finally, remember that it's not just how high your objectives are, but how consistently you hit them. If your service level objective is 90/20, but you base your performance on daily or monthly summaries, you might be getting creamed mid-mornings; and that's when a lot of your customers are calling. If you really want to see how you're doing and what realistic targets might be, produce some service level graphs like those shown in Chapter 7. ■

Whichever combination of methods you choose, you will have more success managing your center just by having a service level target on which to base your planning. Showing senior management what kind of service can be bought for a specific amount of funding is an excellent way to involve them in this decision and to get their buy-in from the beginning.

Realistic Targets, Taken Seriously

If your operation is chronically missing your target, that may indicate a fundamental misconception about the importance of service level. After all, with longer call delays, network costs go up. Excessive delays also increase employee stress levels and error rates, resulting in reduced competitiveness and employee productivity.

You need to focus on a service level objective that your center can realistically achieve. Once you know your center's true capabilities, you must be able to back up your objectives with the right amount of resources. Service level should not be a "goal," something that is nice to strive for. An airline doesn't have the "goal" of reaching Hawaii when it takes off from L.A. It's a concrete objective, supported by adequate resources (fuel, pilots, navigation equipment, etc.).

Service Level Should Be:

• Realistic
• Understood
• Taken Seriously
• Adequately Funded

Why don't some call centers get the resources they need? Sometimes, it's because the money isn't available. Or maybe management at the top believes that it's possible to achieve the service level target with the current level of resources, thinking all that is needed is a little improvement in efficiency. Or maybe the call center manager has failed to educate top management on the link between service level and budget.

Service levels that are impossible to hit are particularly difficult for managers whose job success and salary are tied to meeting the objectives. When senior management hands down an objective without backing it up with adequate resources, these managers are set up for failure.

Part of taking a service level objective seriously means getting the buy-in of everyone who is involved in achieving it. To reach your target, reps, supervisors, managers and those with supporting roles should know what the service level objective is, why it was set where it is and whether or not it is being met. A value system that people do not understand will have little or no impact.

An incoming call center that is serious about service level goals will live by the principle that *answering calls comes first*. Admittedly, that is sometimes easier said than done. There are times when your service level for inbound transactions drops because you have assigned people to catch up on a backlog of critical non-phone work like customer correspondence or research. Further, these activities can turn into inbound calls if they aren't handled within customers' expected timeframes. Consequently, to maintain a consistent and appropriate service level, you also need to establish reasonable response time objectives.

Response Time

Response time is the equivalent of service level for transactions that don't have to be handled the moment they arrive. Response time, like service level, becomes the critical link between the resources you need and the results you want to achieve. Choosing response time objectives involves considering many of the same questions you analyzed when choosing an appropriate service level, e.g., the seven factors affecting tolerance.

An important step in establishing response time objectives is to relay to callers what your objectives are. That means telling them up-front what they can expect. Otherwise, what started out as a fax or e-mail may turn into a phone call: "I'm calling to check up on an e-mail I sent to you. I haven't heard a reply yet, and am wondering..." Consultant Martin Prunty, who is a well-known expert on the future of call centers, says, "You have to be overt about it. Don't leave their expectations to chance, or you'll pay the price." In most call centers, if the original transaction from the customer hasn't yet been handled, reps won't have the information necessary to deal with these calls without duplicating efforts for both the call center and caller.

Here are examples of typical response time objectives:

Type of transaction	Low end of range	High end of range
Customer e-mail	Days to never	Within one hour
Fax	Three days	Three hours
Voicemail	Next day	Within one hour
Letter by Mail	Three days	Same day

This came from a sample we took of several dozen call centers, between May and June 1997. The sample size was small and should not be considered "statistically significant." But it can give you a general idea of the types of objectives being established.

Internal Communications

In some cases, meeting a response time objective requires various internal resources to be available when needed. For example, some incoming messages to help desks that arrive from the Web or by fax require reps to confer with the "internal" help desk or other groups. That has long been the case with inbound phone calls. To achieve established response time objectives, there must also be "internal response time" standards.

For example, internal e-mail works well only when some ground rules are in place. Have you ever received a lengthy, involved e-mail that gave no hint how or even if you were to respond? Or how often have you created and sent an important message you expected a response to, but got no reply because the recipient thought the message was an "FYI" (for your information), requiring no response?

At the least, workgroups need an agreement that specifies how the members of the group will interact with each other. The agreement should stipulate levels of priorities and appropriate responses for each. For example:

1. Urgent messages. Recipients are expected to respond as soon as they get the message. This would be appropriate for customer-driven activities where a quick response time is important. Most voice mail and virtually all e-mail systems allow the sender to designate whether the message is priority.

2. Routine messages. Recipients expected to respond within, say, a day or four hours.

3. Informational messages. These messages require no response. (E.g., "The health club has new hours...")

Internal e-mail messages should have descriptive titles and be written like a newspaper story with headlines first, the main points second and necessary supporting details last. Many of the same principles apply to internal phone calls, faxes and voice mail.

As discussed in Chapter 11, one useful way to identify the resources required to handle a transaction is to chart the handling process step by step. This will identify weak links in the process and help to identify where internal standards are necessary, ensuring that customers are getting the response time promised.

Resource Planning

In chapters to follow, we will cover the planning steps required to handle transactions of both types to meet the service level and response time objectives you have established. These activities will include forecasting, staffing, scheduling and budgeting. None are possible without first establishing the necessary targets.

Points to Remember

• Service level is the performance objective for transactions that must be handled when they arrive (e.g., inbound calls). Response time is the performance objective for transactions that can be handled at a later time (e.g., e-mail).

• Staffing, trunking, scheduling and budgeting are all hinged on your service level and response time objectives.

• Choosing service level and response time objectives is not an exact science, and you will probably adjust your targets when you determine required resources and calculate costs later in the planning process.

• You should view service level in terms of how consistently you meet your objective, half-hour by half-hour. Daily and monthly summaries often conceal important information.

[Chapter 4:

►Acquiring Necessary Data

We're drowning in information and starving for knowledge.
-Rutherford D. Rogers

"C ollect data" is Step 2 in the nine-step planning process. Sound rather mechanical? Even...*boring*? It shouldn't! Acquiring the data you need for call center planning and management will take you to distant corners of your organization and into the farthest reaches of the external environment. It is one of the most involved, politically-charged and outwardly-focused aspects of managing an incoming call center.

Sources of Data

The information necessary to plan and manage an inbound call center comes from many different sources. Consider the systems, departments and external sources of information that a call center for a financial services organization would turn to:

- •ACD
- •VRU
- •Databases

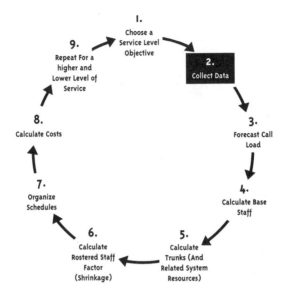

- Workforce management system
- Local telephone network
- Long distance telephone network
- Imaging servers
- Fax servers
- E-mail servers
- Web servers
- Vendors/suppliers
- Marketing department
- Legal department
- Upper management
- Human resources department
- Employees
- Customers
- Product development
- Regulatory bodies
- Economic reports
- The Federal Reserve
- Competition
- Media

Lots of information! Call center systems alone, especially the ACD, crank out reports with a vengeance. In fact, it's all too easy to get buried in information. As consultant Henry Dortmans of Angus Dortmans Associates puts it, "You've got to translate data to information, information to knowledge and knowledge into action."

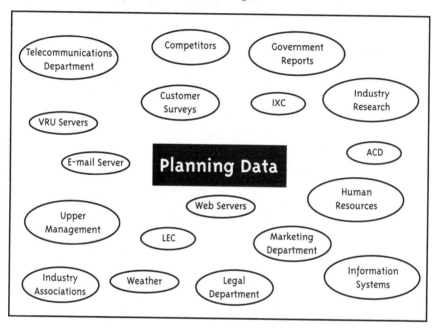

As new ways of handling calls are invented, it is even more critical to anticipate trends, measure the service callers are getting, and their perceptions of that service. Ensuring that your call center is acquiring, assimilating and utilizing the right information at the right times is one of your most important callings as a call center manager. That involves establishing a workable process, getting the tools that you need, and revisiting and refining this planning step often.

A Cross-Functional Process

Different aspects of call center management will require different types of information from different sources. But one thing is for sure: If you view the data-collection step as little more than a straight-forward, mechanical process, you're in trouble.

Many call centers have charged a person or a group of people with forecasting, staffing and scheduling responsibili- ties. As a part of their job, they are given the task of collecting information required for these activities. If they don't get the cross-functional input

> **If you view the data collection step as little more than a straight-forward, mechanical process, you're in trouble.**

they need, they are set up for failure. The organizations that do the best job of planning have developed cross-functional teams that are an integral part of the planning and management process.

Cross-functional planning groups can take many forms. For example, AT&T Universal Card Services has used a "customer listening post," which is essentially a weekly meeting with representatives from departments throughout the organization. Duke Power reorganized their entire organization (not just the call center) around major processes, and included representatives from the call center as a part of these processes. Retailer and catalog company Eddie Bauer set up a forecasting team that includes representatives from marketing and other departments.

An excellent way to identify necessary improvements to your process of collecting and using information is to create a flow chart. The chart can be simple, but should specify:

• The information you need
• What form it should take
• Where it comes from
• Who or what produces it
• How and when it fits into the planning process

The flowchart will identify missing links in your data collection activities and lead to ideas for developing a more integrated, collaborative approach. It should be regularly updated (e.g., quarterly).

Reporting Tools

New developments in call center reporting are creating new opportunities for more closely integrating call center activities with other parts of the organization, getting a handle on what callers are experiencing, and antic- ipating key trends. But good results don't happen just because new information is available.

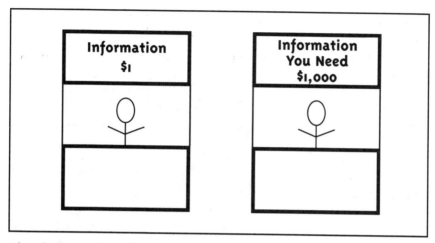

The challenge for call center managers is to identify both opportunities and potential problems information-generating systems provide, and to develop appropriate plans and guidance.

ACD Reporting

One of the key benefits of ACD systems has always been their ability to produce reports. Lots of them. In the early days, reporting was much more limited, and parameters were defined by the manufacturers. Today, a growing number of ACDs have the ability to directly connect to a local area network (LAN), so that the ACD is a more integral part of the organization's information system. With this capability, anyone on the LAN can view, print or store real-time and historical call center information, as defined by system administrators.

Many ACDs also have the capability to export data to a variety of formats, such as relational database programs and spreadsheets. This puts the information into environments that many programmers understand. They can then develop custom reports that combine ACD information with information from other systems.

Further, a key benefit of computer telephony integration (CTI) is the ability to produce reports that give a much deeper view of transactions. In addition to knowing how long calls queue, where they are routed and how long they last, you can analyze other details, such as keystroke sequence, databases searched, on-screen assistance provided, calculations performed, computer response time, etc. CTI capabilities can provide reports that give managers a "three-dimensional" view of activities.

Workforce Management Systems

Well into the mid 1980s, the perspective of ACD manufacturers was that forecasting, staffing and scheduling activities were management issues, and that the roll of the ACD was primarily to process calls. Many ACDs were limited to 24-hour historical reports, most of them defined by the manufacturer.

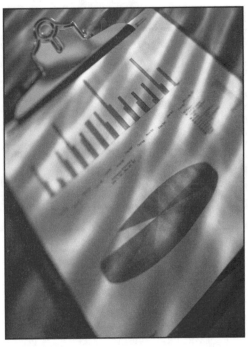

That lack of capability gave rise to a thriving third-party workforce management software industry. Workforce management software picks up where ACD reporting leaves off. It creates forecasts, calculates staffing requirements and organizes schedules. Many are also capable real-time management tools, providing a wealth of reports and updated

Old Reporting Environment	New Reporting Environment
Proprietary	Exportable to other formats and systems
Defined by system manufacturers	User-definable
Limited data storage	Large storage capacity
System-specific	Integrated reports from a variety of systems
Limited number of users	Accessible across the network (as allowed by system administrators)
Limited graphing	Expansive graphing capabilities

information as the day unfolds. What was a relatively small market niche a decade ago is today a growing, lucrative industry with dozens of suppliers.

Should you acquire a workforce management system? There are no hard and fast answers. But generally, if you have a call center with several dozen reps or more and have extended hours with overlapping schedules, the answer is yes. The alternative is to spend a lot of time creating spreadsheets or putting forecasts and schedules together by hand.

However, some managers get their expectations out of kilter and are later disappointed when the software doesn't do everything they thought it would. A workforce management program won't run your business. It won't coordinate with marketing, define agent preferences or develop good strategy. But if used correctly, it can be a time-saving tool that takes a lot of laborious work out of planning and management, improves accuracy and provides useful real-time and historical information.

Beyond Calls

Reporting and management tools for transactions that must be handled when they arrive are excellent. Modern call center systems provide a wealth of user-specified, detailed information.

Unfortunately, that is often not the case for transactions that can be handled later. Even high-end forecasting and scheduling software programs do not yet seamlessly factor these activities into the planning process. You can input them manually, but that assumes you are able to measure them and know what to enter.

There are notable exceptions. Many help desks have software programs that do an excellent job of tracking "open tickets" until a case is complete. And some call centers have developed custom software that tracks response time. But there is a lot of room for improvement.

There are two stubborn perspectives that are hampering progress in this area. First, many of us have assumed the ACD to be the dominant provider of information for so long, it's hard to imagine it any other way. But that framework does not adequately reflect today's environment. Second, vendors are beginning to give users what they want: genuine, open standards and toolkits for custom development. However, few users have taken advantage of these capabilities; most are still waiting for turnkey, "off the shelf" solutions. Whatever your reporting situation, at the very least you'll need to take adequate enough samples in order to perform the resource calculations we will cover in Chapter 6.

Look for more developments in the area of integrated reporting. The ACD-centric perspective will continue to fade. As users continue to clamor for improved reporting capabilities, manufacturers are working on standards that will further deliver on the promise of shared data across an organization and for the full range of activities common in today's inbound environment.

Revisit and Refine This Step

What's the main message of this chapter? *Collecting and utilizing the data you need is a planning step that you should continually reassess and improve.* This aspect of planning should always be a "work in progress." We will cover the specific information you need in the chapters that follow.

Remember to keep your eye on the prize. The purpose of information is to support key activities of the call centers that, in turn, support the governing principles and mission of the organization.

Further, it's important to continually revisit the issue of how you are using information and why. Which information is relevant? Which is useless? How do you want the information formatted and presented? Who should see what? How will the information be used?

Points to Remember

• The data required for call center planning and management comes from numerous internal and external sources.

• Acquiring and using the data you need should be a collaborative, cross-functional effort.

• Develop a flowchart of this step to identify weak or missing links.

• Continually review and improve your reporting systems and methodologies.

[Chapter 5:

----▶Forecasting Call Load...Etc.

The future is really the composite outcome of such a multitude of factors that, beyond a certain level, the precise computations of the highly trained and expensively equipped add little over common sense and a more generalized approach.

-Daniel B. Nickell,
author of *Forecasting On Your Microcomputer*, 1988

Yep, I still agree with that.
-Daniel B. Nickell, 1996

Matching up call center resources with the workload is a critical step in managing a call center effectively. This responsibility goes to the heart of incoming call center management: "Having the right number of skilled people and supporting resources in place at the right times *to handle an accurately forecasted workload*, at service level and with quality."

Here's the scoop: If the forecast is not reasonably accurate, the rest of the planning process will be off the mark. The forecast is the basis for determining staffing needs and requirements for other resources, such as how many workstations are required and how many lines are necessary. It provides the foundation for:

- Calculating base staff required to meet your service level objectives
- Calculating trunking and system requirements
- Minimizing abandoned and blocked calls
- Organizing accurate, workable schedules
- Predicting future staffing and network costs

- Meeting caller expectations
- Enabling an environment in which quality service can be provided

Art and Science

Forecasting is the proverbial mix of art and science. It begins with predicting how many transactions you are going to get in a future period, usually a year. To do that, you look at historical data to determine patterns that reflect when people call, and you consider possible trends that will affect call patterns. You then take that information and break it into the transactions that will be coming to you in different months, weeks of the month, days of the week, and half-hours of the day - or even five minutes of the half-hour, if you are forecasting peaked traffic. Next, you factor in the handling times of the transactions. Finally, you modify results based on conditions not reflected in historical data.

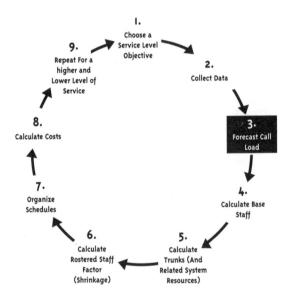

In the call center environment, longer-term forecasts look out a year and beyond. They are used to estimate future annual budgets, establish long-term hiring plans and define future system needs. Shorter-term forecasts project workload out to three months. They are necessary for organizing and adjusting scheduling requirements, anticipating seasonal staffing needs, planning for holidays, and determining imminent hiring requirements. Weekly, daily and intra-day forecasts are short-term tactical forecasts used to tighten up schedules and adjust priorities around current conditions and near-term events.

How far out you forecast will depend on the purpose of the forecast. Regardless, the basic principles and concepts are similar.

Essential Data

The basic historical data you need for forecasting includes how many inbound transactions you have received in the past, when they arrived and how long they took to handle. Four key terms reflect this activity:

Important Definitions

Talk Time: Everything from "hello" to "goodbye."

After-Call Work (Wrap-up): Work that is necessitated by and immediately follows an inbound transaction.

Average Handling Time: Average talk time plus average after call work.

Call Load: Volume x (average talk time + average after-call work)

• **Talk Time** is everything from "hello" to "goodbye." In other words, it's the time callers are connected with reps. Anything that happens during talk time, such as outbound calls or conferring with supervisors or an internal help desk, should be included in this measurement.

• **After-Call Work Time,** also referred to as wrap-up or not ready, is the time agents spend completing transactions after saying goodbye to callers. Legitimate after-call work should immediately follow inbound transactions.

• **Average Handling Time:** Average handling time (AHT) is average talk time plus average after-call work.

• **Call Load:** Call load is the volume of transactions coupled with how long they last. More specifically, it is volume x (average talk time + average after-call work), for a given period of time.

If the historical data you use to build your forecast ignores significant number of callers who got busy signals or abandoned their calls, you will be underestimating demand.

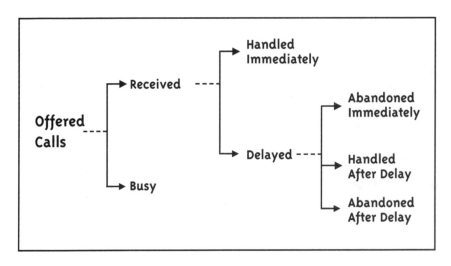

The forecast should reflect "offered calls" discounted for multiple attempts from individual callers. For the purposes of this discussion, offered calls are all of the attempts your callers make to reach you. There are three possibilities for offered calls: they can get busy signals; they can be answered by the system, but hang up before reaching a rep; or they can be answered by a rep.

Abandoned Calls and Busy Signals

Most call center managers opt to count abandoned calls one-for-one, which we generally recommend. The assumption is, if a caller abandons within a given half-hour, they aren't likely to call back that half-hour. Of course, if and when they do call back, they will be counted twice. Consequently, some managers use either judgment or calling number identification information to discount a portion of their abandoned calls from forecasting data. Ideally, the caller's first attempt to reach you is the half-hour in which they should be counted.

Busy signals can be a trickier matter. For every 100 busy signals you generated, was that 100 people who tried to reach you once each, or one persistent soul who tried 100 times? Of course, the answer is somewhere in-between. Busy signals should be discounted for retries, so that the forecast accurately reflects the actual number of individuals who attempted to reach you.

Don't blindly trust the rules of thumb that suggest callers will retry an average three to five times. That may or may not be true in your situation. The number of times someone retries when they get a busy signal is affected by the seven factors affecting caller tolerance.

Busy signals will result when you don't have enough physical capacity to handle the calls or when you've programmed your ACD system to reject calls from entering the queue if the wait backs up beyond a threshold you define. Consequently, data on busy signals may come from your ACD, local telephone company and long distance provider.

Virtually all ACDs have a report called "all trunks busy" (ATB). This will tell you how much of the time and how many times all of your trunks in a specific group were 100 percent occupied. But it won't tell you how many callers tried to reach you when all trunks were busy, so you'll still need additional information from your local and/or long distance network providers.

If you have an ACD that can generate busy signals, it will generally provide a report on how many calls received busies. But that still doesn't tell you how many individuals are represented by those attempts (unless you capture callers' numbers and sift out multiple attempts). You can usually obtain basic reports from your local and long distance providers that give data on how many times busies were generated, for specific time periods.

Within the past few years, some long distance companies have been providing reports that finally solve the retrial mystery. These reports provide actual retrial rates, down to specific increments of time that you specify. Actual numbers are a far cry better than "educated guessing."

Whatever the level of reports you can get, your forecast should as accurately as possible reflect the number of individuals attempting to reach you. If you count every busy signal and abandoned call, the forecast will overestimate true demand. If you ignore busy signals and abandoned calls, your forecast will underestimate demand.

Proportions

The fundamental information you need for call load forecasting includes the three components of call load: talk time, after-call work and volume.

	Calls	Prop.	Average Talk Time	Average Work Time	Average Hndl. Time
08:00-08:30					
08:30-09:00					
09:00-09:30					
09:30-10:00					
10:00-10:30					
10:30-11:00					
11:00-11:30					
11:30-12:00					
12:00-12:30					
12:30-13:00					
13:00-13:30					
13:30-14:00					
14:00-14:30					
14:30-15:00					
15:00-15:30					
15:30-16:00					
16:00-16:30					
16:30-17:00					
17:00-17:30					
17:30-18:00					
Totals/Avgs					

The Fundamental Quantitative Information Necessary For Call Load Forecasting

From this data, proportions can be derived. If you received 1,000 calls for the day, and 60 came in between 10:00 and 10:30, that half-hour's proportion would be 6 percent or .06 (60/1000). Proportions are used to project patterns into the future.

(Note: We discuss forecasting in the context of typical, random call arrival throughout this chapter. In many ways, the forecasting principles are similar for both random and peaked traffic. But the one big difference is in the level of detail you will need from your reports. While half-hour reports are sufficient for random call arrival, you will need historical reports down to much more specific increments of time, e.g., five- or 10-minute segments, in order to adequately forecast and staff for peaked traffic).

This is information your ACD and/or workforce management systems should be collecting *now and forever*. Building on this essential half-hour data, you will accumulate necessary daily, weekly and monthly data. Whatever you do, don't throw data away. You'll never know when you will need information about that campaign in '93. "Hey, how did callers react that time we..."

Repeating Patterns

Virtually all incoming call centers notice at least three dominant patterns in how calls arrive.

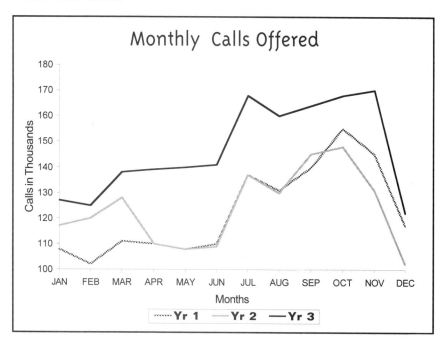

• **Month of year or seasonality**. The graph illustrates data from a financial company. Notice that the most recent year is at a higher plane, but looks similar to the patterns in previous years. Even if your organization is going through dramatic changes, you will usually detect seasonality in your call arrival patterns. Three years of data will provide a good reading on these patterns. If you have additional history, even better. If you don't have three years of data, use what you have; even one year will often reflect what is likely to continue.

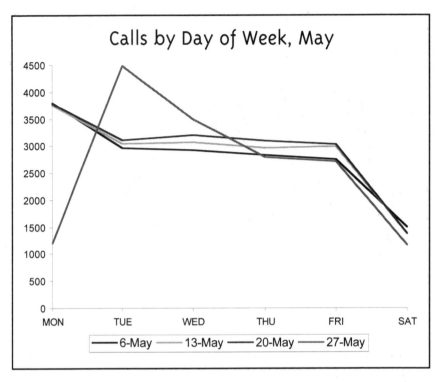

Day of week. The graph is from a telephone company. The first week reflects a holiday on a Monday. The call center was open, but of course, callers were behaving differently than usual. Consequently, that following Tuesday gets more calls than normal, illustrating the "pent up demand" that is common after holidays. Otherwise, the pattern is highly predictable from one week to the next. (Holiday weeks are predictable as well, if you have some history of similar holidays.) As the example shows, as few as four or five weeks worth of history can reveal this pattern.

Half-hour of day. The data for the graph is from a bank. Notice the system outage? That kind of exception from the norm tends to "stick out like a sore thumb." And it raises an important point: exceptions need to be pulled out of the data or they will throw off predictions. A week or two worth of data will often be enough to identify this pattern.

You may have other patterns as well. For example, if you send out statements to your customers on the 5th and 20th of each month, you'll notice day of month patterns. And marketing campaigns will create their

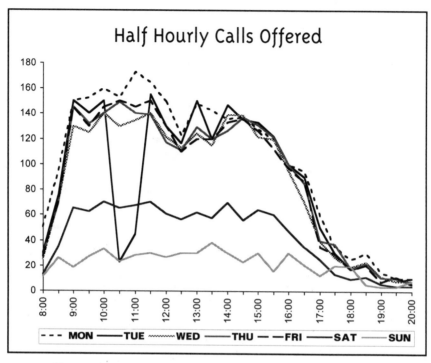

own traffic patterns.

Individuals call for a myriad of reasons, but become part of highly predictable patterns. It's pretty amazing, actually! Hey, whoever said that forecasting was boring?

So, one of the most essential steps in forecasting is to look at your data and identify the patterns that exist. Even if you are using forecasting software, it is still important to graph the "raw" patterns so you can identify exceptions.

Breaking Down A Forecast

Okay, grab a cup of coffee, roll up your sleeves and let's go through a basic approach that illustrates how to break down a forecast. This example starts with longer-term patterns, and works its way down to specific half-hour increments.

The steps involved include:

1. Obtain the number of calls received in the past 12 months, 720,000

Breaking Down A Forecast

720,000	Current year's calls
x 1.12	To add 12% (add after month prop.?)
806,400	Estimated calls in forecast year
x .071	January proportion
57,254	January calls
/ 31	Operation days-January
1,847	Average calls per day
x 1.469	Monday index factor
2,713	Monday's calls
x .055	10:00 to 10:30 proportion
149	Forecasted calls 10:00 to 10:30

Notes:

1) To determine operations days count the days call center will be open.

2) To caluculate day of week index factor, divide day of week proportion by average day of week proportion.

Example January

S	M	T	W	T	F	S
		1	2	3	4	5
6	7	8	9	10	11	12
13	14	15	16	17	18	19
20	21	22	23	24	25	26
27	28	29	30	31		

Example:	Prop.	Avg. Prop.	Index Factor
Monday	.210	.143	1.469
Tuesday	.170	.143	1.189
Wednesday	.165	.143	1.154
Thursday	.165	.143	1.154
Friday	.150	.143	1.049
Saturday	.095	.143	0.664
Sunday	.045	.143	0.315

in this example.

2. Multiply the year's calls by 1.12 to reflect 12 percent expected growth. Factoring in growth at this level assumes that transactions will increase proportionally to the previous years' patterns. If growth will instead be concentrated around marketing campaigns or other events that don't necessarily happen at the same time from year to year, you should factor it in at a more specific level, such as monthly or weekly.

3. Multiply the estimated calls in the year you are forecasting by January's proportion, 7.1 percent. This percentage comes from history and is the typical proportion of the year's calls that January receives.

4. Divide the number of operation days in the month into the estimated monthly calls. This yields average calls per day. In this example, the center is open every day of the month.

5. Adjust average calls per day, using the appropriate daily index factor. The first column in the index factor calculation gives the proportion of

the week's transactions that typically arrive each day. For example, Monday normally gets 21 percent of the week's traffic, Tuesday gets 17 percent and so forth.

The next column reflects the proportion of a week that an operation day represents. For example, if you are open seven days a week, each day is 1/7 or 14.3 percent of a week. If your center is open five days, each day is 1/5, or 20 percent of a week. A day in a six-day work week is 16.7 percent of the week.

The final column is the result of dividing the first column by the second column. These index factors are then multiplied against the average calls per day to estimate traffic by the specific day of week. In this example, Monday's index factor, 1.469, is multiplied against 1847.

6. The final step is to multiply the predicted calls for each day of the week by each half-hour's proportion. In this example, the half-hour 10:00 to 10:30 will get a projected 149 calls.

This process has got to take a lot of time, right? Actually, once you establish a system and an approach, it won't take nearly as much time as you may be thinking. You will get better at it with practice. And forecasting software or, at least, spreadsheets can take much of the labor out of it. But even if it does take time, forecasting is one of the most high-leverage activities in the planning process. You'll spend a lot more time "putting out fires" later on, if you don't have a good forecast.

This is a basic approach, and it's not perfect. But if you are pulling out the exceptions and working with good data, going through this type of process provides a good foundation to build on. You will still need to blend in judgment, coordinate with marketing, etc. After all, past history doesn't always reflect what's going to happen in the future.

You may also need to incorporate other patterns into the forecast. For example, if you send out billing statements twice a month, that will generate traffic a day or two after the mail drop. But the percent increase caused by these events will also fall into predictable patterns, and you can adjust accordingly. You may need to calculate day of month index factors, a process similar to deriving day of week index factors.

Holiday weeks will require their own index factors. But the pattern for one week with a holiday on a Monday will often be similar to another week in the year with a holiday on a Monday. Holidays that fall on various days of the week is another reason to hang on to your historical data.

Holiday Week Index Factors

Examples of Calculating Day of Week
Index Factors For Week With A Holiday
(divide proportion by avg. proportion)

	Prop.	Avg. Prop.	Index Factor
Monday	0	0	0
Tuesday	.290	.167	1.737
Wednesday	.240	.167	1.437
Thursday	.175	.167	1.048
Friday	.155	.167	0.928
Saturday	.095	.167	0.569
Sunday	.045	.167	0.269

Intra-day Forecasts

Intra-day or intra-week forecasts are quick and easy to produce and are often quite accurate. Typically, short-term forecasts are more accurate than long-term forecasts.

Intra-day Forecasting

402	Calls received by 10:30 a.m.
/ .18	Usual proportion of calls by 10:30 a.m.
2,233	Revised forecast for day
x .066	3:30 - 4:00 p.m. proportion
147	Intra-day forecast for 3:30 - 4:00 p.m.

The approach works like this: At some point in the morning, say just after 10:30 a.m., you begin to realize that this is not a typical day. Your reports indicate you have received 402 calls so far, which may be more or fewer than originally expected. Either way, you divide the usual proportion of the day's calls that you would expect by 10:30, 18 percent in this case, into 402. (18 percent came from looking at traffic patterns on previous days and calculating half-hourly proportions.) Bingo, you now know that if the trend continues, you can expect to receive 2,233 calls for the day.

Next, you can break the revised daily forecast down into the remaining half-hours by multiplying historical half-hourly proportions by 2,233. For example, since you would normally expect to get 6.6 percent of a day's calls between 3:30 and 4:00 p.m., you can expect 147 calls during that half-hour.

The assumption behind intra-day forecasting is that the morning will set the tone for the afternoon. However, if you are a utility getting swamped with calls in the morning due to a major power outage, this will be a bad assumption. When the outage is fixed, the calls will go away. In many cases, though, intra-day forecasting is a useful and accurate tool.

Intra-week Forecasting

3,050	Calls received on Monday
/ .23	Usual Proportion of calls by Monday
13,261	Revised calls forecast for week
x .17	Friday's proportion
2,254	Intra-week forecast for Friday

You can use similar logic to create an intra-week forecast.

Sales Forecasts

Some call centers use sales forecasts to verify or improve their call load forecasts. To use this methodology, you need to know the average sales value in the call center and the conversion factor (the number of received calls that result in a sale compared to the total calls received). The conversion factor can be expressed as a whole number or as a proportion. For example, if it takes five calls on average to make a sale, then the expected number of calls would be sales times five (i.e., 5 x 1,000 = 5,000). Alternatively, you could divide one by five to get a proportion and then divide the number of sales expected by that proportion (i.e.,

How Will Next Year Be Different? - Sales

	Jan	Feb	Mar	Apr	May	Jun	Jul	Aug	Sep	Oct	Nov	Dec	Total or Avg.
A. Projected Revenue	—	—	—	—	—	—	—	—	—	—	—	—	—
B. Average Sale Value	—	—	—	—	—	—	—	—	—	—	—	—	—
C. Number of Sales (A/B)	—	—	—	—	—	—	—	—	—	—	—	—	—
D. Conversion Factor 1/(orders/calls)	—	—	—	—	—	—	—	—	—	—	—	—	—
E. Projected Calls (CxD)	—	—	—	—	—	—	—	—	—	—	—	—	—

1,000 / .20 = 5,000).

The subject of sales forecasting is complex and you will need the input and collaboration of the marketing people in your organization. With their help, a sales forecast can provide a good sanity check to ensure that the call center is able to handle the load from marketing efforts.

Direct Marketing Campaigns

Organizations that run direct marketing campaigns often utilize response rates to forecast call load. Usually there is a taper down effect, where

Projecting Calls From A Direct Marketing Campaign

A. Target Audience Size _____

B. Overall Response Rate

(orders/target audience) _____

	Day 1	Day 2	Day 3	Day 4	Day 5	Day 6	Day 7	Day 8	Day 9	Day 10	Day 11	Day 12	Day 13	Day 14
C. Percent Overall Response	—	—	—	—	—	—	—	—	—	—	—	—	—	—
D. Projected Orders (AxBxC)	—	—	—	—	—	—	—	—	—	—	—	—	—	—
E. Conversion Factor 1/(orders/calls)	—	—	—	—	—	—	—	—	—	—	—	—	—	—
F. Number of Calls (DxE)	—	—	—	—	—	—	—	—	—	—	—	—	—	—

volume is relatively high in the initial days of a campaign and then tapers down over time.

One of the things that makes this tricky is that there are often overlapping campaigns going on at any given time. Another is deciding what constitutes an order - is it a single call from a customer or each item ordered? You will need to decide on definitions and stick to them.

Other Types of Transactions

Like inbound transactions that must be handled when they arrive, other types of work (e.g., faxes and customer e-mail) also occur in predictable patterns by volume and average handling time. They also usually have a strong correlation to other forecasts, such as the inbound call load, units of sales or number of customers.

Consequently, many of the same principles apply: look for patterns, break them down into proportions, and use the proportions to project future traffic. You will also need to blend in the appropriate amount of judgment, as discussed in a later section.

Average Handling Time

Many of us have a tendency to refer to call volume as if it's the only criteria in the workload: "How many calls did you get last year? How about yesterday? How about this morning?" Equally important, though, is average handling time which, when coupled with volume, makes up call load. It is call load that matters. Volume alone is relatively meaningless.

As with call volume, average talk time and average after-call work usually fall into predictable, repeating patterns. Similarly, the basic forecasting approach involves utilizing historical reports along with a measure of good judgment. You begin by looking at the average handling time for a recent week, broken down by half-hour. If the week is "typical," the data represented by this pattern is what will likely continue.

The graph of average handling time is from a mobile telephone company. Their average handling time went up in the evenings for several

> It is call load that matters. Volume alone is relatively meaningless.

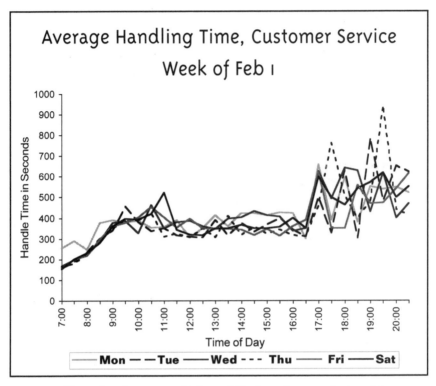

Average Handling Time, Customer Service
Week of Feb 1

reasons. First, they let agents bid on shifts based on seniority. Most reps when given the choice prefer to start and quit earlier in the day, so they had a higher concentration of new reps assigned to the evening shift. (That's not necessarily a bad approach, but it will impact average handling time and must be reflected in the forecast.)

Second, they did not have a good definition for after-call work, and much of it was getting postponed until late in the day. Third, their call mix changed throughout the day, and they got relatively longer calls in the evening.

Average handling time, like call volume, must be incorporated into planning by half-hour. Assuming the same average handling time all day for forecasting purposes will not reflect the environment accurately.

Some relatively simple analysis can go a long way towards tightening up your projections. Here are a few important prerequisites for getting this part of your forecast right:

1. **Look for patterns.** For each answer group, identify how average talk

time and average after-call work vary. You may also discover patterns by day of the week, season of the year, billing cycles and marketing campaigns. For a deeper look at average handling time, make separate graphs for average talk time and average after-call work. This will reveal the patterns for each. You will need these reports when calculating system resources, as discussed in Chapter 6.

2. Train your reps to use ACD modes consistently. Each rep has an impact on the components of handling time (talk time and after-call work) and, therefore, on the data that will be used in forecasting and planning for future call loads. When the queue is building, it can be tempting to postpone after-call work that should be done at the time of the call. This skews reports, causes planning problems and may lead to increased errors. An important and ongoing training issue is to define ahead of time what type of work should follow calls and what type of work can wait.

3. Identify the average handling time for different call types. This presupposes that you have defined and categorized calls by type, that you are accurately tracking calls based on the categories, and that you have

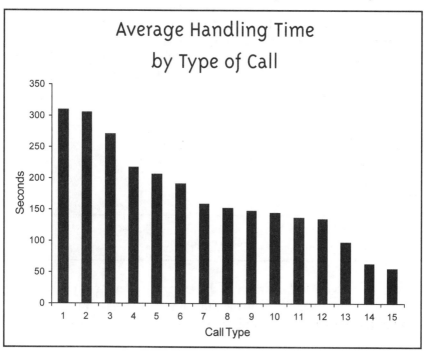

the reporting capability to link average handling time to the categories. A Pareto chart is generally the best way to represent this data.

You can use this information in a number of ways. For example, when you are forecasting an increase or decrease of a specific type of call, you will be able to project the impact on average handling time. A marketing campaign will generate certain types of calls. A new service on the Web, or calls coming through your voice processing system will likely reduce some types of calls reps handle (and may increase others). In each case, you'll be equipped to estimate average handling time.

4. Assess the impact of new agents and process changes. Less experienced agents often require more time to handle calls as they learn how to deal with processes, systems and callers.

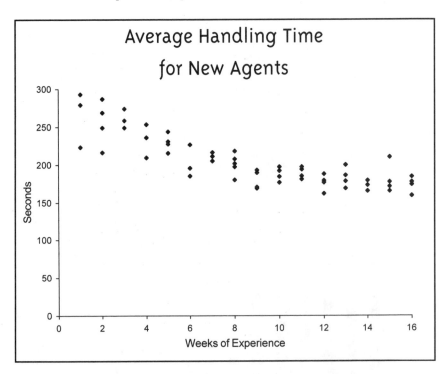

Compare average handling time to the experience levels of your agents. This will enable you to estimate the impact that new hires have on average handling time. It will also be useful in establishing realistic expectations for them.

Beyond the Basics

The major categories of quantitative forecasting include "time series" and "explanatory" approaches. The examples we have used in this chapter are fairly basic, and more advanced alternatives within each category exist. We mention them here to give you an idea of the breadth of possibilities.

Time series forecasting methods include simple or "naive" rules (e.g., the forecast equals last year's same month, plus 12 percent), decomposition, simple time series and advanced time series methods. The governing assumption behind time series forecasting is that past data will reflect trends that will continue into the future. Time series methodologies are common in workforce management software. Most time series forecasts are reasonably accurate when projecting out three months or less.

Explanatory forecasting methods include simple regression analysis, multiple regression analysis, econometric models and multivariate methods. Explanatory forecasting essentially attempts to reveal a linkage between two or more variables. For example, if you manage an ice cream shop, you could statistically correlate the weather (e.g., outside temperature) to ice cream sales. In a call center, you might correlate a price increase to the impact on calling volumes.

Advanced time series and explanatory forecasting methods go beyond the scope of this book. In fact, you can spend a couple of college semesters - make that a career - learning about forecasting. If you would like more information, we recommend that you start with a classic, *The Handbook of Forecasting: A Manager's Guide*, edited by Syros Makridakis and Steven C. Wheelright.

Blending in Judgment

So far, we've discussed quantitative forecasting - in other words, how to use hard data in your forecasting process. Judgmental forecasting goes beyond purely statistical techniques and encompasses what people *think* is going to happen. It is in the realm of intuition, interdepartmental committees, market research and executive opinion.

Judgmental forecasting can be influenced by things like politics and

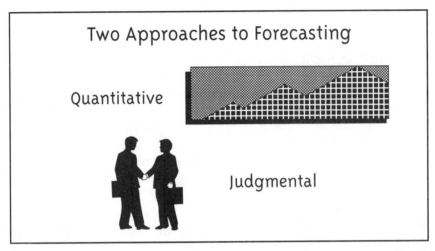

Two Approaches to Forecasting

Quantitative

Judgmental

personal agendas. However, some judgment is inherent in virtually all forms of forecasting. And a degree of good judgment can significantly improve accuracy. The trick is to combine quantitative and judgmental approaches effectively, and to be aware of the limitations of each.

The worksheet, "How Will Next Year Be Different," illustrates one way of applying "common sense and a more generalized approach" to forecasting. In a customer service environment, the number of calls is often primarily a function of the total number of customers or constituents in the organization's universe. It is possible to project calls based on historical data, utilizing the relationships between calling volume and total customers (calls per customer). To the degree that the future repeats the past, this forecast will be accurate.

Part D of the form is where judgment plays a significant role. In this section, you customize the forecast by adding or reducing calls, based on information you develop from your own and others' input. For some of these factors, you may have some hard data that you can use. For others, you'll be making more of an "educated guess."

The factors in Part D are only examples, and you will need to create your own list specific to your environment. For example, if you are a support center for broken down or stranded vehicles, weather would be a key influence on call load.

You will need a routine mechanism or forum for blending judgment into the forecast. A fairly common approach in incoming call centers is a weekly forecasting meeting. These meetings typically include members

How Will Next Year Be Different?
- Customer Service

	Jan	Feb	Mar	Apr	May	Jun	Jul	Aug	Sep	Oct	Nov	Dec	Total or Avg.
A. Projected Customers	—	—	—	—	—	—	—	—	—	—	—	—	—
B. Calls per Customer	—	—	—	—	—	—	—	—	—	—	—	—	—
C. Base Calls (A x B)	—	—	—	—	—	—	—	—	—	—	—	—	—
D. Activity Level Change					CALLS (+ or -)								
1. New Customers	—	—	—	—	—	—	—	—	—	—	—	—	—
2. Media Attention	—	—	—	—	—	—	—	—	—	—	—	—	—
3. Advertising	—	—	—	—	—	—	—	—	—	—	—	—	—
4. New Rate Structure	—	—	—	—	—	—	—	—	—	—	—	—	—
5. New Terms & Conditions	—	—	—	—	—	—	—	—	—	—	—	—	—
6. New Service Procedures	—	—	—	—	—	—	—	—	—	—	—	—	—
7. New Information Required	—	—	—	—	—	—	—	—	—	—	—	—	—
8. New Product Introduction	—	—	—	—	—	—	—	—	—	—	—	—	—
9. General Activity Level	—	—	—	—	—	—	—	—	—	—	—	—	—
10. Product Performance	—	—	—	—	—	—	—	—	—	—	—	—	—
11. Competitors' Actions	—	—	—	—	—	—	—	—	—	—	—	—	—
12. Other	—	—	—	—	—	—	—	—	—	—	—	—	—
E. Total (add 1 through 12)	—	—	—	—	—	—	—	—	—	—	—	—	—
F. Projected Calls (C+E)	—	—	—	—	—	—	—	—	—	—	—	—	—

of the scheduling department and a representation of supervisors and managers from the call center and other departments. The meeting will typically last only 30 or 45 minutes. It often works like this:

• The person in charge of the meeting prepares an agenda of items to be discussed.

• The scheduling person (or team) prepares the quantitative forecast before the meeting.

• During the meeting, the attendees discuss issues that may influence the forecast, such as those in Part D of the worksheet. Each participant brings a unique perspective to the process.

• As each issue is discussed, the forecast is adjusted up or down, based on what the group believes will happen.

The collaborative approach is most effective when key team members who are accountable for staffing take an active role in forecasting (in large call centers, they can be rotated through this process). The forecast not only improves as a result of their perspective, but they gain an understanding of the factors that contribute to staffing. As a result, they more effectively supervise their teams.

Common Forecasting Problems

In 1992, Incoming Calls Management Institute did a study into why some call centers have accurate forecasts and others don't. Ten common problems emerged, and we don't have any reason to believe that these factors have changed much since the research was compiled. They are summarized here, in no specific order. The good news? You can avoid these problems, and the remedies are fairly obvious.

1. **No systematic process in place.** There are often two erroneous beliefs that some managers use to justify the absence of a systematic forecasting process. Some say, "Our environment is too unpredictable. We're growing, we're introducing new products... There is no way we can expect to produce an accurate forecast." However, there are many call centers in highly volatile environments that do a respectable job of forecasting.

Others aren't convinced that forecasting is worth the time. Yep, it takes time - but not near as much as some imagine. Further, a good forecast will save a lot of time later on.

2. An assumption that "the forecasting software knows best." If you have forecasting software, don't blindly relinquish decisions to the program, assuming that it knows best. The software doesn't know what the marketing department is about to do, or that average handling time will be affected by changes you are making to your systems. And if you have busy signals, you will also need to ensure that the system incorporates adjusted offered calls, not just calls received by the ACD system.

Further, it is important to understand the assumptions your forecasting software is making. Some of the techniques it will utilize are user-definable. For example, you can program the system to give more weight to recent historical data, or you can tell it to ignore data that varies beyond X percent of the norm. It's a great idea to have the vendor provide a flow chart of the methodology the system is using and decision points where your input is necessary.

3. Not forecasting at the agent group level. Even a perfect forecast of the aggregate call load will be of limited use if you route calls to specialized groups. If you have a group of French-speaking agents handling services A,B and C, you will need to forecast calls from French-speaking callers who need help with those services.

4. The forecast is taken lightly. If the forecast has been ridiculously inaccurate in the past or if no one understands the assumptions used in the process, it will not be given the prominence it needs in the planning steps to follow.

5. Events that should be exceptions become a part of the forecast. Utilities tend to get lots of calls when storms knock out power, the travel industry gets swamped during airline price wars, and many call centers have, on at least one occasion, dealt with calls from an unannounced marketing campaign. (Have you ever sheepishly asked a caller, "What does the ad say we are offering?")

Those preparing the forecast have to be aware of the root causes of calls in order to make a good judgment on what is likely to continue (and therefore should be built into the forecast) versus the exceptions.

6. Good ties with other departments don't exist. Most of what happens in a call center is caused by something going on outside the call center. The forecast is doomed if strong ties with other departments don't exist.

7. Planning is done around goals, not reality. If staffing is based on a talk time of 180 seconds when actual talk time is more like 195 seconds, the resulting staff calculations and schedules will be based on a pipe dream. Sure, maybe talk time *ought* to be 180 seconds, and improved training, streamlined procedures and better systems would make that possible. But fudging on reality in the planning process is no way to achieve better results or build confidence in the forecast.

8. No one is accountable. As vital as a good forecast is, there is often no one who spearheads the effort. Someone needs to be responsible for bringing the various types of input together, ensuring that it is integrated into the forecast, and investigating which assumptions were off when the forecast is not accurate.

9. Agents are mixing flexible activities into the after-call work mode. If agents are not using the ACD modes consistently, especially after-call work, then accurate forecasting will be elusive.

10. Not making the connection with staffing. Forecasts mean nothing unless they are tied to staff and trunks required. That is the subject of Chapter 6.

Look Back and Adjust

How accurate should your forecast be? Large agent groups (100 or more reps) generally see relatively stable call arrival patterns and should strive for plus or minus 5 percent (or better) of call load down to the half-hour level. Small groups (15 or fewer reps) often have more volatile patterns and should shoot for plus or minus 10 percent. Those in-between should strive for something close to 5 percent. This is not to suggest you can't do better. But if your forecast is much further off the mark, your staffing calculations, schedules and budgets will be unacceptably inaccurate.

The call centers that produce accurate forecasts are not necessarily those that have the most stable environments. Rather, they have a group of people (or an individual) who have made accurate forecasting a priority. They have taken responsibility, established good ties with other departments, pulled in the data required, and established a forecasting process they are continually improving. They set accuracy goals and monitor progress. They consider accurate forecasting to be mission-critical.

As the saying goes, "The proof is in the pudding." Forecasting takes practice. You will never learn all there is to know about it. One of the most important steps you can take to improve accuracy is to compare your forecasts to actual results and then ask, "Why?"

Points to Remember

• Forecasting is a blend of art and science, and incorporates both quantitative and judgmental approaches.

• The forecast should accurately predict all three components of call load: talk time, after-call work and volume. Volume alone is meaningless.

• The forecast should reflect adjusted offered calls, or the individuals who try to reach you.

• There are a variety of quantitative forecasting methodologies. Time series forecasting is popular for inbound call centers.

• You need a mechanism, such as a collaborative weekly meeting, to blend good judgment into your forecasts.

• You should create a forecast for each agent group.

• A good forecast provides a solid foundation for the planning steps that follow.

[Chapter 6:

Determining Base Staff and Trunks Required

Having the right number of skilled people and supporting resources in place at the right times.

-Incoming Calls Management Institute

The key to achieving service level and response time objectives ultimately comes down to having the right people in the right places at the right times, supported by the right system resources. With a reasonably accurate forecast, base staff and trunking calculations are usually straight-forward.

However, there are two caveats to getting this part of planning right: 1) you will need to use the right methodology in your calculations, and 2) trunking should be calculated in conjunction with staffing because staffing impacts delay, which affects the load trunks must carry.

In this chapter, we will dispel the common myths about staffing and trunking. We'll look at the mechanics of correct calculations and how existing software tools can be applied to the task. We will also cover important definitions and measurements related to this aspect of planning.

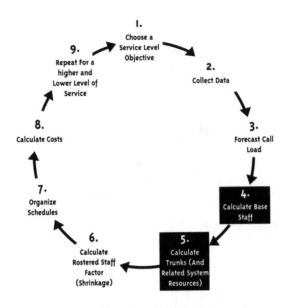

The Relationship Between Staffs and Trunks

To understand the association between staff and trunks, you need to know some key definitions. When interpreting the diagram of the definition, assume a "straight-in" environment, where callers dial a number and are routed directly to the agent group handling the calls. (This example assumes no VRU involvement).

• Delay: Delay is everything from when the trunk is seized to the point at which the caller is connected to a rep.

• Agent load: Agent load includes the two components of handling time, talk time and after-call work.

• Trunk Load: Trunk load includes all aspects of the transaction other than after-call work, which does not require a circuit. The "caller's load" is the same as the trunk load, other than the short time it takes for the network to route the call to the call center.

Notice that agent load and trunk load both include talk time. However, trunk load carries the delay, which is not a direct part of the agent load. And the agents handle after-call work, which is not carried by the trunks.

This realization leads to two important considerations when

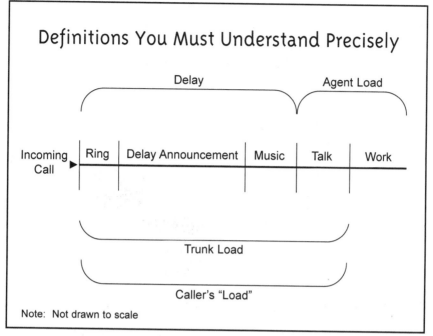

Definitions You Must Understand Precisely

| Ring | Delay Announcement | Music | Talk | Work |

calculating staff and trunks:

1. Staff should be calculated in conjunction with trunks. The more staff handling a given call load, the less delay callers will experience. In other words, staffing impacts delay; therefore, it directly impacts how many trunks are required. There is no way to know base trunking needs without knowing how many staff will be handling the projected call load.

2. There is no single staff-to-trunk ratio you can count on. You may have heard the rule of thumb that you need 1.5 trunks per agent (e.g., 15 trunks for every 10 agents). If that's the ratio you end up needing, it's purely chance. There is no ratio that can be universally applied. The reasons? For one, after-call work, which occupies reps but doesn't require trunks, is different from one call center to the next.

Second, caller tolerances vary widely among organizations, as influenced by the seven factors affecting tolerance (Chapter 2). If you have a high service level, the trunks will carry little delay. If your service level is low, the trunks will have to carry more delay and, consequently, you will need more trunks.

There's a better way to determine resources than to depend on ratios

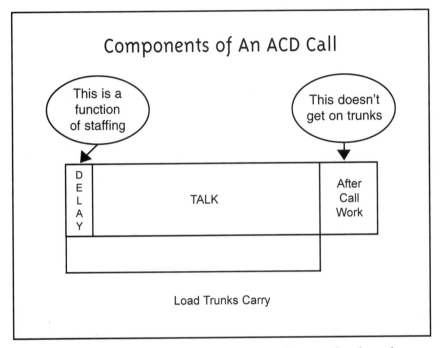

that may not work: calculate staff, then calculate trunks *the right way.*
Whatever the staff-to-trunk ratio turns out to be, that is what will work
for you.

Integrate Budgets

Despite the inextricable relationship between staff and trunks, call centers
have traditionally paid for these resources out of different budgets.
Telecommunications costs are paid out of one budget, and staffing and
other costs often come out of another. Unfortunately, that will cause
inaccurate budget projections and could lead to what the late quality guru
W. Edwards Deming called "sub-optimizing," where one aspect of the
operation is optimized in a vacuum while overall costs and performance
suffer. Staff and trunks are a classic example of the need to look at the
big picture.

"Wrong" Ways to Calculate Staff

To calculate how many staff you need, why not use this formula? Take the average handling time of a call (average talk time + average after-call work) and multiply it by the number of calls forecasted. Then, divide the result by 1,800 seconds (the total seconds in a half-hour). You may even build in extra time, such as an added 10 percent or 20 percent, assuming reps will actually need a breather now and then.

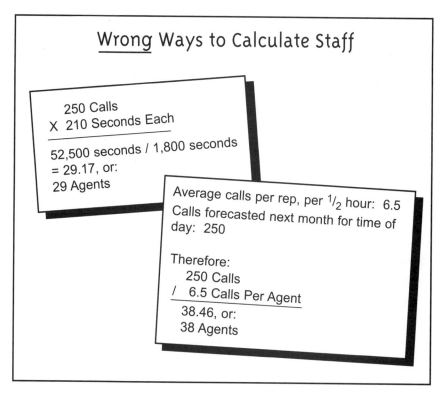

Wrong Ways to Calculate Staff

250 Calls
X 210 Seconds Each
_____
52,500 seconds / 1,800 seconds
= 29.17, or:
29 Agents

Average calls per rep, per ½ hour: 6.5
Calls forecasted next month for time of day: 250

Therefore:
250 Calls
/   6.5 Calls Per Agent
_____
38.46, or:
38 Agents

Or what about this formula? Determine the actual average calls per agent in a group. Then, divide that into the number of calls forecasted. Or use target objectives, as in "our reps ought to be able to handle X calls per half hour, therefore..."

These methods may sound logical, and some call center managers - quite a few, actually - use them. Unfortunately, they are dead wrong. They do not relate the outcome to a target service level. Further, they are based on moving targets. The average group productivity (calls that the group can handle) is not a constant factor. Instead, it is continually fluctuating because it is heavily influenced by vacillating call loads and the service level objective. But the biggest problem is that these approaches ignore a fundamental driving force in incoming call centers: *Calls bunch up!*

This figure illustrates a possible queuing situation (it's not as complicated as it first looks!).

Simulation of Queuing Situation

	Arrival		One Agent Case		Two Agents Case	
(1) Arrival Number	(2) Time of Arrival		(3) Time Call is answered	(4) Waiting Time	(5) Time Call is answered	(6) Waiting Time
1	0:04.3		0:04.3	0	0:04.3	0
2	0:04.4		0:07.3	2.9	0:04.4	0
3	0:15.7		0:15.7	0	0:15.7	0
4	0:17.3		0:18.7	1.4	0:17.3	0
5	0:21.1		0:21.7	0.6	0:21.1	0
6	0:22.1		0:24.7	2.6	0:22.1	0
7	0:25.4		0:27.7	2.3	0:25.4	0
8	0:26.3		0:30.7	4.4	0:26.3	0
9	0:27.4		0:33.7	6.3	0:28.4	1.0
10	0:27.5		0:36.7	9.2	0:29.3	1.8

Average Delay............2.97   .28

In this scenario, 10 calls arrive in a half-hour, and each call is assumed to last three minutes. The second column shows when each of the 10 calls arrives. The third column gives the time each call is answered, and column four is the waiting time (the difference between when a call arrives and when it is answered).

For example, call number two arrives 4.4 minutes into the half-hour, but has to wait 2.9 minutes before being answered because the first call is still in progress. With one agent, the waiting times build throughout the half-hour and beyond, and service is poor. With two agents, it's a different story; service is much better and waiting times are minimal.

If sorting out staffing for random call arrival is this involved with two agents, imagine a scenario with 15 agents. Or 115! The point is, if you want to determine staffing correctly, you need the right tools. You need a method that takes the usual randomness of call arrival into consideration. That means using the Erlang C formula (or a variation of it). It can also mean using computer simulation.

Staffing the "Right" Way

The widely-used Erlang C formula was developed in 1917 by A.K. Erlang, a Danish engineer with the Copenhagen Telephone Company. Erlang C can be used to determine resources in just about any situation where people might wait in queue for service - whether it is at a ticket counter, a bank of elevators or toilets in a stadium. Erlang C is currently built into virtually all of the commercially available workforce management software packages.

Erlang C calculates predicted waiting times (delay) based on three things: the number of servers (i.e., reps); the number of people waiting to be served (i.e., callers); and the average amount of time it takes to serve each person. It can also predict the resources required to keep waiting times within targeted limits, and that's why it is useful for incoming call centers.

As with any mathematical formula, Erlang C has built-in assumptions that don't perfectly reflect real-world circumstances. For one, it assumes that "lost calls are delayed." In plain English, that means that the formula

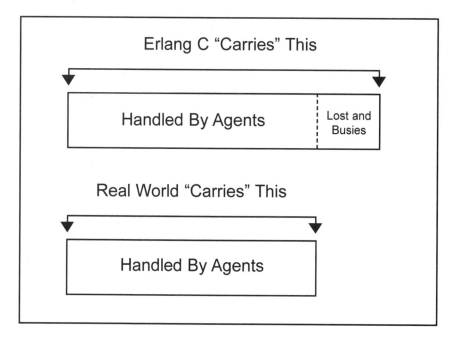

assumes that calls are queued. No problem with that. The problem is, it assumes callers queue as long as it takes to get an answer, or that nobody will abandon. *OOPS!*

Erlang C also assumes that you have infinite trunking and system capacity or that nobody will get a busy signal. But some call centers have quite a problem with busy signals. *OOPS again!*

The result is, in a nutshell, Erlang C may overestimate the staff you really need. If some of your callers abandon or get busy signals, your reps won't have to handle all of the calls Erlang C is including in its calculations. For a given level of staff, Erlang C predicts that conditions will be worse than they really are. Erlang C also assumes you have the same level of staff on the phones the entire half-hour. In reality, if service level starts taking a nose-dive, you may be able to add reinforcements on short notice.

Variations on Erlang C

Several companies provide traffic engineering formulas that are variations of the traditional queuing formulas. For example, workforce management supplier Pipkins developed the "Merlang" formula, a variation on A.K. Erlang's original work. Industry veteran Mike Hills, president of software concern HTL Telemanagement, developed the Hills B formula, which adjusts for Erlang C's tendency to overestimate staffing needs. "Erlang C is fatalistic and can overestimate required staff by 20 percent," says Hills. "No formula is perfect. But we have built-in assumptions that better model the real environment." ■

So, just how bad is Erlang C, anyway? "Erlang C is fairly accurate for good service levels," says Mike Hills, a software developer and recognized expert in traffic engineering. "However, for poor service levels, Erlang C overestimates how bad it really is. Reality will be nowhere as bad as Erlang C predicts."

Then, why is Erlang C so popular? As you might guess, there are defensible reasons to use it. For one, it's a planning tool, and most call centers are *planning* to have good service levels. When service level is decent, you should theoretically have little in the way of lost calls or busy signals. If you *do* have a lot of calls disappearing or getting busy signals, it's probably because you don't have enough staff to handle the load. In that case, who's worried about over-staffing? As your staffing more accurately reflects the workload demand, Erlang C will inherently become more accurate.

Advantages of Erlang C	Disadvantages of Erlang C
• Assumes random call arrival and that calls queue if a rep is not immediately available. • Is accurate at good service levels, where abandoned calls and busy signals are minimal. • Is easy and quick to use and available in software form from a wide variety of sources. Illustrates call center tradeoffs well (e.g., when service level goes up, occupancy goes down). • Is the basis for staffing calculations in almost all workforce management software programs.	• Assumes no abandoned calls or busy signals. • Assumes "steady state" arrival, or that traffic does not increase or decrease beyond random fluctuation within the time period. • Assumes you have a fixed number of staff handling calls throughout the time period. • Assumes that all agents within a group can handle the calls presented to the group.

Further, if you try to adjust for abandoned calls and busy signals, and retry rates are higher than you estimate, you could wind up underestimating staff. (And frankly there's a little industry secret...shhh...some call center managers have decided that a little over calculation as a safety net isn't such a bad thing. They figure that they fail to get full effective use of their already authorized headcount anyway, due to staff turnover and the time it takes to hire and train replacements.)

Erlang C is designed for straight-forward environments, like sales calls going here and customer service calls going there. But the realities of today are not so straight-forward. You may have complex routing contingencies in place, such as agent groups that overlap, skill-based routing and complex network inter-flow.

Enter computer simulation. What simulation does for call centers is

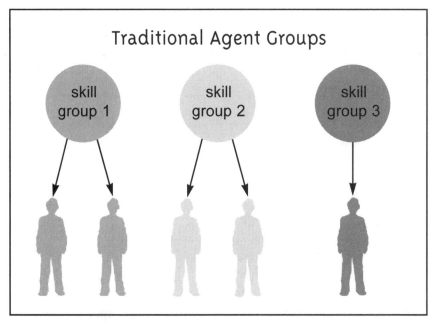

Traditional Agent Groups

skill group 1

skill group 2

skill group 3

comparable to what flight simulators do for airplane manufacturers. Boeing spent a lot of time simulating the design of their 777 aircraft. And they crashed a lot - on computer. By the time the real thing came out, they knew the ins and outs of good design.

Similarly, you can use simulation to resource your call center without making too many real live mistakes. Simulation programs are all the talk right now, and the vendors who provide this software (e.g., Bard Technologies, Systems Modeling Corporation, TCS, Rockwell and others) are riding a wave. Others who provide workforce management systems are also designing packages based on simulation.

However, computer simulation has some downsides. First, simulation is designed for modeling, design and verification, and is generally not meant to be a forecasting and scheduling tool. It's usually provided as a stand-alone system (although Rockwell's simulator is built into their ACD). As a result, you will still need your forecasting and scheduling software.

Second, simulation software takes a lot more time to set up and use than Erlang C. Like a flight simulator, you have to run it over and over to identify potential results. That is a phenomenon of its added flexibility, and the time spent will be time saved if you have a complex environment

Advantages of Computer Simulation	Disadvantages of Computer Simulation
• Can be programmed to assume a wide variety of variables, such as overflow, overlapping groups and skill-based routing. • The assumptions can include lost calls and busy signals. • May be programmed to use the terminology of your ACD vendor, for ready translation into your environment.	• Takes time to set up and use, and requires a relatively advanced user. • Is a stand-alone tool that is generally not integrated with forecasting and staffing modules. • Is generally more expensive than stand-alone Erlang C programs.

that requires a simulator's perspective. But it takes time to feed variables into the program and interpret the results.

Currently, Erlang C is still predominant in workforce management software. But a growing number of call centers are utilizing simulation.

So, what should *you* use? For fairly straight-forward environments with good service levels, Erlang C remains an accurate tool. And the variations on Erlang C, such as Hills B, may provide additional accuracy in some circumstances. If you have a complex environment (i.e., several languages to handle), there is something to be said for a combination of Erlang C, intuition and experience. But we recommend that you look into simulation.

Whatever methodology you use, remember that no formula or program can perfectly predict the future. As Hills says, "As much as I love it, traffic engineering is only a guide - not omnipotent."

Basic Staffing

For most of us, Erlang C in its raw beauty is unwieldy at best and totally unusable at worst. That's what prompted various sources to publish Erlang C tables before computers came along. But using an Erlang C table isn't that easy either because you have to take factors from the table, multiply them against the "holding time" and so on, to get usable answers. And using an Erlang C table is anything but self-evident if you

---

Erlang C

$$P\,(>0)= \cfrac{\cfrac{A^{N}}{N!}\cdot\cfrac{N}{N-A}}{\displaystyle\sum_{x=0}^{N-1}\cfrac{A^{X}}{x!}+\cfrac{A^{N}}{N!}\cdot\cfrac{N}{N-A}}$$

Where

A = total traffic offered in erlangs

N = number of servers in a full availability group

P(>0) = probability of delay greater than 0

P = probability of loss -- Poisson formula

---

want to relate staffing to service level. Thank goodness for software!

(Note, in the examples to follow, we are using an Erlang C program provided by Incoming Calls Management Institute. Similar Erlang C "calculators" are available from ACD vendors and software companies.)

Erlang C requires you to input four variables:

• **Average talk time, in seconds.** Input the projected average for the future half-hour you are analyzing.

• **Average after-call work, in seconds.** Input the projected average for the future half-hour you are analyzing.

• **Number of calls.** Input the projected volume for the future half-hour you are analyzing.

• **Service level objective in seconds.** If your service level objective is to answer 90 percent of calls in 20 seconds, you will input 20 seconds. If it's 80 percent in 15 seconds, plug in 15 seconds. In other words, the program needs the Y seconds in the definition, "X percent of calls answered in Y seconds."

Input the numbers, and "Voila!" the output provides a wealth of information and insight into the dynamics of incoming call centers.

Probably the first column you'll look at is labeled "SL," which is

Erlang C For Incoming Call Centers

Incoming Calls Management Institute
Annapolis, Maryland

Average talk time in seconds: 180   Average after call work in seconds: 30
Calls per half hour: 250   Service level in seconds: 20

TSRs	P(0)	ASA	DLYDLY	Q1	Q2	SL	OCC	TKLD
30	83%	209	252	29	35	24%	97%	54.0
31	65%	75	115	10	16	45%	94%	35.4
32	51%	38	74	5	10	61%	91%	30.2
33	39%	21	55	3	8	73%	88%	28.0
34	29%	13	43	2	6	82%	86%	26.8
35	22%	8	36	1	5	88%	83%	26.1
36	16%	5	31	1	4	92%	81%	25.7
37	11%	3	27	0	4	95%	79%	25.4
38	8%	2	24	0	3	97%	77%	25.3
39	6%	1	21	0	3	98%	75%	25.2
40	4%	1	19	0	3	99%	73%	25.1
41	3%	1	18	0	2	99%	71%	25.1
42	2%	0	16	0	2	100%	69%	25.0

service level. That's the X percent to be answered in the Y seconds you input. In the first row, the number 24 means that you'll answer 24 percent of the calls in 20 seconds. The next row is 45 percent, meaning 45 percent answered in 20 seconds.

Let's say your objective is to answer 80 percent of calls in 20 seconds. Keep going down the rows and...hey, where's 80 percent? The answers go from 73 percent to 82 percent. But where's 80 percent? You guessed it - the program is calculating staff required, and people come in "whole numbers," so some rounding is involved. Since 82 percent meets your standard, that's the row you would then concentrate on.

Next, glancing across that row you can see that you need 34 agents (first column), average speed of answer will be 13 seconds (third column), etc. In other words, each column provides insight and information into the service level you choose.

Here's what the column headings stand for:

• **TSRs** - Number of telephone sales or service representatives required to be on the phones. Throughout the book, we are using the terms agent and rep interchangeably. That's the number of people you need plugged in and handling calls - in this case 34 reps.

• **P(0)** - Probability of a delay greater than 0 seconds. In other words, the probability of not getting an immediate answer. In the example, 29 percent of calls will be delayed. That means that 70 percent won't be delayed, but will instead go right to an agent.

• **ASA:** Average Speed of Answer. With 34 reps handling calls, ASA will be 13 seconds. ASA is the average delay of all calls, including the ones that aren't delayed at all. In this example, 250 calls are included in the calculation. Remember in Chapter 3, we suggested ASA is often misinterpreted? Here's why. If, according to column two, P(0), 70 percent of the calls will get an immediate answer, that tells you that 70 percent of the input in the ASA calculation is made up of zeros. Actually, 13 seconds is the correct mathematical average, but it's anything but a typical experience. Most callers get through quicker than that, and some wait far longer.

• **DLYDLY:** Average Delay of Delayed Calls. This is the average delay only of those calls that are delayed - 43 seconds in this example. DLYDLY is a better reflection than ASA of what's actually happening to the calls that end up in queue. But keep in mind, it's still an average. Some calls wait five seconds and others may wait several minutes. If calls end up in queue any amount of time, they will be included in the calculation.

• **Q1:** Average number of calls in queue at any time, including times when there is no queue. The label is a misnomer, because Q1 incorporates all calls into the calculation, including those that don't end up in queue.

• **Q2:** Average number of calls in queue when all reps are busy or when there is a queue. In the example, an average of six calls are in queue, when there is a queue. Again, this is an average, and some of the time there will be more than six calls in queue, some of the time less. But this figure can provide useful guidance for what to look for when monitoring real-time information. It can also be useful for estimating the "queue slots" required by some ACD systems.

• **SL:** Service Level. The percentage of calls that will be answered in the number of seconds you specify.

• **OCC:** Percent agent occupancy. The percentage of time agents will spend handling calls, including talk time and after-call work. The balance of time, they are available and waiting for calls. In the example, occupancy will be 86 percent. Notice the tradeoff: when service level goes up, occupancy goes down. We will discuss this dynamic in Chapter 8.

• **TKLD:** This column is the hours (erlangs) of trunk traffic, which is the product of (talk time + average speed of answer) x number of calls in an hour. Since Erlang B and other alternatives used for calculating trunks often require input in hours, these numbers can be readily used as is. The actual traffic carried by trunks in a half-hour will, in each row, be half of what is given.

The mechanics of staffing are easy enough. Plug in your numbers and Erlang C gives answers. It's the interpretation that takes a bit of thought and application.

If you have never used an Erlang C program, we recommend that you get one and experiment with it. You will learn more about call center dynamics and tradeoffs in half an afternoon than it once took someone years of using tables or - heaven forbid - the raw formula to learn.

So far, you have calculated staff required to handle a specified mix of inbound transactions that must be handled when they arrive, for one half-hour of the day. You will also need to calculate base staff for each half-hour of the day and for every unique group of agents - sales, customer service and other types of groups you have. In Step 6, we will discuss how to factor in breaks, absenteeism and non-phone activities so that the schedule (Step 7) reflects the total staff you need.

Other Transactions

Recall the two major categories of inbound transactions defined in Chapter 3: First, those that must be handled when they arrive; and second, those that can be handled at a later time. Staffing for transactions that must be handled when they arrive should be calculated using Erlang C or computer simulation. Those transactions include inbound voice calls, inbound video calls, and transactions from the Web that are handled when they arrive or that require an immediate call back.

To calculate the staff required for transactions that do not have to be handled when they arrive, you can often get adequate results with more traditional methods of industrial planning. For example, if you have 50 customer e-mail messages to respond to that require an average three minutes processing time, there is 50 x 3 or 150 minutes of workload to handle. Since there are 60 minutes in an hour, the work will require 150/60, or 2.5 base staff hours. That's assuming 100 percent efficiency (which is not realistic), so you will need to adjust base staffing estimates upward. You also need to consider inaccuracies in staffing and plan for a margin of error.

(Note that some traffic engineers recommend using Erlang C when response time objectives are less than an hour. The assumptions of Erlang C are valid, because the work arrives randomly and is "queued" until handled).

The response time objectives you set for these transactions (Step 1) will dictate when this work must be scheduled. For example, if you promise a next-day response, you'll need to forecast the transactions for a day and ensure that enough staff are scheduled to handle the work within 24 hours. If you promise an hour response, you'll need to schedule enough staff to handle the transactions that arrive each hour within the next hour. You'll also need to factor in necessary breaks and other activities (Step 6).

Consequently, meeting response time objectives requires:

- Setting response time objectives.
- Forecasting these transactions, within time-frames specific enough to calculate base staff required.
- Calculating base staff needed.
- Factoring in breaks and other activities that will take staff away from the work.
- Factoring these staffing needs into overall schedules.

Staffing for Non-Traditional Groups

Today's inbound environment is often characterized by complex transactions and sophisticated routing alternatives. You may be utilizing skill-based routing, overlapping agent groups, sophisticated network environments and other configurations that go beyond simple ACD groups. Your environment will dictate the staffing methodology that will yield the best results.

Skill-Based Routing

Skill-based routing matches a caller's specific needs with an agent who has the skills to handle that call, on a real-time basis.

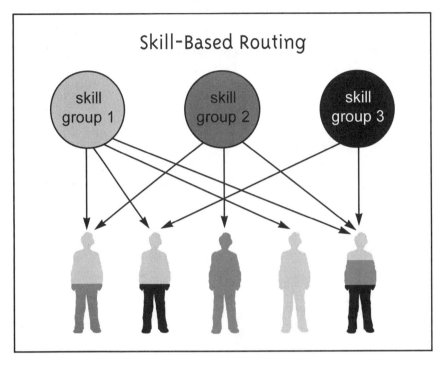

In this environment, Erlang C's assumption of traditional ACD groups no longer fits. But computer simulation can help fill the gap.

The basic requirements for skill-based routing include:

- Identify and define the skills required for each call type.
- Identify and define individual agent skills.
- Prioritize agent skills, based on individual competency levels.
- Devise and program into the ACD an appropriate routing plan.

You will essentially create two "maps" when you program your ACD for skill-based routing. One will specify the types of calls to be handled and the other will identify the skills available by agent. As an example, the maps for a technical support center handling calls across Europe might look like this:

Map 1

English-speaking callers who need assistance with modems.

English-speaking callers who need assistance with printers.
English-speaking callers who need assistance with fax machines.
English-speaking callers who need assistance with PCs.

French-speaking callers who need assistance with modems.
French-speaking callers who need assistance with printers.
French-speaking callers who need assistance with fax machines.
French-speaking callers who need assistance with PCs.

German-speaking callers who need assistance with modems.
German-speaking callers who need assistance with printers.
German-speaking callers who need assistance with fax machines.
German-speaking callers who need assistance with PCs.

And so on. The second map might look like this:

Map 2

Tom - Speaks English, Dutch and French. Trained on modems and printers.
Angelique - Speaks French and Italian. Trained on printers, PCs and fax machines.
Erik - Speaks Swedish, French and English. Trained on modems and PCs.
Maria - Speaks Spanish, Italian and French. Trained on printers and fax machines.

Consider a simple case that illustrates the basic steps in staffing for skill-based routing. Assume you have two languages to handle, English and Spanish. And let's say that you have four call types to handle, orders and

Agent Skills

Caller Types (Based upon VRU menu selections)	Agent Type 1	Agent Type 2	Agent Type 3	Agent Type 4	Agent Type 5	Agent Type 6	Agent Type 7	Agent Type 8	Agent Type 9
Orders - English	x	x						x	x
Orders - Spanish				x		x		x	x
Tech Support - English		x	x		x				x
Tech Support - Spanish			x			x	x		x

technical support calls in each language. The agent skills are illustrated in the first table.

Next, let's assume that your plan is to route calls to the least skilled agent who can handle the call because you want to preserve your more experienced or skilled agents for less common or more complex calls. Consequently, the routing plan would look like this:

Routing Plan				
Call Routing Hierarchy	Order-English	Order-Spanish	Tech Support-English	Tech Support-Spanish
Skill Choice 1	Agent Type 1	Agent Type 4	Agent Type 5	Agent Type 7
Skill Choice 2	Agent Type 2	Agent Type 8	Agent Type 2	Agent Type 6
Skill Choice 3	Agent Type 8	Agent Type 6	Agent Type 3	Agent Type 3
Skill Choice 4	Agent Type 9	Agent Type 9	Agent Type 9	Agent Type 9

You would set up the simulator the same way you would program the maps into your ACD. You tell it what types of calls you are going to get and the skills of your group. You will also plug in the same data required by Erlang C: volume of each transaction you expect, and corresponding talk time and work time estimates. Additionally, you can specify caller tolerance levels by type of call, trunking configurations and other conditions.

We used this data to run three different scenarios, all using the same call load and service level objective:
- Conventional ACD groups (one group for each call type)
- Skill-based routing
- Universal agents (a fully cross-trained group)

As the results in the table indicate, skill-based routing is more efficient than separate, segmented groups. Also note that universal agents, where each agent is fully cross-trained and speaks both languages, is the most efficient arrangement.

In general, skill-based routing works best in environments that have small groups where multiple skills are required. It can also help to quickly integrate new agents into call handling, by sending only simple

Results of Each Scenario			
Time Period	Separate Groups By Language and Call Type	Skill-Based Routing Scenario	Universal Agents
09:00-9:30	30	27	24
09:30-10:00	43	41	39
10:00-10:30	64	62	59
10:30-11:00	58	56	52
11:00-11:30	44	41	40
11:30-12:00	31	28	27

calls to them. It also has the potential to improve efficiency by matching up callers with "just the right agent."

Skill-based routing has some disadvantages, though. In application, it seems to be Murphy's Law that the agent with just the right skill is on break at the wrong time. Mapping out skills and programming routing scenarios is one thing. Getting people in the right place at the right times can be quite another. Small, specialized groups are tough to manage. And they can eliminate the efficiencies of pooling, common to conventional ACD groups.

Further, routing and resource planning becomes more complex. Be prepared to run simulation enough to learn what's workable in your environment. You also need to develop contingency plans, for when the call load of a specific call type is greater than expected, or when you don't have the specialized staff you planned for (e.g., because of sickness).

Skill-based routing is a powerful capability. But it must be managed well - that means going through the planning process diligently. You'll need a good forecast and solid staff calculations. Veteran call center consultant Todd Tanner offers good advice: "You've got to develop people in your call center who understand modeling projections, and the impact of a wide variety of variables on staffing calculations. You need these skills in-house so that you are equipped to respond to rapidly changing circumstances."

Also remember to work toward pooled groups, to the degree your circumstances allow. All things equal, an environment with proficient, cross-trained agents will always be the most efficient.

Network Environments

Networked environments, like skill-based routing, can introduce complex contingencies into staffing calculations. The method you use for calculating staff will depend on the type of networked environment you have.

Generally, you will have a network that is structured in one of three ways:

1. Percent allocation. With this configuration, the network is set up to allocate calls between sites, according to thresholds you define. For example, you may program 25 percent of your calls to be routed to one site, 35 percent of the calls to go to a second site, and the balance, 40 percent, to go to a third site.

Erlang C will generally provide good results in this environment. Even if you change call allocation throughout the day based on evolving circumstances, Erlang C will be an effective planning tool. As with ACD groups in a single site, you will forecast the call load you anticipate and run Erlang C calculations for each site.

2. Network inter-flow. Networks that are designed to inter-flow calls are a step up from straight percent allocation. In this type of environment, network circuits link the individual sites. Calls initially presented to one site can be simultaneously queued at other sites, based on thresholds you define. As circumstances allow, calls can then be sent from an original site to a secondary site.

Contingencies will vary based on how you program the environment. The criteria that determine how calls are inter-flowed can run the gamut, from availability at each site to the types of calls you are handling. For example, you might immediately send high-priority calls to available agents in any site, but queue lower priority calls longer in initial sites to avoid excessive transmission costs. Consequently, simulation can help to model and test the environment under different conditions.

3. Virtual call center. In a true, virtual environment, each call is routed to the first available agent (or longest waiting agent). Other contingencies notwithstanding, this environment represents a traditional ACD group regardless of where agents are, and Erlang C will produce accurate calculations.

Long Calls

Long calls pose another staffing challenge. Thirty-minute reporting periods provide an adequate level of detail and accuracy for most inbound call centers. However, some call centers, particularly those in help desk environments, handle calls that are complex enough that average handling time approaches or exceeds 30 minutes.

When long calls are not distributed as Erlang C assumes, they may violate the assumptions of the formula. Compounding the problem is the fact that ACDs often count calls in the period in which they begin, but report average handling time in the period in which they end. Consequently, reported averages can be skewed.

Maggie Klenke, of workforce management company TCS, has studied and lectured on this challenge extensively, and she recommends that report intervals may need to be adjusted upwards, i.e., to hours. This minimizes the effects of skewed averages. She also believes that "common sense needs to be balanced with statistics." For example, if long calls are an anomaly, you might opt to adjust your statistics before using your reports to project staffing needs. And to avoid a service level that ends up in the swamp, you might force higher staffing in hours when long calls arrive.

Most Erlang C programs will allow you to define the interval you want to examine, e.g., hours instead of half-hours. Alternatively, you can program a simulator to model the mix of calls you are taking. You will also need to consider how you manage long calls.

For example, Klenke points out some of the benefits of establishing a second tier of staff to handle complex calls: Calls to the initial group can be treated normally, all callers reach someone quickly, and those with simple questions don't have to wait for the second tier. Further, those with complex problems may be more willing to wait for service, and reps handling these calls can do so under less pressure. Be sure to also manage the service level of the second group, or service in both tiers will suffer.

Peaked Traffic

Peaked traffic, as discussed in Chapter 2, is a surge beyond random variation within a half-hour, which poses a unique staffing challenge. For the purposes of this discussion, there are two types of peaked traffic - the type you can plan for and incidents that are impossible to predict.

The calls that utilities get just after a major power outage will surge far beyond normal random variation. Similarly, if a national news program unexpectedly provides your telephone number to the viewing audience as part of its story, you will get unannounced peaked traffic. And it will be quite an experience.

The problem is, you can't predict these events, and you're probably not willing to staff up for them just in case they happen. So staffing for unexpected peaks falls more in the categories of real-time management or disaster recovery planning.

On the other hand, peaked traffic that you are expecting belongs squarely in the realm of fundamental call center planning. Forecasting, staffing and scheduling to meet a specified service level still apply. However, planning must happen at much more detailed periods of time, often in five- or 10-minute increments. For a given service level, peaked traffic requires more staff than random traffic, and agents will have a lower occupancy over a half-hour period.

Most use Erlang C to calculate base staff for predicted peaks. If you expect 200 calls in a five-minute span, that's the equivalent of 1,200 calls

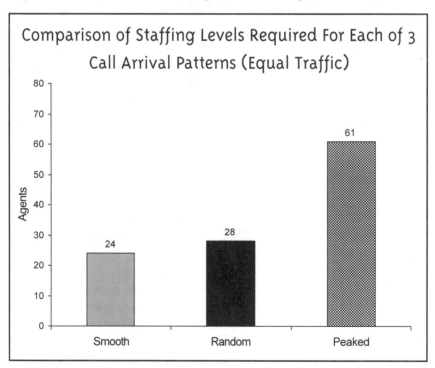

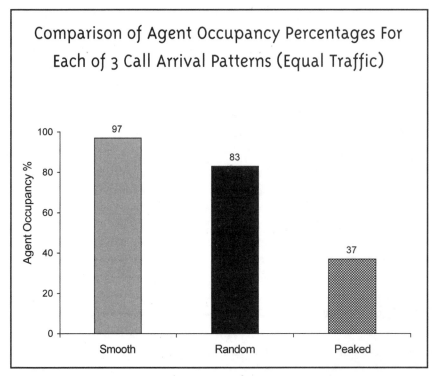

Comparison of Agent Occupancy Percentages For
Each of 3 Call Arrival Patterns (Equal Traffic)

in a half-hour. If you use an Erlang C program based on half-hour data, you will assume 1,200 calls for the calculations. Alternatively, some Erlang C software allows you to specify the time-frame you choose, and can accomodate short intervals.

But some common sense is required. If you have 75 people to handle the 200 calls, and the calls come in at virtually the same time, you know that the first 75 are going to get immediate answer. The next 75 are going to have to wait, and the average wait will be similar to the average handling time of the first 75 calls. The last 50 calls will have to wait something like two times the average handling time of the calls.

The situation can be similar to a bus dropping people off in front of Disneyland. Those reaching the gates first get quick service. For others, service levels can be dramatically different, depending on where they end up in the line. Consequently, how peaked the traffic is (how concentrated it is within a small period of time) will dramatically impact service level.

Calculating Trunks

You will need enough trunks to carry the delay callers experience (the time from the moment calls arrive at the telephone system until reps say "hello") and the conversation time (talk time), for the period you are analyzing. The general method for calculating trunks is as follows:

1. Forecast the call load (work load) to be handled for the busiest half-hour in the foreseeable future.

2. Compute the number of reps required to handle the forecasted call load at your service level objective.

3. Determine the trunk load, according to the call load you will be handling and the service level you can realistically achieve. The trunk load represents how much time in *hours* callers are in queue or connected to reps *over an hour*.

4. Determine the number of trunks required to handle the calculated trunk load, using an appropriate formula. Erlang B is widely used, but there are other alternatives you can choose from. Each has built-in assumptions. With any of the formulas used for calculating trunks, you will need to specify the probability of busy signals you can live with, because if you specify none, you'll need as many trunks as there are calls! But if you can

Formula	Assumptions
Erlang B	Assumes that if callers get busy signals, they go away forever, never to retry. Since some callers retry, Erlang B can underestimate trunks required.
Poisson	Assumes that if callers get busy signals, they keep trying until they successfully get through. Since some callers won't keep retrying, Poisson can overestimate trunks required.
Retrial Tables	Used less frequently by traffic engineers, but correctly assume that some callers retry and others will go away.

Sample Erlang B Table

Carried Traffic in Erlangs (hours)

Probability of busies:	0.01	0.02	0.05	0.10
Carried Traffic in Erlangs (Hours):				
25.0	36	34	31	28
25.5	36	34	31	28
26.0	37	35	32	29
26.5	38	36	32	29
27.0	38	36	33	29
27.5	39	37	33	30
28.0	39	37	34	30

** This table provides rows of answers based on increments of .5 hours of traffic (i.e., 25 hours, then 25.5 hours, etc). Most Erlang B tables feature smaller increments (i.e., 0.25 hours) and are therefore more precise.

tolerate even a small probability of busy signals, e.g., 1 percent, then the number of trunks required becomes much more realistic. In the sample Erlang B table, you can see that you will need 38 trunks to handle 26.8 hours of traffic with a 1 percent probability of busy signals.

If you have more than one trunk group, you will allocate the trunk load among your trunk groups, before calculation. For example, if 25 percent of the traffic will arrive on a trunk group that handles local calls and the other 75 percent on a group that carries toll-free traffic, you will need trunks to handle 6.7 hours of traffic in the first group (.25 x 26.8 hours) and 20.1 hours in the second (.75 x 26.8 hours).

You may have a VRU that callers go through before they reach an agent (to enter their account number, route themselves, etc.). If so, the time

Erlang B

$$P = \frac{\dfrac{A^N}{N!}}{\displaystyle\sum_{x=0}^{N} \dfrac{A^x}{x!}}$$

Where

A = total traffic in erlangs

N = number of trunks

P = grade of service

callers spend in the VRU will have to be factored into the calculations. And if trunks are shared among different agent groups, that would also be a consideration. Regardless, the basic concept holds true: staffing impacts trunking requirements. Delay is key - the fewer people you have for a given call load, the more trunks you'll need.

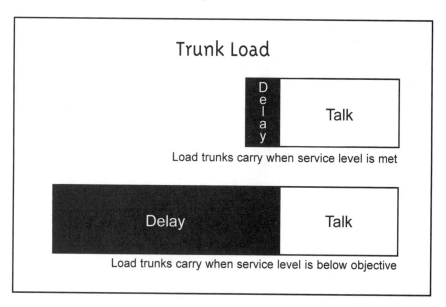

Our purpose here is to illustrate the relationship between staff and trunks, and introduce the basics of calculating the trunks you need. There are many possible trunking scenarios that go beyond the scope of this chapter, and we highly recommend that you get the help of a competent telecommunications professional to help you engineer your system. But ensure that they understand the relationship between trunks and staff. And make sure that staffing and trunking are coordinated activities, both in calculations and in your budgets.

Points to Remember

• Staffing and trunking are inextricably related and should be budgeted for and calculated together.

• The Erlang C formula is commonly used for calculating base staff and is easy-to-use and widely available.

• Computer simulation is more difficult to use than Erlang C, but can more accurately model complex environments.

• No staffing methodology is perfect, and it is important to understand the assumptions each makes and to blend in a good dose of common sense.

• Base staffing reflects "on phone" requirements. Steps 6 and 7 will incorporate other activities that keep agents from the phones, so that schedules are realistic and reflect total staffing needs.

[Chapter 7:

Scheduling Efficiently and Sufficiently

Where are they?

-Anonymous Call Center Manager

Scheduling is more of a challenge in today's environment than it was in call centers of yesteryear. A number of trends have contributed to this complexity. Modern call centers support a broader range of products and services than they did in the past. Technology has enabled many simple transactions to be automated, leaving reps with more varied and demanding calls, which often necessitate more off-line research, follow-up and training. And customers are utilizing a variety of communications media other than the telephone (i.e., e-mail, fax and VRU services) to interact with organizations.

Nonetheless, the core objective of staffing and scheduling remains the same as in the past: get the right people in the right places at the right times. This involves accurately forecasting the workload and correctly calculating base staff requirements. It then requires accurate rostered staff factor (shrinkage) calculations and schedules that realistically reflect the growing variety of events and activities that tug on reps' time.

From one perspective, a schedule is a high-level forecast. It incorporates all of the previous planning steps and predicts who needs to be where, doing what and when. It is also a "game plan" that is designed for people to follow. Consequently, you need both a schedule that accurately matches agents to the workload and good schedule adherence (we will discuss schedule adherence in Chapter 12).

The Scheduling Challenge

Before we head into the next two planning steps, let's take stock of where we are in the planning process. You chose service level and response time objectives (Step 1), acquired necessary planning data (Step 2), and forecasted the workload associated with the various types of work you must handle (Step 3). You then calculated base staff and trunks required (Step. 4 and 5).

A. 's point, if you graph out half-hour staffing requirements for any day of the week, you will see that you need different levels of reps every half-hour. And, you'll need different levels of staff for each day of the week and different seasons of the year. Scheduling for an average half-hour of the day, average day of the week or average month of the year will mean being either overstaffed or understaffed much of the time. Consequently, schedules need to reflect the workload as it changes throughout the day, week and year.

There is also another big scheduling challenge. Have you ever looked at a supervisor monitor or done a count out on the floor and wondered, "Where is everybody?" We have a hunch that every call center manager has asked that question at one time or another!

You can accurately forecast the workload, know exactly how many people you need on the phones, and still miss your service objectives by a long

Consequences of Being Overstaffed

-Unnecessarily high staffing costs
-Under-utilization of staff
-Boredom of staff
-Loss of credibility in budgeting

Consequences of Being Understaffed

-Unhappy callers
-Abandoned calls
-Longer calls
-More errors and re-work
-Higher telephone network usage and costs
-Staff stress and burnout

shot because you don't have the staff you expected in the right places at the right times. Consequently, schedules need to realistically reflect the many things that can keep reps from actually being at their desks, taking calls.

Most call center managers know that. Some, however, incorrectly add a fixed percentage to base staff, such as 15 percent or 20 percent. That approach will not be sufficiently accurate, because the things that keep staff off the phones *fluctuate* throughout the day and week. Breaks vary through-out the day. Absenteeism is usually higher just before and after weekends, and non-phone work will ebb and flow.

> *Thank you for holding. Currently our reps are either:*
>
> - *On a break*
> - *At lunch*
> - *Making personal calls*
> - *In a meeting*
> - *In the bathroom*
> - *Rebooting their computer*
> - *Researching something*
> - *Responding to correspondence*
> - *Sick*
> - *On vacation*
> - *Catching up with e-mail*
> - *Getting supplies*
> - *Stuck in after-call work*
> - *In training*
> - *Or, talking with other callers.*
>
> *Your call is important to us. Please continue to hold.*

As a result, you will need to account for these activities in a way that reflects their variation. That means calculating rostered staff factor (RSF).

Accounting for Shrinkage

Rostered staff factor, alternatively called an "overlay" or "shrink factor," is a numerical factor that leads to the minimum staff needed on schedule over and above base staff required to achieve your service level and response time objectives. It is calculated after base staffing is determined and before schedules are organized.

As far as we know, airline reservation centers began using the term rostered staff factor in the '70s. You'll see the term in call center literature, and you need to know what it means. But we think it sounds a bit stuffy, so we're going to use the term shrink factor. After all, shrink factor inherently describes the phenomenon - you schedule 50 people, but that

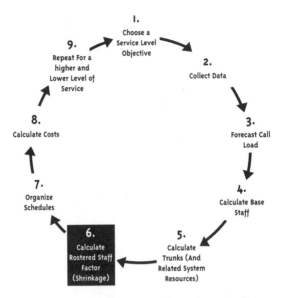

number shrinks to something like 35 who are actually on the phones handling transactions!

Calculating shrink factor is a form of forecasting. The major assumption is that the proportion of staff off the phones will be similar to what is happening now. In other words, if one person is on break in a group of 10, 10 people will be on break in a group of 100.

Basic Steps

An illustration of how to calculate shrink factor is shown in the following table.

Rostered Staff Factor (Shrinkage) Calculations

	Base Staff Required	Absent	Break	Training	On Schedule	Rostered Staff Factor
08:00-08:30	28	3	0	4	35	1.25
08:30-09:00	30	3	0	4	37	1.23
09:00-09:30	37	3	4	4	48	1.30
...						
...						

$$\text{Rostered Staff Factor} = \frac{\text{On Schedule}}{\text{On Phone}}$$

The mechanics boil down to five steps:

Step 1: Enter the base staff required by half-hour. What base staff includes will depend on the structure of your groups. If you have separate agent groups for transactions that must be handled when they arrive and transactions that can be handled at a later time, the base staff entered represents one of those groups. You will need shrinkage calculations for each group.

On the other hand, if you set up groups that handle both types of transactions, base staff is first calculated for both types of work separately (using the appropriate methodologies covered in Chapter 6) and then added together. You would then calculate the shrink factor for the combined group.

Step 2: Identify the things that routinely keep agents off the phones. The next three columns reflect the numbers of staff absent, on break and in training, as they now occur. These categories are just examples, and you can include research, outbound calls (those that are not part of talk time or after-call work) and other activities. You may also want to further subdivide the categories. For example, absenteeism can be divided into planned absenteeism, such as vacations, and unplanned absenteeism, such as sick leave.

Step 3: Add base staff to the number of reps that will be off the phones, each half-hour. The "on schedule" column is the sum of the entries in previous columns, by half-hour.

Step 4: Calculate shrink factor. The last column is derived by dividing the staff required on schedule by staff required on the phones, for each half-hour. The proportions are the mechanism you will use to project future shrinkage.

Step 5: Use the shrink factors when organizing future schedules. The result of these calculations is a set of factors reflecting expected shrinkage by half-hour. You multiply them against the number of people you will need on the phones when assembling future schedules. Bingo, the schedules more realistically reflect the staff you need to schedule, so that you have the right number of people on the phones when the dust settles.

For example, if you are putting together a schedule for two weeks from now, and you need 32 people on the phones between 8:00 - 8:30, you will need to schedule 40 reps (32 X 1.25) for that half-hour - plus any staff required to be working on projects, in meetings or anything else not included in the shrinkage calculation.

What to Include

Are we suggesting, from the example, that you can *forecast* absenteeism? Yes - at least it shouldn't be a total surprise. Granted, you won't be able to predict when the flu will sweep through. But take a look at absenteeism by day of week, and it will likely be higher before and after the weekend. That means Monday and Friday to many. Since weekends in some Middle Eastern countries occur on Thursday and Friday, call centers there notice that absenteeism is often highest on Wednesdays and Saturdays. And if you are open 24 hours a day, absenteeism for a given shift will likely be higher around whatever the "weekend" is for that shift.

Absenteeism, like the other factors, needs to be anticipated for specific times of the day. Strategies such as staggered schedules and part-time agents mean that absenteeism will vary by time of day.

While breaks and absenteeism should almost always be included in shrink factor calculations, other activities require some analysis and judgment. For example, should training be included? If training schedules frequently change and/or require differing proportions of staff, keep training information out of shrinkage calculations and instead factor it into schedules on a case-by-case basis. But if training happens in predictable proportion to the staff required on the phones, include it.

Improving Accuracy

Why bother with shrinkage proportions if you know how many staff you will need simply by adding the columns together? The answer is, without these calculations, you will spend about half your waking hours adding columns together. Shrinkage calculations not only improve accuracy, they are a big time-saver.

Larger call centers will pick up some accuracy by going through this planning step in 15-minute increments. In smaller centers, half-hour periods are sufficient, but you should use numbers that are conservative. For example, if you have two people on break the first 15 minutes of the half-hour, and four on break in the second half of the period, use four in the calculations.

If you calculated staff for hour increments, due to long calls (as discussed in Chapter 6), you can also generally calculate shrinkage by hour, since scheduled breaks and lunch tend to get moved around by long calls. If you find that hours are not picking up the activity accurately, drop to half-hour increments.

If you are handling peaked traffic, you can usually use half-hour increments for shrinkage even though you calculated base staff for shorter periods. Naturally, you will plan any activities that are flexible around the inbound peaks.

In many incoming call centers, shrink factor falls between 1.1 and 1.4 throughout the day, meaning that a minimum of 10 percent to 40 percent additional staff are required on schedule over those required on the phones. But don't trust rules of thumb; you will need to produce your own calculations. If non-phone activity is included in shrinkage, and there is a lot of it, shrink factor can be as high as 2.0, meaning that you'll need to schedule two people for each agent required on the phones. This is fairly common in some help desks that have extensive off-line research.

We recommend that you initially produce a table of factors for each day of the week and for each agent group you will be scheduling. Then, adjust the calculations as circumstances dictate (i.e., for vacation season or major changes in training schedules).

A Prerequisite to Effective Budgets and Schedules

Frankly, the phenomenon of shrinkage *really bugs* some financial people. And understandably so. "You mean to tell me we need to hire 42 people so we can have 30 on the phones handling calls?" (In our defense, *they* go on breaks, take vacations and handle a variety of tasks too, but don't try that argument!). There's simply no substitute for showing them what's going on and why the extra staff are required. As a result, shrinkage calculations are necessary to communicate budget requirements effectively.

An added advantage of making this effort is that it will force you to examine these activities - should they be happening when and to the degree they are? Some changes may provide better coverage or make scheduling easier or more acceptable to agents. Like any aspect of planning, examine how accurate your shrinkage predictions are compared to actual results, and adjust accordingly.

After you have calculated shrinkage, you know your staffing requirements accurately down to specific times of day. The next challenge is to identify scheduling alternatives and parameters so that you can organize schedules that closely match staffing requirements.

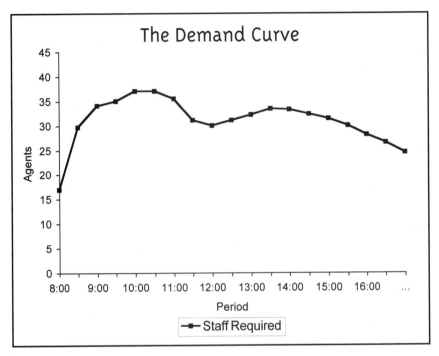

Scheduling Alternatives

Considering that staffing needs fluctuate significantly throughout the day, month and year, what alternatives exist for having an adequate number of people in place without being overstaffed much of the time? After all, we don't know of too many people who like to work half-hour shifts!

Fortunately, quite a few alternatives exist. Here, we've listed some of the strategies inbound call centers are using. Not all will be available for you. This aspect of planning involves putting the cards on the table - identifying the scheduling approaches that are feasible in your environment.

• **Utilize conventional shifts.** Many call centers have a core group of agents that work traditional five-day-a-week shifts during normal hours (e.g., 9:00 a.m. to 5:00 p.m.).

• **Stagger shifts.** For example, one shift begins at 7:00 a.m., the next at 7:30 a.m., the next at 8:00 a.m., until the center is fully staffed for the busy mid-morning traffic. This is a common and effective approach. Be sure to tweak these shifts as necessary because calling patterns can subtly move out from under what were good schedules.

• **Adjust breaks, lunch, meeting and training schedules.** Even slight changes to when these activities are scheduled can mean that a few more people are handling inbound transactions at just the right times. And that can make a big difference (review the staffing calculations in Chapter 6 and notice the impact of just one person on service level when it is low!). This alternative is available to virtually every incoming call center.

• **Forecast and plan for regular collateral work.** If you can accurately forecast incoming call loads (and you can), then you can forecast collateral work (various non-phone activities). Collateral work provides flexibility, if it is planned for and managed well. The objective is to have all hands on deck when the call load is high, and assign the flexible tasks to slower periods. Even if your agents are already swamped 100 percent of the time, manage this area well. After all, there are degrees to how bad things can get!

• **Schedule part-timers.** Some call centers are prevented from using part-time help by union agreements or logistics (e.g., complex call center services requiring extensive training). But when available and practical, this is a popular and common strategy.

• **Establish internal part-timers.** This approach is sometimes called the "reinforcement method." When phone answering duties are combined with other types of tasks, such as correspondence, outbound calling or data-entry, the agents assigned to these collateral duties can act as reinforcements when the calling load gets heavy. This is like being able to bring in part-timers on an hourly, half-hourly or even five-minute basis.

• **Create a swat team.** This takes the reinforcement method one step further. Vanguard, a large mutual fund company, keeps service level high by calling in "reservists," non-call center employees, to help when the call volume soars. Even the company's chairman, John C. Bogel, has been known to step in and help with calls.

This approach is not common, but it is gaining acceptance. Are your calls important enough to warrant at least some additional help from people elsewhere in the organization? Setup is not trivial. Plan on tackling training, scheduling, pay and cultural issues.

• **Offer concentrated shifts.** We humans are a diverse lot. Given the choice, some of us prefer to work fewer days, with more hours per day.

Others prefer to work fewer hours in a day, even if that means a six- or seven-day work week.

"Four by ten" shifts are particularly popular with many agents (four days on for 10 hours each, with three days off). But an important consideration is whether they can handle the longer hours without losing effectiveness. Ironically, short, easy calls (e.g., directory information) are tedious, and toughest to handle for long hours. Longer calls, even if complex, provide more variety and an environment more conducive to extended hours.

• **Offer overtime.** No additional training is required and many agents will volunteer for the extra work. But overtime can be expensive as an ongoing strategy. Further, as with concentrated shifts, an important consideration is whether agents can remain effective in extended hours.

• **Give agents the option to go home, without pay.** This is a popular strategy on slower days, and there are usually enough agents willing to take you up on it. It's something referred to as LWOP (leave without pay, pronounced "el-wop").

• **Offer split shifts.** Split shifts, where agents work a partial shift, take part of the day off, then return later to finish their shift, are not common. But don't count this alternative out all together. We've seen it work handsomely in some situations. If you hire college students, for example, they may prefer to work in the mornings and evenings, leaving afternoons free for classes.

A group of agents in one of Met Life's call centers volunteered to work in the mornings and come back for the less popular evening shift. They were happy to have the free midday time to play golf. Not a bad arrangement!

• **Arrange for some agents to be on call.** Although this strategy is also impractical for many and is not common, it can work in situations where events cannot be precisely predicted (i.e., catalog companies during the initial days of a new promotion). Typically, agents must either live near the call center or be equipped to telecommute.

• **Set up a telecommuting program.** This is not a scheduling alternative, per se, but it can provide an environment in which unpopular shifts can be more palatable and enable agents to begin handling the workload on short notice. JC Penney, Holland America Cruise Line and American

Express are just a few of the growing number of organizations that have successfully implemented call center telecommuting programs that are well beyond the trial stage.

WearGuard and Cross Country Motor Club Form Unique Staffing Alliance

WearGuard Corp., manufacturer of rugged work clothes and uniforms, has teamed with Cross Country Motor Club, an automotive roadside assistance company, in a unique staffing experiment. The two Boston-area companies' call centers recently began sharing reps to help each other meet seasonal needs and avoid employee layoffs.

The program was kicked off in 1996 when 35 WearGuard reps took calls from Cross Country customers, from March through August. The following October through January, Cross Country's slow period, 35 Cross Country reps handled calls for WearGuard. The program continues annually. Says Dea Harrington, vice president of operations for Cross Country, "It's like having a remote call center when you need it."

Before the staffing experiment, WearGuard had to add staff during their busy season, then lay off most of those people when business slowed down. Now, because the company takes Cross Country calls, call volume never slows down entirely, allowing WearGuard to keep some of those people. Ditto for Cross Country.

One of the biggest benefits of the arrangement is lower training costs for both centers because they don't have to constantly hire new people. As Barbara Piepenbrink, director of sales and customer service for WearGuard explains, "In the past, we brought in a new group each year who worked with us for just three months. It was like throwing money away."

To put the staffing partnership in place, the two call centers had to work through several wage and benefit issues as well as training and technology hurdles. Thanks to several months of planning, and the help of talented telecom people from both organizations, these issues were resolved.

> The partnership may not be for everyone. Says Harrington, "If we [the two companies] didn't have the same beliefs, it would never have worked." Piepenbrink adds, "Cross Country reps are like our employees. They understand our culture and are trained and supervised...by our own people. The result is better customer service." ■

• **Use hiring to your advantage.** An important criteria when hiring new reps should be the hours they can (or can't) work.

• **Send calls to a service bureau.** Service bureaus represent one of the fastest growing segments of the inbound call center industry. In the past, they were viewed by many call center managers as call processing "factories." The prevailing wisdom was, send simple, routine calls to outsiders, but don't send them complex customer service calls. Today, service bureaus of all types and capabilities are available. Some can handle calls of virtually any type or degree of complexity.

Case in point, Hewlett-Packard, Microsoft, and many others handling involved customer support calls now send part of their traffic to outside service bureaus. They work with them to staff and schedule agents, ensure quality and track activity. This trend follows the path many manufacturers have taken: keep strategy and analysis activities in-house, but outsource the tasks that somebody else can do better or cheaper.

• **Collaborate with similar organizations.** We believe there is a lot of opportunity for partnerships such as the one that WearGuard and Cross Country Motor Club have formed (see case study).

• **Sacrifice service level for a planned period of time.** It may be unrealistic for some customer service centers to meet service level objectives during the initial weeks of a new product introduction, or during the busiest season. Consequently, some plan to "sacrifice" service level for three to six weeks and rely on customers to understand. This must be carefully planned, and to be acceptable to callers, it must fall within the realm of their expectations.

Sometimes we hear defeatist attitudes related to staffing and scheduling: "Hey, they're going to give us what they are going to give us" (see next chart). But there are many scheduling alternatives available, even in relatively restrictive environments. Further, would senior

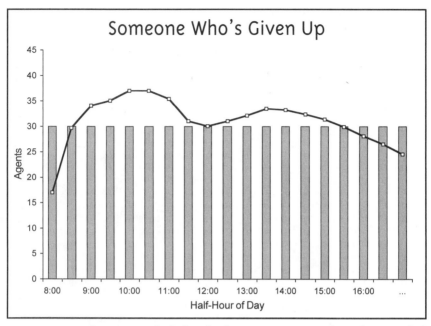

management be persuaded by budgetary requests based on solid planning? The answer is often an unequivocal "yes."

Putting the Pieces Together

As you identify scheduling alternatives, there are a number of other parameters to consider. For example, how far in advance will you determine schedules (the "schedule horizon")? If you schedule further out, say for two or three months from now, your schedules will be less efficient. They will be locked in place, even if call load deviates from the forecast. But a big plus is that they will be more agreeable to your staff, who prefer to know their work schedules well in advance. On the other hand, if you use a shorter time-frame, the scheduling process will be less popular with some agents, but schedules will likely be more accurate. So, this issue is a balancing act.

You will also need to carefully consider union and legal requirements. Restrictions on part-time staff, hours worked and overtime pay will impact the alternatives you can use. If you are in a union environment, union representatives should be involved in scheduling decisions up-front.

Scheduling is inherently an iterative process, meaning that it involves a certain amount of trial and error. Traditionally, scheduling has been geared towards matching up schedules with the inbound call load. A well-tuned schedule might look like the illustration, "Matching Supply with Demand."

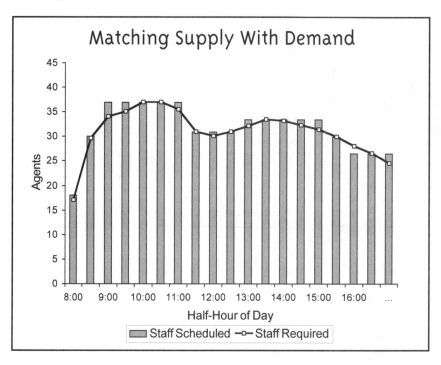

However, with more types of work to handle, many call centers are using an "envelope" approach. This strategy recognizes that some types of work have to be handled at specific times of the day, and other types of work allow more flexibility. The idea is to move in and out of the various types of work as circumstances dictate. This is sometimes referred to as a "blended environment," whereby agents handle a variety of tasks. (The term "call blending" also refers to a system capability that automatically switches agents from inbound calls to outbound, and vice versa, as real-time circumstances allow.)

Some try to tap into the envelope strategy by winging it. But that won't work. You still need to go through base staff and shrinkage calculations. And you'll also need schedules that, as accurately as possible,

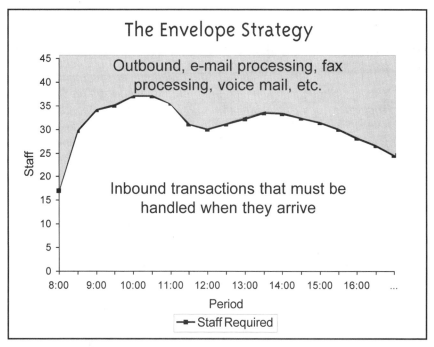

account for both types of work. But with good planning, this approach can be very effective.

Scheduling software can be a big help in shuffling the pieces and generating schedules according to the parameters you establish. Conversely, it can turn out schedules that people look at and say something like, "Are you kidding? There's no way we can adhere to that."

As in other aspects of planning, you'll need to make sure the software is considering all of the alternatives and parameters unique to your environment. You will also need to be realistic about agent preferences. If you involve agents in identifying scheduling possibilities up-front, they will often generate ideas you didn't consider and will better accept and adhere to the schedules that are produced. At the risk of sounding like a broken record: this, like other planning steps should be a collaborative effort; it involves a great deal more than mechanics.

How Did it Go?

Want to really know how well scheduling is going? Make a line graph of service level, as it was during a recent week. The line charts that follow represent agent groups in three different call centers (note, the hours and days of operation are different for each). Each chart covers a specific week, and each line represents a different day.

Because these graphs display actual results by half-hour, versus results for a single day or averages for a week or month, they can expose recurring problem areas.

The first graph illustrates a fairly consistent service level that is centered around the call center's target of answering 85 percent of calls in 30 seconds (minus a few short-lived problem areas). A consistent, on-target service level such as this is what you are striving for. If the graph doesn't look consistent, keep in mind that because service level is a high-level report, these graphs won't show stable, repeating patterns usually inherent with handling time or volume graphs.

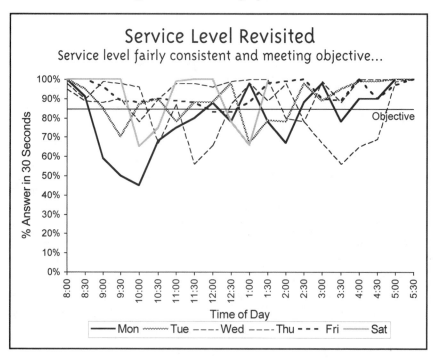

The next graph illustrates a service level that isn't so hot. You can see that service level is relatively consistent from day to day, but well below the call center's objective of answering 75 percent of calls in 20 seconds.

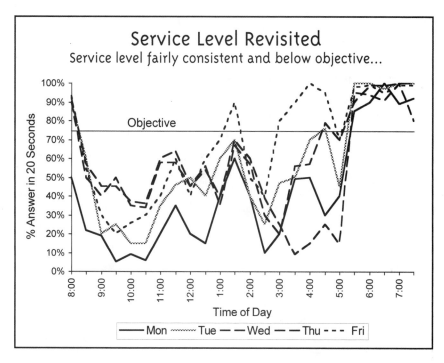

It dips mid-morning, mid-afternoon, and some around lunch time - probably the result of breaks and lunch.

The afternoons are consistently more...well, inconsistent. Our hunch is, call-related or non-phone work is building up through the first part of the day and being squeezed into the afternoons, often at the expense of service level. Monday (probably the busiest day of the week) takes a beating. Service level also drops Thursday afternoon, possibly the result of meetings, training or some other activity that occupies part of the staff. Based on these observations, you should investigate the following:

• Can breaks and lunch be adjusted to provide better coverage during the mornings and afternoons? For example, can you move lunch to a later time for some agents? Granted, you have to be reasonable - few would want to take a break at 9:00 a.m. or eat lunch at 3:00 p.m. But even slight adjustments can yield significant results.

• Is phone-related and non-phone work being forecasted and managed as well as possible? Do supervisors and agents know when to move from handling incoming calls into other types of work? Do they have real-time information on service level? Can some of the work be shifted into the evening when service level is high?

• Are there any scheduling strategies available that would provide better coverage on Monday? Are there any activities on Monday (non-phone work, meetings, training, etc.) that can be moved to another day? Is there any way to provide better coverage Thursday afternoon (maybe not; this may be the best time for the event that is affecting service level)?

• Do the resources exist to achieve the service level target, especially on Monday? Consistent results such as these can indicate that, when all is said and done, the group is doing about as well as it can. In that case, only additional staff or a reduction of call load is going to improve results.

The next figure reveals an erratic service level that is usually below management's objective of 80 percent answer in 20 seconds. This may be an indication that the resources to meet the objective are adequate, but that they aren't in the right places at the right times.

There are probably inconsistencies in how agents are handling the workload. Further, agents may not understand or have information on service level. Some of the issues to investigate include:

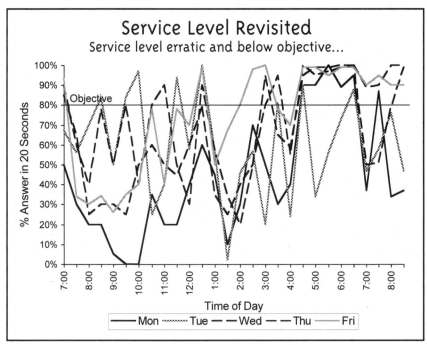

• Is non-phone work being forecasted and managed as well as possible? Can some of the non-phone work be moved into the evening when service level is generally better?

• Do supervisors and agents have real-time information on service level so they know when to sign-off or go into other work modes versus when to "plug in" and help handle the queue?

• Do agents use the after-call work mode consistently? Do they know what constitutes after-call work or are they mixing other activities into this mode?

• Are there scheduling strategies available to provide better coverage on Mondays?

• Is staffing adequate to achieve service level, assuming breaks, training and non-phone work are being scheduled as appropriately as possible?

Staffing and scheduling is an art which takes time, practice and collaboration to master. As the environment becomes more complex, this step becomes more important. The results you are getting are telling, and you'll learn a lot by making the effort to compare what actually happens to what was scheduled to happen.

Points to Remember

• Scheduling is both a forecast and a game plan. It requires accurate planning and good schedule adherence.

• Shrink factor (rostered staff factor) accounts for the things that routinely keep agents from the phones and should be calculated down to specific increments of the day.

• Many scheduling alternatives exist, even in relatively restrictive environments. You should regularly reassess which alternatives are feasible in your call center, and how you can use them.

• Service level graphs by half-hour reveal how well schedules are matching up agents to the incoming workload and will expose recurring problem areas.

Part Three:

Understanding Inbound Dynamics

There are important fundamental principles that govern how incoming call centers behave. Understanding them is key to everything from making a case for the budget you need to managing the call center in "real-time."

Chapter 8:   How Incoming Call Centers Behave

Chapter 9:   Conveying Call Center Activity to
              Senior Management

Chapter 10:   Managing Service Level in Real-Time

[Chapter 8:

How Incoming Call Centers Behave

Every why hath a wherefore.

-Shakespeare, *The Comedy of Errors*

As surely as the laws of physics define the parameters for air travel, fundamental principles govern incoming call centers. When these principles are misunderstood or ignored, the results are often poor or volatile service levels, inappropriate staffing, excessive costs and unhappy callers.

Six "immutable laws" are at work in any incoming call center. They are immutable in the sense that they are unchangeable, always have been with us and always will be with us. Understanding these dynamics is key to cultivating an effective planning process, setting fair standards, preparing accurate budgets, and communicating call center activities to upper management and others.

When Service Level Goes Up, Occupancy Goes Down

As discussed in Chapter 3, service level is expressed as "X percent of calls answered in Y seconds." Occupancy is the percent of time during a half-hour that those reps who are on the phones are in talk time and after-call work. The inverse of occupancy is the time reps spend waiting for the inbound calls, plugged in and available.

As the following table illustrates, a service level at 80 percent of calls answered in 20 seconds (82/20 to be precise) equates to an occupancy of 86 percent. If service level drops to 24 percent answer in 20 seconds, occupancy goes up to 97 percent.

Six Immutable Laws in Incoming Call Centers

1. For a given call load, when service level goes up, occupancy goes down.

2. Keep improving service level and you will reach a point of diminishing returns.

3. For a given service level, larger agent groups are more efficient than smaller groups.

4. All other things equal, pooled groups are more efficient than specialized groups.

5. For a given call load, add staff, and average speed of answer will go down.

6. For a given call load, add staff, and trunk load will go down.

The relationship between occupancy and service level is often misunderstood. The incorrect logic goes something like, "If reps really dig-in, service level will go up and so will their occupancy." In reality, if occupancy is high, it is because the reps on the phone are taking one call after another and another, with little or no wait between calls. Calls are stacked up in queue and service level is low. In the worst scenario, occupancy is 100 percent because service level is so low that all callers spend at least some time in queue.

When service level gets better, occupancy goes down. Therefore, average calls taken per individual also will go down. That suggests that setting standards on number of calls is inherently unfair, because reps can't directly control occupancy. Further, that would conflict with an important objective: ensure that enough reps are available to handle calls so service level objectives are achieved. (We will discuss individual performance standards in Chapter 12.)

Occupancy is driven by random call arrival and is heavily influenced

Avg. Talk Time: 180 sec; Avg. Work Time: 30 sec; Calls: 250				
Agents	SL% in 20 Sec.	ASA	Occ.	Trunk Load (in hours)
30	24%	208.7	97%	54.0
31	45%	74.7	94%	35.4
32	61%	37.6	91%	30.2
33	73%	21.3	88%	28.0
34	82%	12.7	86%	26.8
35	88%	7.8	83%	26.1
36	92%	4.9	81%	25.7
37	95%	3.1	79%	25.4
38	97%	1.9	77%	25.3
39	98%	1.2	75%	25.2
40	99%	0.7	73%	25.1
41	99%	0.5	71%	25.1
42	100%	0.3	69%	25.0

by service level and group size (see the third immutable law). Some managers can't stomach this reality - heaven forbid any "unproductive" time. However, the time reps spend waiting for calls is sliced into 12 seconds there, two seconds there, and so on - a factor of how calls are arriving.

In most call centers, reps handle various non-phone tasks when the inbound call load slows down. In fact, blended environments make a lot of sense because no one has a perfect forecast all of the time, and schedules don't always perfectly match staff to the call load (see Chapter 7). But don't be misled. When non-phone work is getting done, there are either A) more reps on the phones than the base line staff necessary to handle the call load at service level, at that time, or B) the service level objective is sacrificed. In other words, don't try to force occupancy higher than what base staffing calculations predict it should be.

What's Too High?

As any rep knows, extended periods of high occupancy are stressful. Studies suggest that from 88 to 92 percent occupancy is where reps begin

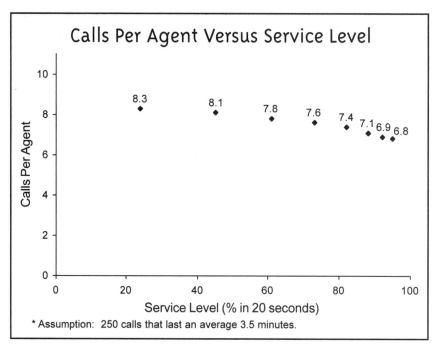

Calls Per Agent Versus Service Level

* Assumption: 250 calls that last an average 3.5 minutes.

to burn out, if the condition lasts for an extended time (i.e., several half-hours in a row). Most call center managers agree, but unfortunately, a high occupancy tends to feed on itself. Taking breaks is a natural reaction to high occupancy, and this tends to compound the problem.

As an example, consider this scenario. Jen, Ben and Mary are three of 32 reps plugged in and taking calls. The queuing formula Erlang C predicts that the average occupancy for the half-hour for 32 reps will be 91 percent and service level will be just above 60 percent answer in 20 seconds.

Jen: Boy, it's call after call this morning. I need a breather! I don't have a scheduled break for awhile so, let's see... I think I'll head to the water cooler for a couple of minutes.

OOPS. Now there are only 31 reps on the phone. If traffic keeps arriving at about the same clip, service level will drop and occupancy will go...up. Ben begins to ponder...

Ben: Things sure are busy today, just one call after another. And this caller sure is friendly. Wish everyone was this pleasant. I wonder what the weather is like where she is...

So, Ben takes a little bit longer on the call, service level drops another notch, and occupancy goes up more. Mary really begins to feel the load...

> When adherence to schedule improves (goes up), occupancy goes down.

Mary: This call doesn't really require wrap-up, but...!

This is the proverbial "vicious cycle." If things are chronically backed up, service level will consistently be low and occupancy will be high. The real fix, of course, goes to the fundamentals of managing a call center - a good forecast, accurate staffing calculations and schedules that match people to the workload.

Occupancy Versus Adherence To Schedule

Notice an important distinction that this law reveals. When adherence to schedule improves (goes up), occupancy goes down. Why? Because when reps are available to handle more calls, service level will go up. And when service level goes up, occupancy goes down.

The terms adherence to schedule and occupancy are often incorrectly used interchangeably. They not only mean different things, they move in opposite directions. Further, adherence to schedule is within the control of individuals, whereas occupancy is determined by the laws of nature, which are outside of an individual's control.

The Law of Diminishing Returns

Economists identified the law of diminishing returns many years ago as it applies to manufacturing environments, but it also significantly impacts incoming call centers. Let's define it this way: When successive individual telephone reps are assigned to a given call load, marginal improvements in service level that can be attributed to each additional rep will eventually decline.

The next figure is based on the data from the first table (based on Erlang C). It shows that 30 reps at the given call load will provide a service level of just over 23 percent in 20 seconds. Keep in mind, these numbers will not be exact - at that low of a service level, many of the calls may get cleared via busies and abandonments, so Erlang C may

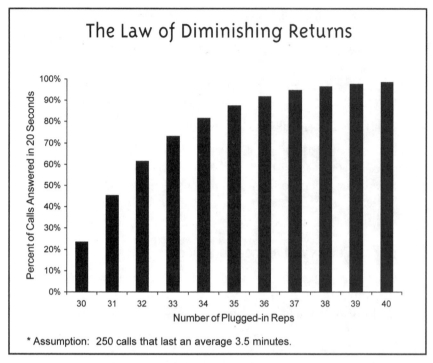

The Law of Diminishing Returns

*Assumption: 250 calls that last an average 3.5 minutes.

exaggerate how bad things will be. But the exact results notwithstanding, service level will be poor.

With 31 reps, things improve dramatically. Service level jumps to 45 percent, a quantum improvement. Adding one more person yields another big improvement. In fact, adding only four or five people takes service level from the depths of poor service to something respectable. That, of course, means a commensurate drop in average speed of answer (ASA) and trunk load.

The same principle is true for larger groups, as the next table shows. Each person has a significant positive impact on the queue when service level is low, even in groups with hundreds of agents.

Call centers who struggle with a low service level will like this law because it often doesn't take a lot of resources to improve things dramatically. On the other hand, those who want to be the "best of the best" in terms of service level find that it takes a real commitment in the staffing budget. The relationship between varying levels of resources and service level ought to be demonstrated in the budgeting process.

Viewed from a different angle, if you have the right number of people

	SL%			Trunk Load
Agents	in 20 Sec.	ASA	Occ.	(in hours)
117	7%	607	100%	437.0
118	24%	135	99%	175.0
119	39%	68	98%	138.0
120	51%	42	97%	123.5
121	61%	29	96%	115.9
122	69%	20	96%	111.4
123	75%	15	95%	108.4
124	80%	11	94%	106.3
125	85%	9	93%	104.8
126	88%	7	93%	103.7
127	91%	5	92%	102.9
128	93%	4	91%	102.2
129	94%	3	90%	101.7
130	96%	2	90%	101.4
131	97%	2	89%	101.1
132	97%	2	88%	100.8
133	98%	1	88%	100.7

Avg. Talk Time: 180 sec; Avg. Work Time: 30 sec; Calls: 1000 in 1/2 hr.

handling calls to begin with, but just a few of them unplug or go unavailable at an inopportune moment, things begin to back up. Think of what a stalled car blocking just one lane can quickly do to a busy expressway. This phenomena has been referred to as "falling in the swamp."

Swamp-Avoidance Strategies

Here are a few ideas to avoid this pitfall:

• Train every rep on how important they are. Everyone needs to be aware of how much they contribute, even if they are tempted to feel like just one of many!

• Provide real-time queue information to reps. Readerboards from a variety of manufacturers provide current data on the queue, and most have color-coded information for easy interpretation or to make the point (red means "help!"). Another alternative is detailed real-time information delivered to

> Everyone needs to be aware of how much they contribute, even if they are tempted to feel like just one of many!

displays on phones or computer screens. We will discuss real-time information in more detail in Chapter 10.

• Fix the basics, if necessary. If things are predictably and consistently backed up, occupancy will be high and you will have to be sensitive to the need for more breaks, even though they add to the problem. The real fix is in improving the planning process and making an effective case for the necessary resources.

Ultimately, there is a fine line between a service level that's good for everybody (callers and reps alike) and one that snowballs out of control, zapping the productivity and fun out of the environment.

Small Improvements, Big Results

From another perspective, this law reveals why improvements to call processes can yield such dramatic results. Some examples we have witnessed include:

• A consumer resource center for a major manufacturing company improved call tracking in its database system, clarified codes and rep training on call tracking, and assigned a small team to prepare reports for the quality assurance, marketing and consumer relations departments. While sales went up, call volume dropped by 7 percent, the result of preempting calls at the source. Service level has improved by 30 percent during busy half-hours.

• An insurance company, which upgraded their computer hardware to provide quicker response time, cut nine seconds off average handle time. Service level went up from 60 percent answer in 20 seconds to about 80 percent answer in 20 seconds during busy half-hours.

• A financial company, which added additional services to its existing VRU, reduced traffic to its customer service group by around 5 percent. Service level improved by over 15 percent during busy half-hours. (Note:

new VRU and Web services won't necessarily reduce the number of calls requiring live answer. We'll discuss this more in Chapter 13.)

Larger Groups Are More Efficient

Average group productivity (transactions that a group handles) is not a constant factor. Instead, it is constantly fluctuating because it is determined by the number of calls to handle and the service level objective. Therefore, if you hold the service level constant, and provide the correct number of staff on the phones to achieve it, you'll find that average productivity is relatively lower at lower call volumes and relatively higher at higher call volumes. Since the number of calls is changing throughout the day, so is average group productivity. (When we use the term "group," we are not referring to supervisory groups or teams, we are referring to call answering groups or queues, which could contain many supervisory groups.)

Calls in 1/2 Hour	Service Level	Reps Required	Occupancy	Avg. Calls Per Rep
50	80/20	9	65%	5.6
100	80/20	15	78%	6.7
500	80/20	65	90%	7.7
1000	80/20	124	94%	8.1
Assumption: Calls last an average 3.5 minutes.				

Why? Mathematically, larger groups of reps are more efficient than smaller groups, at the same service level. Therefore, larger groups assigned to heavy mid-morning traffic will be more efficient than smaller groups handling the lighter evening load. So, calculating staff the wrong way - assuming fixed productivity at different call volumes - will be highly inaccurate (see next chart).

This is yet another reason why setting standards on the number of calls reps handle is an inherently unfair way to measure productivity. Attempting to compare groups or sites in a networked environment may also be misleading (the exception would be a network that finds the longest waiting rep, regardless of location - a true virtual group).

Despite mathematical efficiencies, there is a point where groups

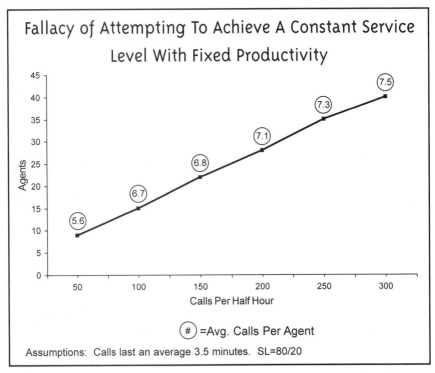

Fallacy of Attempting To Achieve A Constant Service Level With Fixed Productivity

(#) =Avg. Calls Per Agent

Assumptions: Calls last an average 3.5 minutes. SL=80/20

become large enough that occupancy becomes too high for reps to handle. Some managers believe that the number of agents in a single group should be limited to 125 to 150 people. However, there are plenty of call centers (i.e., Microsoft, USAA, United Airlines and others) that have much larger groups.

A better approach than establishing a strict limit to group size is to watch occupancy and take appropriate measures when it edges above 90 percent. For example, in the scenario on page 135, scheduling 130 plugged-in reps is recommended, even though the required service level may be exceeded. Callers sure won't mind, and your reps will have a fighting chance at being able to function at the end of their shift!

The Powerful Pooling Principle

The powerful pooling principle is a mathematical fact, based on the laws of probability, and is well rooted in telecommunications engineering practice. It states: Any movement in the direction of consolidation of resources will result in improved traffic-carrying efficiency. Conversely, any movement away from consolidation of resources will result in reduced traffic-carrying efficiency.

Put more simply, if you take several small, specialized agent groups, effectively cross train them and put them into a single group, you'll have a more efficient environment.

Note in the table on page 137, which compares service level to group size, 15 reps are required to provide a service level of 80/20. Only 124 reps

The Powerful Pooling Principle

• Handle <u>more calls</u>, at the same service level, with the same number of agents

• Handle the same number of calls, at the same service level, with <u>fewer agents</u>

• Handle the same number of calls, at a <u>better service level</u>, with the same number of agents

are necessary to handle a load 10 times as large, *not* 150 (10 x 15 reps).

The pooling principle should be a consideration from the highest levels of strategic planning (How many call centers should we have? How should existing call centers be networked?) down to moment-to-moment decisions about overflowing calls between groups.

In one sense, pooling resources is at the heart of what ACDs and networks do. In fact, when ACDs first came into the market in the early '70s, the big challenge was to get users to abandon the "clientele" approach.

A clear trend today, though, is the recognition that different types of callers often have different needs and expectations, and that different reps with a mix of aptitudes and skills are required. New capabilities in the intelligent network and in intelligent ACDs give call centers the means to pool resources as well as segment and prioritize their customer base. Skill-based routing is a notable example (see Chapter 6).

But, have we gone full circle? In 30 years, have we moved from specialization to consolidation and then back again to specialization? Can we have specialization without foregoing the benefits of the powerful pooling principle?

It depends. Consider two perspectives. As the case study in Chapter 6 demonstrated, skill-based routing can yield efficiencies over specialized, individual groups. However, when not managed well, the number of contingencies can multiply beyond the center's ability to understand and handle them. The interplay can become stupefying. And, the whole notion of call answering groups and traditional ACD organization can begin to erode.

One thing is for sure: As real and pervasive as the pooling principle is, it is not an all-or-nothing proposition. There is a continuum between pooling and specialization.

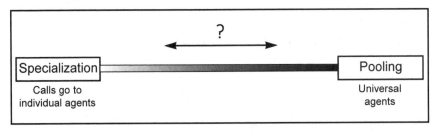

Your objective should be to get as close to the pooled end of the spectrum as circumstances allow. This requires developing a detailed flowchart, along with a certain degree of experimentation. More specifically, it means hiring multilingual agents, expanding responsibilities for reps, and improving information systems so agents are equipped to handle a variety of transactions.

Add Staff and ASA Goes Down

Anyone who has ever waited in line knows that if there were a few more toll booths or a few more people behind the counter, the line wouldn't be so long. And when someone behind the counter goes on break (invariably, just as you enter the queue!), the wait will increase.

The same principle is at work in incoming call centers. When more reps are plugged in and handling inbound transactions, assuming they are proficient and equipped to do so, the queue will be shorter. Fewer reps mean a longer queue. This principle leads to the next immutable law...

Add Staff and Trunk Load Goes Down

When more telephone reps are assigned to a given call load, trunk load goes down. The converse is also true: When fewer reps are available to handle a given call load, trunk load goes up because delay increases (see discussion on trunks in Chapter 6).

In an inbound call center, each person connected to your system requires a trunk, whether they are talking to a rep or waiting in queue. If you have toll-free service (or any other service which charges a usage fee), you are paying for this time. Telecommunications costs are inextricably wrapped in staffing issues. If service level is continually low, the costs of network services will be sky-high.

Look again at the first table in the chapter, and examine the tradeoffs between staffing levels and service level, ASA, occupancy and trunk load. If 42 reps are handling calls, ASA will be less than a second. If 30 reps are handling calls, ASA is predicted to be over 200 seconds. In short, the number of staff you have determines ASA, and ASA is a key variable in trunk load, and therefore toll-free costs.

Now, let's do a bit more analysis. As demonstrated, the trunk load will be 26.8 erlangs (hours) at a service level of 80/20. To make this easy for comparison's sake, assume that you get the same call load two half-hours in a row so that you will need the number of reps shown for the entire hour. You can then easily compare hourly staffing costs to hourly network costs.

Assume that each rep costs $15 per hour and that your toll-free service costs 12 cents per minute ($7.20 per hour). Using these costs, 34 agents will cost $510 per hour (34 x $15) and the toll-free service will cost $192.96 per hour (26.8 hours x $7.2 per hour) for a total of $702.96 per hour.

Now, use the same approach to analyze any of the other service levels. If you have only 30 reps available to handle calls, total costs will climb to $838.80 per hour, or $450 per hour for the staff and $388.80 per hour for the toll-free service. For 38 reps, total costs are $752.16 per hour, or $570 per hour for staff and $182.16 per hour for toll-free service. The graph illustrates these figures.

In short, staffing affects toll-free service costs. Saving a nickel on staffing levels can result in spending a dime on the network. There may also be other considerations - busies and abandonments (likely at low

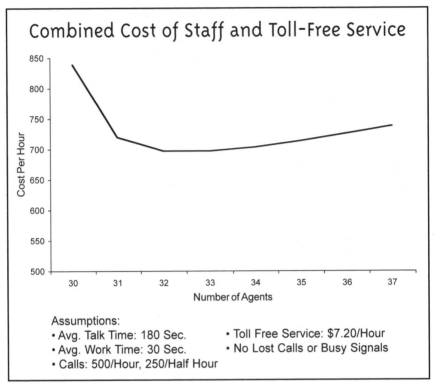

Combined Cost of Staff and Toll-Free Service

Cost Per Hour (y-axis): 500, 550, 600, 650, 700, 750, 800, 850

Number of Agents (x-axis): 30, 31, 32, 33, 34, 35, 36, 37

Assumptions:
- Avg. Talk Time: 180 Sec.
- Avg. Work Time: 30 Sec.
- Calls: 500/Hour, 250/Half Hour
- Toll Free Service: $7.20/Hour
- No Lost Calls or Busy Signals

service levels), and answer-delay (whereby the ACD doesn't immediately return "answer-supervision" to the long distance carrier) may lower toll-free costs. Nonetheless, the tradeoff between staff and network costs is direct and reasonably predictable.

The direct expense of putting callers in queue is called the "cost of delay." It is expressed in terms of how much you pay for your network service each day just for callers to wait in queue until they reach a representative. We recommend that you plot the cost of delay each day.

Making a graph of your cost of delay is relatively simple. First, take the total delay (time callers spend in queue before reaching reps) as reported by your ACD for the day and convert that to minutes or hours. Next, multiply the minutes or hours of delay by your average per minute or per hour network service cost. The final step is to walk to the wall (where you've prominently displayed the chart!) and draw in the new point. The process takes only a few minutes.

The graph will be a constant reminder that poor service is not cheap,

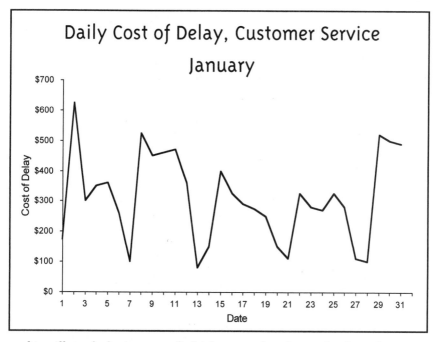

Daily Cost of Delay, Customer Service
January

and it will catch the interest of a higher-up when he or she drops by..."You mean that's what we're paying just for callers to wait? Why, we could use that money for..."

The main message in all of this is: As you estimate staffing levels necessary to handle your forecasted workload, you should also incorporate network costs. If your service level is struggling, improving it will mean reduced delay, which often translates into lower overall costs. Of course, a less measurable (but very real) benefit of reducing delay is the positive impact on callers' perceptions, and the commensurate improvements in good will, customer retention and positive word of mouth about your organization.

Knowing these tradeoffs will lead to better decisions. And you'll be equipped to diffuse the faulty logic, "We aren't achieving a very good service level because we had to cut costs."

Points to Remember

• There are six important immutable laws at work in any inbound call center.

• A common theme runs through these laws: do a good job of matching staff with the workload or *bad things* will happen.

• The impetus doesn't fall solely on those who do the planning and scheduling. Designing and managing an incoming call center requires a big picture perspective and the collaborative effort of all involved.

• A good understanding of these principles is fundamental to a workable planning process, accurate budgets, fair standards and good strategy.

[Chapter 9:

→Conveying Call Center Activity
to Senior Management

Talk low, talk slow and don't say too much.

-John Wayne

C all center management has the responsibility of succinctly, but adequately, conveying call center activity to senior management. And that can be quite a balancing act! There's a lot going on in call centers, and simplified summary reports often gloss over important details. Complex reports filled with pages of numbers may give more information, but senior managers may not have the time - or the expertise - to read and understand complicated call center statistics.

Conveying call center information in a thorough, but straight-forward format is critical if your reports are to be read and understood. For many call center managers, determining what to include and how to present the material can be one of the most difficult tasks they face. But when done correctly, these reports will give senior management an accurate understanding of what is going on in the center, what resources are needed and what objectives are realistic.

In this chapter, we will review the essential areas of the reporting process, which will help you find the right balance in producing and communicating critical reports.

Ten Things Senior Management Should Understand About Incoming Call Centers

Call centers have become recognized as a major force in competitiveness, are significantly impacting the allocation of organizational resources and are transforming economies. As a result, "selling" senior management on the call center concept has become much easier for most call center managers.

A prerequisite to getting good support from senior management, and from managers in other key areas, such as marketing, information systems, telecommunications and human resources, is that they have a basic working knowledge of how incoming call centers tick. Here's a summary of 10 things that, at a minimum, they need to know about call centers.

1. Calls bunch up. As discussed in Chapter 2, calls arrive randomly (or as peaked traffic). Senior management needs to know that planning for a workload that arrives randomly is different than planning for workload in other parts of the organization. Callers decide when they will call, and the work will not arrive in a nice, even flow. Reps can't complete work in advance and set finished work aside. Consequently, staffing and productivity issues must be considered in this context.

2. There's a direct link between resources and results. You may need 36 people on the phones to achieve a service level of 90 percent answer in 20 seconds, given your call load. But if you have 25 and are told to hit 90/20, that's not going to work. That's an example of mutually exclusive objectives. It behooves the call center manager to constantly reinforce the fact that a certain level of resources are required to achieve a specified result (see Chapter 6).

3. "Staffing on the cheap" is expensive. If you provide toll-free service for callers, you are paying for the time they spend waiting in queue (see Chapter 8). But there are less measurable, but very real costs you will also incur that senior management needs to be aware of. High occupancy, which if chronic, leads to burnout and turnover. Further, average handling time will increase as more callers comment about the long wait and as reps need more "breather" breaks because there is no time in between calls.

4. There's generally no industry standard for service level. No one service level makes sense for every call center (see Chapter 3). Different organizations place different values on customer service, and each will have different staffing costs, network costs, and numbers and types of callers. Instead of looking for industry standards, determine a service level that makes sense for your organization, according to your callers' needs, your objectives and your cost structure. (The exception is in regulated industries that have mandated service levels.)

5. When service level improves, productivity declines. As discussed in Chapter 8, when service level goes up, occupancy goes down. Senior management should understand that the better the service level you provide, the more time your reps will spend waiting for calls to arrive.

6. You will need to schedule more staff than base staff required. If you hear senior management complaining, "You mean we need to hire 30 people so that we can have 25 people on the phones handling calls?" then you need to explain why. They need to recognize that schedules should realistically reflect the many things that can keep reps from taking calls (Chapter 7).

7. Staffing and telecommunications budgets should be integrated. Staffing and trunking issues are inextricably associated, as discussed in Chapter 6. Call center budgets should consider both staffing and telecommunications costs and their impact on one another.

8. Buy the best systems you can afford. Senior managers should be aware that equipment and software generally make up less than 15 percent of a call center's budget over time. These are valuable tools, and it makes sense to buy the system that has more capacity, better reports and more advanced features. Few have regretted buying too much, but many regret being encumbered day after day by a system that doesn't quite meet their needs.

9. Telecom and IS people should support call centers, not manage them. When they wield too much control, it usually stems from the assumption that call centers are "technology operations." Indeed, call centers are laden with systems, but senior management should understand that the systems must be managed from within, with the support of telecommunications and IS. Case in point: If you don't have an ACD manual and aren't allowed to change call routing instructions, that's a symptom of control in the wrong hands.

10. Summary ACD reports don't give the real picture. Interpret summary ACD reports with caution - they can be very misleading. For example, daily reports of service level may look good, but the report conceals the fact that you got walloped in the morning and had agents sitting idle much of the afternoon. Even half-hour reports can be misleading. They report average staffing for specific periods, but reality unfolds moment by moment, day by day.

Reporting Call Center Activity

A variety of reports is necessary to paint a clear picture of what's going on in an incoming call center. To be correctly interpreted, the reports often must be viewed in terms of how they are interrelated. Keep in mind, any measurement by itself is potentially

Seven-Step Reporting Framework

1. Determine your objectives
2. Identify supporting information
3. Put information in a user-friendly format
4. Clarify information that could be misleading
5. Annotate exceptions
6. Augment reports with "show and tell"
7. Organize an ongoing forum for discussing and acting on the information

misleading. The trick is knowing what to present to upper management and how to help them interpret information without burying them in a mountain of details.

The following seven-step framework will help you prepare meaningful reports for upper-level management.

1. Determine the objectives. What are the objectives for the reports? If nobody knows for sure, then it's time to assemble a team for a working discussion. A cross-section of upper management, call center managers, supervisors and agents should be involved. Topics can include:

- Workload handled and workload forecasted
- Customer satisfaction and quality measurements
- Costs and revenues
- Resource utilization (staffing and scheduling needs)

- Queue reports (service level, abandonment, etc.)
- Access alternatives (e-mail, VRU, video, phone, etc.)

Don't worry whether or not you have the reports to support the objectives you identify. Your objectives - not the reports you happen to have - should drive this process.

It's often useful to preface this exercise with a question like, "If we could wave a magic wand, what would we want to know about our call center?" The objectives your team comes up with will be enlightening and will provide much needed direction for the steps that follow.

2. Identify supporting information. List the possible alternatives under each of the objectives you identified in Step 1. Include reports from the ACD, database computer, voice processing system, telecommunications network, e-mail servers, customer surveys, and other systems, as well as information from other departments.

The challenge now becomes one of selection. Stephanie Winston, author of the popular book, *The Organized Executive*, advises that "a report should not simply be a compendium of facts, but a judgment tool for management; the right information presented in the right way to the right people."

To pare down the lists, Winston suggests asking a variety of questions: Is the report really necessary? What questions does it answer? Which reports would you dispense with if you were charged for them? Could several reports be combined?

3. Put the information in a user-friendly format. Once you have a list of desired reports, the next step is to compile them into a simple, understandable format. This often means creating graphs of the information. This may take more pages, but a 10-page report of graphs is often quicker to read and easier to comprehend than two pages of detailed numbers in rows and columns.

Some data needs to be combined to give the full story. For example, service level should be interpreted with blockage and abandonment. Put these reports together, and use the same general format for headings, periods of time covered and chart types.

4. Clarify information that could be misleading. As Winston Churchill declared, "There are three kinds of lies - lies, damned lies and statistics." You can make many reports say whatever you want them to say. For example, you can prop up service level by generating controlled busy signals or taking messages for later callbacks.

Further, cumulative summary reports can conceal important information. A manager might report that the center's average speed of answer for April was 18 seconds. What really happened is that the call center got hit hard on some days, but had idle capacity the rest of the time. This would not be evident from the summary report.

Similarly, some managers use weighted averages to combine the reports of multiple small and large groups into one set of numbers. In that case, small groups have less impact than larger groups on service level. But the small groups may handle important transactions, and their results should not get rolled up with other information.

The point is, are the reports telling you what you need to know or are they masking what is really happening?

5. Annotate exceptions. There will be points that are clearly out of the norm. Don't leave them hanging. Sometimes you need to explain what happened and why. Why did service level drop and average speed of answer go through the roof March 15-17? Drop in a footnote to give the answer: "March blizzard - call load 35 percent higher than normal."

6. Augment reports with "show and tell." Giving upper management a report to read on what happens on Monday mornings versus bringing them into the call center to *observe* what happens is the difference between night and day. You need to do both. We are convinced it is virtually impossible to understand call center reports without spending time in the call center.

7. Organize an ongoing forum for discussing and acting on the information. Many call center managers struggle with that awful feeling of sending out reports and never getting a response. You need to establish a mechanism for discussing reports and adjusting plans on an ongoing basis.

Example Reports

There are many ways that call center information can be presented. Here are a few ideas of how to report common activities.

Service Level

While many call centers diligently crank out reports on service level (or its close cousin, average speed of answer), the information is often presented as daily or monthly summary reports. As discussed, that can conceal the real story.

One way to get around this problem is to illustrate how often you are hitting your service level target versus being under or over the objective. Consider using a "100 percent stacked bar chart." To create this chart,

Input For 100% Stacked Bar Chart

Group 1												
Day of Month, May	3	4	5	6	7	8	10	11	12	13	14	15
Above SL Objective	4	8	4	10	8	6	2	8	8	8	6	10
At SL Objective	8	12	14	10	12	18	6	10	12	8	14	10
Below SL Objective	12	4	6	4	4	0	16	6	4	8	4	4

specify the number of half-hours each day you were within your target service level range (i.e., 70 percent to 90 percent answer in 20 seconds), the number of half-hours you were above the range, and the number of

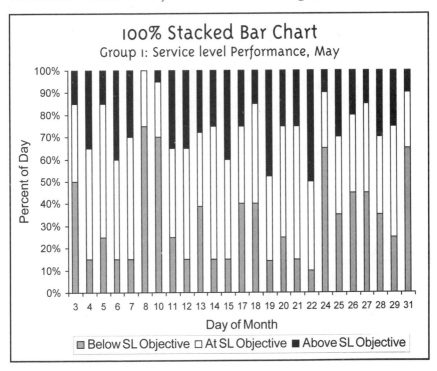

151

half-hours you were below the range, for each day.

Next, use the graphing capability in a spreadsheet, ACD or workforce management software to produce the chart. The scale up the side equals 100 percent of a day, and the graphing capability in your software will automatically allocate the percentages. For example, on the third of May, the center was below service level 12 out of 24 half-hours or 50 percent of the time. The advantage of this chart is that the reader can quickly decipher how consistently service level is being met.

The chart's downside is that it doesn't tell you how many calls were affected by your performance. When you are below the target, it's probably during key half-hours with the heaviest workloads. One way to get around this is to use the necessary ACD reports to graph the number of calls answered each day within 10 seconds, 20 seconds, 30 seconds, and so on.

Transactions by Type

Ever noticed that the Pareto principle almost always applies to the transactions you are handling? Chances are, about 20 percent of call types account for about 80 percent of the call load. It's critical to know what is driving demand and track changes. A Pareto chart is a bar chart that

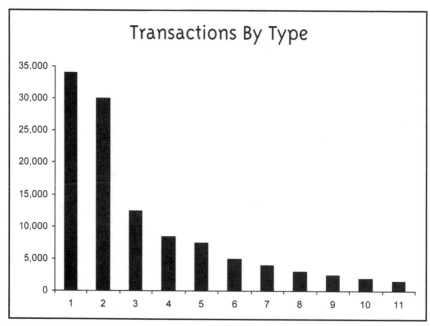

ranks categories. This type of analysis leads to pivotal questions, such as, should the call center be getting so many calls of that type? Where can automation handle some of the load? Would better product literature or expanded Web services prevent calls at the source?

Calls By Group

With multiple groups of agents and automated access alternatives, it's important for senior level managers to know what the trends are. Simple line charts are often the most effective.

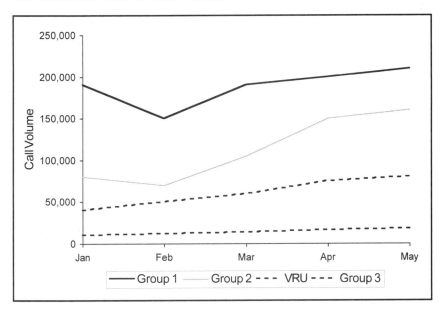

This type of chart gives the reader a quick grasp of what would otherwise be hard-to-decipher numbers.

Executive Summary

As mentioned earlier, it's useful to develop a standard report format. You should also include a one-page executive summary that recaps key data and summarizes your recommendations.

Presenting Budgets

A good budget clearly relays what is happening in the call center and what your objectives are. It should also reflect your organization's mission, and how the call center supports those objectives. This demonstrates to senior management that you have an understanding of the "big picture" when it comes to securing the financial and other support you need to operate successfully.

An important principle in call center budgeting is to highlight the tradeoffs. Because of the many variables, it's useful to create three budgets: one based on your target service level and response time objectives, another that identifies costs for lower objectives, and another for higher objectives. These costs will, of course, come from previous planning steps.

Often you will find that costs are actually higher for the lower objectives. Creating three budgets will preempt any inaccurate speculation and give you more confidence in the case you are presenting.

Effective Budgeting

-Identify what is happening now
-Define your objectives clearly
-Prepare three budgets
-Present your budget formally
-Prepare for the "big questions"
-Keep it short, use pictures and practice
-Demonstrate that present resources are being used effectively
-Put the call center into perspective
-Point out the things that cannot be numerically measured
-Don't treat the budgeting process as a once-a-year event
-Revisit the budget: How accurate was it?

Once you are ready to review your budget with senior management, consider presenting it formally. The idea of a formal presentation may not strike your fancy, but consider the advantages: 1) It can be the catalyst for getting all decision makers together at one time. 2) All attending will hear the questions and comments of the others, saving time and raising the general level of understanding more quickly. 3) You will be motivated to get organized.

To help you build confidence, be prepared to answer the "big questions":

•What did we spend on the call center in total last year?
•Where is the money going?
•Can the current staff handle the growth this year?

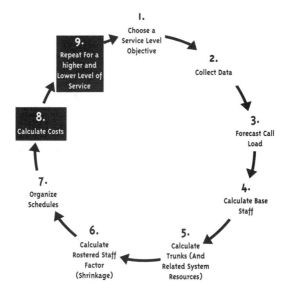

- What are your ideas for reducing costs?
- What are others in our industry doing?

Keep your presentation short and uncluttered. Use pictures and graphs where possible. Provide backup material as necessary, such as actual ACD reports - but only as backup and not as a part of the main presentation.

The most effective budget presentations are those which include specific requests. For example, will you need four additional agents by May and nine more by July to achieve your objectives? Ask for it, then be prepared to prove that the resources you already have are being used as effectively and efficiently as possible.

Another effective presentation approach is to bring statistics to life. We are seeing more budgets that put the call center in perspective, and include real examples, such as "We handled 510,150 calls last year. Sue Mayer, one of our customers in Savannah, Georgia, was one of those calls. When she called, she was frustrated that..."

When making the presentation, point out the things that can't be measured. By nature, budgets revolve around numbers. However, as the late quality guru W. Edwards Deming warned, "Many important things are simply unknown and unknowable." For example, in a customer

FRANK & ERNEST by ® Bob Thaves

FIRST NATIONAL
BANK
+ ASSETS: $370,000,000 AND
SOME VERY NICE HOLD MUSIC

With permission of Bob Thaves

service environment, what is the dollar impact of an unhappy customer? What happens to turnover when you lower occupancy? The answers are important but difficult to predict.

Budgeting works best when it is one facet of ongoing, effective communication. Don't treat it as a once-a-year event. It should be part of a continuous effort. Revisit it often, and, as with other aspects of planning, make adjustments as necessary.

Anticipating Growth

Growth remains one of the biggest challenges facing the call center industry. Even as many organizations have grappled with painful cutbacks and downsizing in recent years, most call centers have continued to grow, albeit with significant budget pressures.

What does growth have to do with conveying call center activity to senior management? A great deal. As long as your call center is growing, you will be confronted with this issue over and over. Senior management will understandably want to know why the call center represents a growing percentage of the organization's expenses, and where the money is going.

Liberfone Rediscovers an Old Adage

Remember the old adage: "If you improve service, callers will use more of it"? It's been proven true over and over in incoming call centers.

Liberfone, a new mobile telephone service provider in The Netherlands, has an excellent call center under the direction of

Wouter Tiems, a veteran in the call center industry. Liberfone regularly studies the calls they receive by type, and noticed that they often get the same types of calls from new customers.

Along with improving customer literature, Liberfone decided to initiate a two-month trial, in which agents made outbound calls to new customers, both to welcome them and to answer five of the most common questions they are likely to have (based on historical data). Among other benefits, such as reducing fraud and verifying account details, Liberfone expected to reduce inbound calls by at least 30 percent.

The result? Inbound traffic *grew* by 25 percent! "We lowered the 'entrance barrier' to our call center substantially," reasons Tiems. "We obviously showed the customer that we had a group of capable and friendly employees that were very helpful."

Tiems also points out that Liberfone created happier customers and improved loyalty. As a result, they plan to begin a similar campaign again soon. But the expectations for the next campaign are more realistic. They continue to work towards preventing unnecessary calls at the source in every way possible, but realize customer satisfaction - not call reduction - will likely be the main payoff of the outbound program. ■

An important principle in managing growth is to do an analysis of the likely impact of growth in advance. The objective is to avoid surprises so you aren't going into the budget process "behind the power curve."

Accurate growth projections often take the form of a document that illustrates projected costs and time-frames, such as 10 percent growth in call load, 20 percent growth, 30 percent growth, and so on (up to at least two times the current size).

Your analysis should consider each major call center component and answer important questions such as, when will you need a new ACD cabinet? More VRU ports? More trunking capacity? More space? Additional supervisors or analysts? What is the ideal lead-time for each increment of growth? How long does it take to recruit, hire and train reps?

Because the document is a projection, it won't precisely predict required resources. It's not a budget, per se. But it will illustrate required lead-times and key decision points necessary to keep up with calling demand. As industry consultant Laurie Solomon puts it, "This analysis gives you the information you need to minimize costly surprises and thrown-together solutions."

Points to Remember

• Senior management needs a basic knowledge of incoming call center principles.

• Call center managers must develop a reporting framework that gets the message across clearly.

• Call center managers must develop a budgeting process that builds credibility and clearly demonstrates tradeoffs and decision points.

• Anticipating the impact of growth is critical, and should be a part of the communication and budgeting process.

[Chapter 10:

Managing Service Level in Real-Time

Hurry? I have no time to hurry.

-Igor Stravinsky

The planning is done, the schedules are in place - and the calls are pouring in. Now what? Even with good forecasts and accurate schedules, random call arrival means that call centers inherently operate in a "demand-chasing" mode. Each moment, there are either more calls to be answered than resources available, or more resources than calls. Because supply and demand are rarely equal, demand must be chased with the supply of answering capabilities.

Further, there are those times when planning goes haywire. The forecast may be a bit on the low side. Callers may behave differently than expected. Marketing or some other part of the organization may do something that affects the call load without telling you in advance. Unscheduled activities or unplanned absenteeism can cause unexpected staffing problems. In short, even the most accurate call center planning must be augmented by effective "real-time" management: monitoring events as they happen and making adjustments as necessary.

Real-time management should compliment call center planning. When the planning is done, it's the moment-by-moment decisions and actions that will enable you to maintain an appropriate service level. Effective real-time management includes establishing a good foundation, monitoring real-time developments and implementing a workable escalation plan.

A Good Foundation

An important prerequisite to effective real-time management is to establish a good foundation *before* the calls come crashing in. This involves clearing up potential misconceptions among staff, putting the right tools in place, and establishing workable objectives and a good planning process. In other words, it means ensuring that you aren't creating many of the crises you are reacting to.

Service Level and Quality

One important principle is to make sure that everybody understands the complimentary relationship between service level and quality. Supervisors and reps sometimes see little connection between what they do here and now and what those in planning roles do. They may feel that the pressure of the moment forces them to make tough tradeoffs between seemingly competing objectives.

Although service level and quality seem to be at odds in the short-term, poor quality will negatively impact service level over time, by contributing to repeat calls, escalated calls and other forms of waste and rework. So, the emphasis should be on handling each call correctly, regardless of how backed up the queue is.

Current Display...

Doomed..........We're Doomed....We're Doomed....We'

But supervisors and reps may believe they are getting mixed signals from management: "Hey, you train us to do a quality job, but then you put a lot of emphasis on service level. You put queue displays all over the place and get unhappy when service level drops. What do you really want?"

The answer: "Both!" Look at the calls in queue, make sure people are plugged in and in the right mode, and do what's possible to arrange flexible activities around the incoming call load. But handle each call right the first time no matter what's happening with service level.

The Impact of Each Person

Everybody in your call center needs to be aware of how much impact each agent has on the queue. Review the "Law of Diminishing Returns" in Chapter 8. The message from that discussion, as it relates to real-time management, is clear: when the queue is backed up, each person makes a big difference.

This issue sheds light on the importance of training reps on how a queue behaves (e.g., how fast it can spin out of control) and providing them with real-time information so they can adjust priorities as necessary. Real-time information can be delivered via:

- Supervisor monitors
- Wall or ceiling-mounted readerboards
- Displays on telephones programmed to give queue statistics
- Graphically displayed queue information in a window on each person's workstation
- Don't have the latest technology? We know of a few call centers that still post regularly updated results on easels or white boards throughout the center (not an ideal solution, but it's better than nothing!).

Queue information must be complimented with appropriate training so reps know what to look for and how to react.

You also need to establish clear expectations on adherence to schedule. Many call centers diligently track adherence factor, which is a measure of how much time reps spend plugged in and available to take calls. Often, it's viewed only as an issue of how much. Equally important, though, is when reps are plugged in and available to take calls. A key responsibility of supervisors and team leaders is to ensure that people are plugged in when they are most needed. (We will discuss adherence factor more in Chapter 12).

Auto-Available and Auto-Wrap-up

Most ACD systems can be programmed for either "auto-available" or "auto wrap-up." With auto-available, reps are automatically put into the available mode after they disconnect a call. With

> There is no way you can anticipate in advance how much time after-call work will take for an individual call.

auto-wrap up, they are automatically put into the after-call work mode.

It usually makes sense to program your system to put agents into the mode they will most often need to be in, after talk time. This can save precious seconds and minimize the need for agents to manually put themselves in and out of modes.

Some managers program their ACD to put agents into the after-call work mode for a predetermined amount of time. This is usually a bad idea. There is no way you can anticipate in advance how much time after-call work will take for an individual call. If your objective is to give people breaks due to a heavy call load, you are adding more time to each call, further backing up the queue.

It's a much better idea to give agents control over the mode, and let them take short breaks when necessary. (There is one exception to this rule: some ACDs require a small window of time after a call is discon-nected, i.e., a few seconds, to enable agents to put themselves into the after-call work mode.)

Another alternative you have when programming your ACD is to use a feature generally referred to as "call-forcing." Call-forcing is a terrible, autocratic-sounding term, but it is actually a valuable capability. With this feature, calls are automatically connected to agents who are available and ready (thus, obviating the need for them to manually answer calls). Agents must be wearing headsets (a great idea anyway), and are notified that a call has arrived by a beep-tone (zip tone).

Studies indicate that call forcing can cut four to six seconds off each call. And agents usually like the feature. It chops what would be an extra step out of the process, and they remain in control -if they aren't ready for the next call, they can stay out of the available mode.

Consistency

Ensure that agents maintain a consistent approach to handling calls, regardless of queue conditions. Each rep has an impact on the components of call load, and therefore, on the data that will be used in forecasting and planning for future call loads. When the queue is building, it can be tempting to postpone some of the after-call work. As discussed in Chapter 5, this skews reports, causes planning problems and may lead to increased errors.

The solution is to define ahead of time which types of work should follow calls and which types of work can be completed later. Then, train agents and supervisors accordingly.

Accurate Resource Planning

Real-time management can never make up for inadequate planning. The nine-step planning process (covered in Chapters 3 through 9) should be as accurate as possible. This includes:

• Establishing service level and response time objectives that everybody understands.

• Accurately forecasting all three components of call-load - talk time, after-call work and volume.

• Calculating base staff requirements.

• Planning for and managing non-phone activities.

• Building schedules that match staff with the workload as closely as possible.

Monitoring Real-Time Developments

The second major principle in real-time management is to monitor developments and identify trends as early as possible. The trick is to react appropriately to evolving conditions. Random call arrival means that, at times, it will look like you are falling behind even though you are staffed appropriately. But if you *are* experiencing a genuine trend, you need to move quickly. Time is of the essence.

Interpreting Reports

Service level is "rolling" history. The ACD has to look at what happened to the last X calls (e.g., 20), or occurred in the last X minutes (e.g., five minutes) in order to make the calculation. That suggests, even though service level is a primary focus in call center planning, it is not a sensitive real-time report.

(Note, with many ACDs, you can define these thresholds. You may need to experiment some. Set them high enough that the reports aren't jumpy, but low enough that they provide information that is as current as possible. "From the beginning of the half-hour" or "150 calls" is too much history, and the reports will have little real-time value. But the last 60 seconds or five calls is too little history, and reporting will be volatile. Also note that "screen refresh" does not correlate to the timeframe used for calculations. Your monitors may display updated information every five to 10 seconds, but that has nothing to do with how much data your ACD uses for the calculations that require rolling history.)

Service level will tell you what has already happened, given recent unique call volume, random arrival, average handling time and staff availability patterns. But it's important to realize that what is being reported is not necessarily an indication of what is about to happen.

On the other hand, the number of calls presently in queue is a real-time report, as is longest current wait and current agent status. Understanding the distinction between reports that are genuinely real-time versus those that must incorporate some history explains apparent contradictions.

For example, service level may indicate 65 percent answer in 20 seconds, even though there are no calls in queue at the moment. Keep watching the monitor, though, and service level will begin to climb. Alternatively, service level may look high at the moment, even though an enormous amount of calls recently entered the queue. Give it a few minutes and, unless circumstances change, it will be at the bottom of the barrel.

There will be at least several minutes delay before service level reflects the magnitude of a trend. As a result, for service level to have meaning, it must be interpreted in light of the recent past, calls in queue and current longest wait. If you focus only on service level, you could misread the situation.

Since the number of calls in queue foretells where service level is about to go (unless conditions change), it should be a primary focus, along with longest current wait. As circumstances dictate, you would then assess the state reps are in - signed off, auxiliary, handling

Monitoring Real-Time Reports
1. Number of calls in queue
2. Longest current wait (oldest call)
3. Service level/average speed of answer
4. Agent status
5. Escalation plan...

calls, etc. - and make appropriate adjustments.

In sum, focus on real-time reports in this order:

1. Number of calls in queue. This is the real-time report most sensitive to changes and trends. Look at this first.

2. Longest current wait (oldest call). This is a real-time report, but behaves like a historical report (e.g., many calls can come into the queue, but longest current wait will take some time to reflect the problem). This report gives context to number of calls in queue. For example, if there are far more calls in queue than normal, but longest current wait is modest, you are at the beginning of a downward trend. Now is the time to react.

3. Service level, average speed of answer, average time to abandonment and other measures of the queue and caller behavior. These reports provide additional context to number of calls in queue and longest current wait. For example, if service level is low, but there are few or no calls in queue, then you have hurdled the problem and service level will begin to climb. Don't sweat it.

4. Agent status. This real-time report indicates how many agents are available and what modes they are in. Some call center mangers suggest that agent status should be at the top of the list. Their argument is that if agents are where they need to be, there wouldn't be much of a queue in the first place.

There is some logic in that argument. However, we put agent status after other reports because it can be difficult to interpret unless you know something about the queue. So what if few agents are taking calls, if few calls are coming in? In that case, you would want agents to be working on other tasks.

In the end, the debate on the order of reports doesn't matter much, because you should monitor and interpret them together. With the right training on what real-time information means and the activity it is reporting, experienced reps and supervisors can scan and decipher these reports quickly.

Display Thresholds

Some ACD and wall display systems allow you to establish various priority thresholds. For example, you can color code information yellow when the queue begins to back up, and red when it's in bad shape. Alternatively, some ACDs, particularly older models, do not have queue displays on phones, but provide blinking lights. The lights can be programmed to blink more rapidly as the queue builds.

The problem is, the thresholds are often set arbitrarily. Further, reps often do not understand what is expected from them at different levels. If that's the case, real-time information will raise everybody's stress level. And your agents might feel like it's their fault that they can't clear up the queue. Proper programming and training are necessary.

Generally, the first threshold should be set for one call in queue. Reps should proceed normally, and no tactical adjustments are required. The second threshold should indicate that there are more calls in queue than the average expected for the desired service level (see "Q2" in Chapter 6). Routine adjustments should be made (e.g., postpone flexible work) to get the calls answered. The next threshold should indicate that there are more calls in queue than the reps can handle. In this case, more involved real-time tactics (e.g., calling in reinforcements) are required.

You can program some systems to adjust thresholds as calling loads change (10 calls in queue may be no problem during a fully staffed shift, but would be a nightmare for two people handling calls at 3:00 a.m.). If your system doesn't have that capability, you'll have to either manually

adjust threshold settings (impractical in most cases) or program them for typical half-hours and realize they provide only rough guidance.

Coordination

Ever had this happen? Someone looks at the real-time reports and everything is fine, so they decide to unplug and begin work on a project or take a break. But enough others have the same idea at the same time that the queue spins out of control. Interpreting real-time information when there is no queue is almost as tricky as identifying trends when there is a queue.

Consequently, most large or networked call centers have a designated "traffic control" center that coordinates activities. The traffic controller's authority can range from making informed suggestions on priorities to flatly dictating what can and can't happen at any given time.

Whatever the size of your call center, you will need someone with the whole field in view to monitor conditions. This person (or team) may also produce and interpret intra-day forecasts (see Chapter 5) and make adjustments to system or network thresholds.

A Workable Escalation Plan

To achieve your service level and response time objectives in real-time, you will need to make appropriate tactical adjustments as conditions change. An important principle in effective real-time management is to outline a workable escalation plan that is in place *before* a crisis. Most call centers use a tiered approach.

Level 1

The first level of action involves routine, common sense adjustments that enable you to get the calls answered. Agent status becomes the focus, and many use a variation of the time-honored phrase: "Everybody take a call!" This is generally directed towards people on the floor who are not currently handling calls. It can also be for reps stuck in after-call work.

At this level, agents make routine adjustments to work priorities. Flexible tasks are postponed. If you have a secondary group handling correspondence, outbound calls or data-entry, they can be temporarily assigned to the inbound traffic. You might also overflow calls to agents in other groups (who are trained to handle the calls).

Make sure your reps understand that speeding up their rate of speech will not help. Callers can usually sense they are rushed, and will often dig in their heels to slow things down. However, they shouldn't go beyond what is necessary to completely satisfy the caller's stated objectives and handle the call with quality.

Level 2 and Beyond

If the workload still outpaces the staff required to handle it, the call center can move on

Real-Time Tactics

- "Everybody take a call"
- Assist people who are stuck in talk time or after-call work
- Postpone flexible work
- Record appropriate system announcements
- Bring in secondary groups
- Adjust overflow or network parameters
- Reassign agents to groups that need help
- Adjust the placement of delay announcements
- Use supervisors wisely
- Bring in agents who are on call
- Send calls to outsourcers
- Mobilize the swat team
- Adjust call routing priorities
- Take messages for callback
- Generate controlled busy signals

to more involved real-time alternatives. For example, it may be feasible to reassign agents from one group to another.

Another possible Level 2 activity is to change system announcements so that they off-load what would otherwise be routine calls. Utilities use messages such as, "We are aware of the power-outage in the Bay Ridge area, caused by nearby construction. We hope to have power restored by 11:00 a.m. We apologize for the inconvenience. If you need further assistance, please stay on the line, one of our representatives will be with you momentarily..."

(More routinely, calls can be directed elsewhere: "Thank you for calling ABC airline. If you would like to use our automated flight arrival and departure system, please press..." Some call centers also give callers the ability to check the status of an order, listen to specific product information, or hear answers to commonly asked questions while they wait and without losing their place in the queue.)

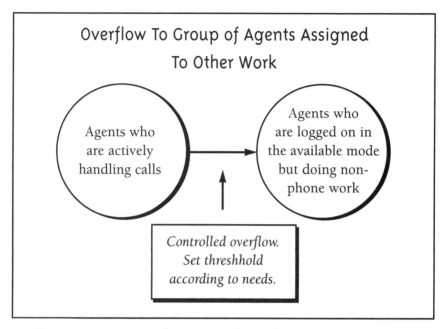

Overflow To Group of Agents Assigned To Other Work

Agents who are actively handling calls

Agents who are logged on in the available mode but doing non-phone work

Controlled overflow. Set threshhold according to needs.

Sometimes, you can foster empathy with system announcements: "Due to the snowstorm blanketing the East Coast, we are operating with fewer of our associates than normal. However, your call is very important to us. We apologize for the delay and will be with you just as soon as possible. Thank you for your patience." This tactic will backfire if it's overused or stretches the truth.

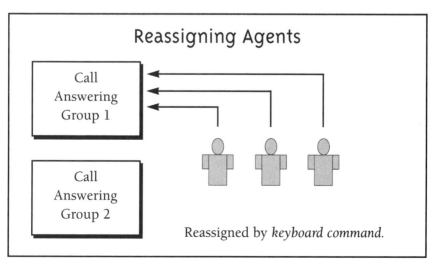

Reassigning Agents

Call Answering Group 1

Call Answering Group 2

Reassigned by *keyboard command.*

You might also be able to improve circumstances by changing call routing thresholds between groups or sites.

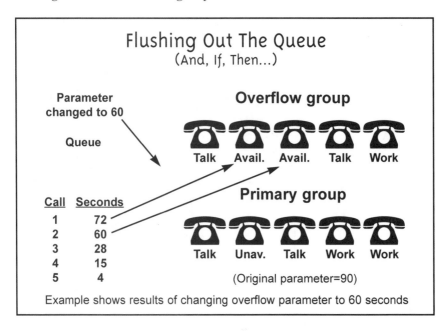

Flushing Out The Queue
(And, If, Then...)

Parameter changed to 60

Overflow group

Talk   Avail.   Avail.   Talk   Work

Queue

Primary group

Call	Seconds
1	72
2	60
3	28
4	15
5	4

Talk   Unav.   Talk   Work   Work

(Original parameter=90)

Example shows results of changing overflow parameter to 60 seconds

Most modern ACDs are capable of "if-then" programming logic to automate this process. But there are cases that may require some adjustments. And if you have a network that sends fixed percentages of calls to various sites, you may need to adjust these thresholds.

It may make sense for supervisors and managers to help handle calls. However, this approach must be well thought-out, because if they are unavailable when reps need help, the situation could further deteriorate. Some union agreements restrict supervisors and managers from taking calls, but if allowed, this can be an effective tactic.

Some call centers take messages for later callback. However, this approach doesn't work well for most. (Consider the new challenges created: How do you insure that the callbacks are timely? What do you do when you reach Junior, who informs you that Mom or Dad is gone? What is your policy when you reach the caller's voice mail? Or secretary?) This strategy can work in call centers that handle complex calls and have defined customers who are easy to reach. But you may have to experiment with it to find out whether it's workable in your environment.

Other Level 2 tactics include calling in a swat team, bringing in agents who are on reserve, routing some calls to established outsourcers, adjusting the placement of delay announcements and generating controlled busy signals.

In sum, establishing an effective escalation plan involves:

• Identifying feasible real-time tactics (ahead of time)

• Determining the conditions in which each should be implemented (ahead of time)

• Monitoring conditions (real-time)

• Deciding on adjustments necessary (real-time)

• Coordinating and communicating changes to all involved (real-time)

• Implementing the tactics (real-time)

• Assessing how well the escalation plan worked (after-the-fact)

An important but sometimes neglected aspect of real-time management is to analyze what happened, once the crisis has passed. How well did your escalation plan work? Were the right tactics deployed? This analysis will help you fine-tune your escalation plan and improve the planning process.

Delay Announcements

Most inbound call centers provide delay announcements to callers who wait in queue. The first announcement recognizes callers, explains the delay and promises that the calls will be answered.

The typical behavior of callers who abandon can provide insight into the use of delay announcements.

Due to our complete inability to staff appropriately, your call will be delayed...and so will many others.

Callers who hang up when they hear the first delay announcement are called "fast clear-downs." They may have dialed the wrong number or they may just be the type to hang up

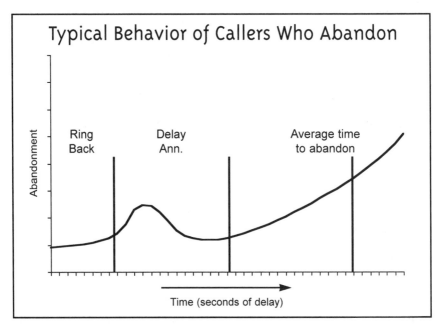

Typical Behavior of Callers Who Abandon

when it's confirmed that they are in a queue.

Sometimes, repositioning the first delay announcement will lower abandonment. For example, if the delay announcement is normally set to come on after 10 seconds of ringing, moving the threshold to 20 or 25 seconds will give your reps more time to get to callers before they become fast clear-downs. Further, because callers don't mentally register that they are in a queue until they hear the announcement, they may wait longer.

Will this work for you? You'll have to try it to find out. Keep in mind, this technique will actually increase average speed of answer and reduce service level. But you have a higher value in mind: get to as many callers as possible before they give up and hang up.

You may also be able to reduce abandonment by adjusting the position of the second delay announcement. For example, if average time to abandonment is 55 seconds and the second delay announcement is set for 60 seconds, you might hang on to more callers by programming it to play earlier. The purpose of the second delay announcement is to give callers who are about to abandon renewed hope that you will get to them: "We haven't forgotten you. One of our telephone representatives will be with you momentarily. Thank you for waiting."

The first and second delay announcement are valuable, but repeating

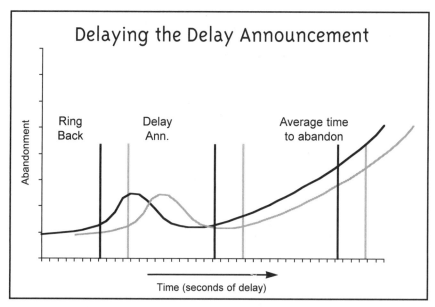

Delaying the Delay Announcement

delay announcements tend to make things worse. Callers have to mentally tune in every time the announcement is played, which, over time, can make them cynical: "Yes, I know this call is important to you

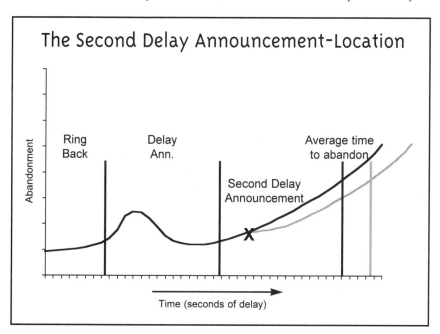

The Second Delay Announcement-Location

and that you'll be with me momentarily. You've told me eight times so far."

Abandons or Busy Signals?

What if things are really rough? What if you get more calls than expected and have exhausted all other alternatives? Should you continue to let callers into the queue?

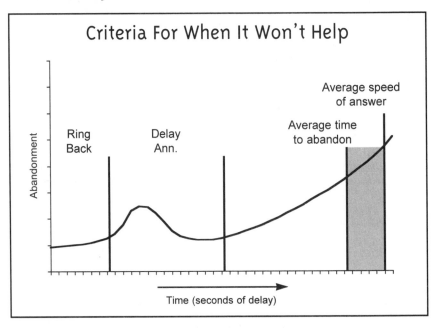

The unsavory choice may be to give callers busy signals or let them enter a long queue, only to abandon anyway.

Some call centers could never consider using busy signals. Emergency services are a notable example. But for others, generating a busy signal may occasionally be an acceptable alternative. Callers who get busy signals are more likely to make immediate and repeated attempts to reach you than those who abandon.

Two reports, average speed of answer and average time to abandonment, provide useful direction. If ASA is four minutes and ATA is two minutes, then you might begin to block some calls from getting into the queue to force ASA down.

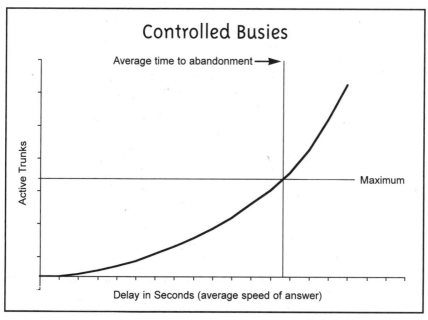

Several technical alternatives exist that allow you to block calls from entering the queue. With older systems, call center managers had to be creative. For example, they could overflow calls to "dummy" answer groups that were busied out. They could also play an "all circuits are busy" message (which is not a good approach because you or your callers will have to pay for the calls, if toll charges apply). Today, many systems are capable of "controlled" busy signals, whereby the system blocks calls according to the thresholds you program (e.g., seconds in queue or number of calls waiting).

Matching ASA and ATA is by no means a sure-fire approach. Keep in mind, if percent abandonment is low (i.e., 2 percent or 3 percent), then ATA is irrelevant. When percent abandonment goes up, ATA typically goes up (and becomes more meaningful) because it includes a broader sample of callers in the calculations.

Further, ASA and ATA measure two different populations; ASA includes callers who wait until they reach agents, while ATA consider only those who abandon. Both reports tend to be moving targets, and can fluctuate widely within a few minutes. And callers who get blocked a number of times before reaching the queue tend to be more tenacious and will usually wait longer for a rep.

All of this to say, *this approach must be used judiciously*. Busy signals are compelling because they make reports look better and take the pressure off your agents. But some managers depend on them as a crutch for inadequate staffing. That's poor customer service, and it defeats the mission of the call center. This tactic should only be used in extreme or short-lived situations.

Planning and Practice

The call centers that do the best job of real-time management have a few things in common. They plan the escalation procedure ahead of time and define the thresholds that will determine when each tactic should be implemented. They continually review and refine their escalation plan. When the dust settles, they take the time to go back and analyze what happened, what worked and where there were problems. And they continually improve their planning process, so they are not leaving those on the floor with mission impossible.

Real-time management takes planning, coordination and practice. It's also gratifying. One of the rewards of working in a call center is to step up to a challenge, then be able to look back at the results...and smile.

Points to Remember

• Establish a good foundation ahead of time so that you are not creating many of the crises you are responding to.

• Provide real-time information to reps and supervisors, and train them on how to interpret the information.

• Plan the escalation procedure ahead of time and define the thresholds that will determine when alternatives are deployed.

• Establish a person or a team to coordinate real-time tactics.

• Review and refine your escalation plan on an ongoing basis.

• Continually improve your planning process. Real-time management will never be an effective substitute for accurate resource planning.

Part Four:

Rethinking Quality and Productivity

The subjects of quality and productivity have been reassessed with every passing management movement and are hotly debated in call center management circles today. But progressive inbound call centers have made a dramatic shift in recent years from bull-pen style call "factories" to environments marked by high skill levels, agent-empowerment and an incessant focus on ever-increasing caller expectations.

Chapter 11:   Service Level with Quality

Chapter 12:   Assessing Performance in a New Era

[Chapter 11:

Service Level With Quality

It will not suffice to have customers that are merely satisfied.

-W. Edwards Deming

Time and again, the business world has been captivated by still another revolutionary management concept that its proponents say holds the answer to quality and productivity challenges. Remember Excellence? Then there was MBO (management by objectives). Then came One Minute Managing, Situational Leadership, Management by Walking Around and Theory Z. More recently, TQM (total quality management), then Reengineering planted their flags. Go back even further, and you'll find Scientific Management, Human Relations and other management movements.

Some managers have become justifiably cynical. We heard one jokingly refer to her "total quality reengineering program." Another had a sign on his desk:

"We are reshaping our total quality reengineering focus to further augment our global core competencies through enhanced customer delight."

He was kidding, of course. But some people even suggest that "quality" is a phase that has run its course. There's got to be a balance.

No one would argue that quality as an attribute of products or services or the need to satisfy customers will ever be passé. And many of the tools and methodologies that the modern quality movement has produced will be valuable long into the future.

So, where's the wheat versus the chaff? Naturally, new ideas and new movements will come along. Each will produce lots of money and speaking engagements for its proponents. Each will eventually be usurped by new trends. And most likely, each will leave some new kernels of perspective and know-how that will outlive the labels.

Here, we're going to take the safe road (we think), and summarize five principles that are quietly but significantly transforming the most forward-thinking call centers.

> **Five Important Principles**
>
> - Quality is built around customer expectations
> - Quality and service level work together
> - The process is where the leverage is
> - Use the tools to find and fix root causes
> - Skills and knowledge will make the difference

Quality and Customer Expectations

The dual objectives of the modern quality movement are to meet (and exceed) customer expectations and to reduce costs resulting from poor quality. To put it another way, three key quality issues are: 1) define customer expectations, 2) identify how you can meet and exceed them, and 3) use the fewest possible resources to do so.

Pretty simple, in theory. But some of the tougher challenges that call centers face include:

> **Important Quality Issues**
>
> - What are customer expectations?
> - Are we meeting them?
> - Are we using the fewest possible resources?

• What is the call center really capable of producing? There is an abundance of objectives and standards, for service level, individual productivity, customer satisfaction and many others. But do the standards have any bearing on quality or true productivity? Do they fit into reality?

• Where should ongoing improvements and investments be made? While major problems - e.g., inaccurate workload forecasts, poor schedules, and demoralized staff - are usually apparent, more subtle problems can be difficult to identify and fix.

• Who is responsible for what? The telephone system (e.g., connection speed, queuing capabilities), telephone trunks, information retrieval (e.g., computer response time, software design), agents (e.g., training, motivation), and callers (e.g., their expectations, behavior, reasons for calling) all play a role in the call center process. Who or what is responsible for productivity and quality, and to what degree?

• Should the existing process be scrapped in favor of a totally new design and approach?

• Probably the biggest challenge all types of organizations are grappling with: Callers quickly get used to improvements in service, then expect and demand them. Further, innovative improvements made by service leaders quickly become a part of general customer expectations, raising the bar for every organization.

What are caller expectations? The following general list is substantiated by customer surveys from many organizations. You can use this list as a guide to create your own focused customer survey questions. Naturally, the specifics vary, depending on the circumstances. We have no reason to believe these expectations are going to change significantly,

Typical Customer Expectations
•Be accessible
•Treat me courteously
•Be responsive to what I need and want
•Do what I ask promptly
•Don't make me deal with poorly trained and ill informed employees
•Meet your commitments, keep your promises
•Do it right the first time
•Follow up
•Tell me what to expect
•Be socially responsive
•Be ethical

any time soon. But the definitions for things like being accessible, being responsive and meeting commitments will evolve.

Quality and Service Level

The following list identifies the components of a quality call.

What Is A Quality Phone Call?

- Caller is satisfied
- All data entry is correct
- Call necessary in first place
- Agent provided correct response
- Caller received correct information
- Agent captures all needed/useful information
- Caller not transferred around
- Caller doesn't get rushed
- Caller has confidence call was effective
- Call center's mission is accomplished
- Unsolicited marketplace feedback is detected and documented
- Caller doesn't feel it necessary to check-up, verify or repeat
- People "down the line" can correctly interpret the order
- Agent has pride in workmanship
- Caller did not get busy signal
- Caller was not placed on hold for too long

These items apply almost universally. Take a few minutes to study the list and think through how each criteria applies in your environment.

Next, using this framework, think about the possible repercussions if quality is lacking. For example, what happens if the caller is not satisfied? What happens if data is entered incorrectly? What happens if the agent does not provide the correct response? You're probably considering things like repeat calls, unnecessary service calls and escalated calls.

The next list identifies possible costs when quality is lacking. Unlike the previous list, not all of these items will apply in every situation. For example, if you are an insurance company, the cost of handling product

Costs When Quality Is Lacking

- Escalation of calls and complaints to higher management
- Repeat calls from customers
- Callbacks to customers for missing or unclear information
- Cancellations
- Cost of closing accounts
- Handling product returns
- Unnecessary service calls
- Wrong problems get fixed
- Calls to customer relations
- Negative publicity from angry customers
- Diversion of agents to activities that should be unnecessary
- Agents taking the heat for mistakes made by others
- Bad moves, adds and changes
- Shipping expenses to re-ship, express mail
- Loss of referrals
- Cancellations causing inaccurate inventory status

returns won't apply. Similarly, tax collection agencies don't incur the cost of closing accounts (to the chagrin of some who would love to close their accounts if they could). But repeat calls, escalated calls and diversion of agents to activities that should be unnecessary *do* apply.

Next, consider these issues within the context of service level and staffing. What portion of average talk time represents waste and rework? How about after-call work? What percent of calls were unnecessary in the first place? And what amount of time are agents spending on activities that should be unnecessary?

It becomes very clear, good quality will have a direct and positive impact on service level. Quality service pays for itself because it helps to eliminate the many costs incurred when quality is lacking.

Errors and rework are

> Reducing errors and rework has a positive impact on service level, morale, customer satisfaction and costs.

often part of a downward cycle. They consume valuable staff time, which can lead to insufficient staff to handle the incoming workload. Insufficient staff then leads to a low service level, high occupancy, unhappy callers and increased stress. Those

Impact of Reducing Defective Calls

- Quality up
- Production of good calls up
- Capacity up
- Lower costs
- Profit improved
- Callers happier
- Agents happier

things contribute to errors and rework, completing the cycle. So, reducing errors and rework has a positive impact on service level, morale, customer satisfaction and costs.

The Call Center Process

Another basic tenet of the quality movement is continuous process improvement. The best call centers make the effort to understand their processes and are working to improve them.

An incoming call center itself is a "process" or "system of causes." Taking a larger view, the incoming call center is part of a larger process, the organization. In a lesser view, each agent group in an incoming call center is a system of causes unto itself, as are individual agents in a group.

The central focus of the process illustrated in the next figure is average holding time on trunks, which is a high-level process that includes both talk time and delay. Note that most of the items are the responsibility of management, not the agents. Also notice that just about everything is interrelated, so the causes of performance problems are often difficult to isolate and measure. The diagram is only one of many ways to depict the incoming call center process.

This picture leads to a conclusion that is at the heart of the modern quality movement: There is little use exhorting reps to improve quality, without making improvements to the system itself. Most of the things that contribute to quality are out of their hands, such as having good training, the right tools, accurate information and a logical work flow. The system of causes - the process - is where the leverage is! Some call center managers try to force change by setting strict standards for agents.

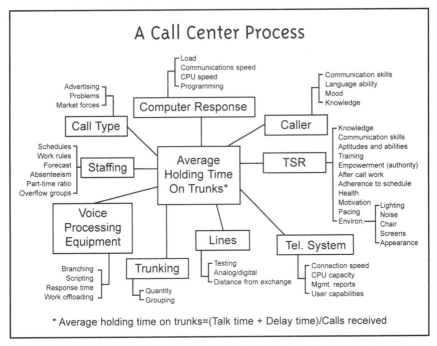

A Call Center Process

* Average holding time on trunks=(Talk time + Delay time)/Calls received

But that will not improve the system and is usually detrimental.

Key Performance Indicators

To effectively run an incoming call center, you need key performance indicators that measure overall call center activity. The 10 KPIs listed here are useful for tracking performance over time and assessing the impact of process changes. However, quality improvements must happen at a deeper level.

1. Average Call Value (For Revenue-Producing Call Centers). This measure is generally calculated by dividing total revenue generated by number of calls. This is a top priority in sales and reservations environments.

2. Customer Satisfaction. Most call centers conduct surveys via outbound calls or by mail to randomly selected callers. Some contract with outside firms to conduct surveys and prepare the results, while others do the surveys in-house. A growing number of call centers are automating some surveys, whereby callers are transferred into a VRU that guides them through a series of questions and allows them to respond via the keypad on their telephone. Others are enabling customers to provide focused feedback, from the Web.

3. Service Level. As discussed in Chapter 3, the best managed call centers take service level and response time seriously and budget the resources to meet these objectives consistently.

4. Percent Abandoned. If callers hang up before you get a chance to talk to them, you are missing the opportunity to make them happy, sell to them and solve their problems. However, as discussed in Chapter 2, abandonment is difficult to accurately forecast and is often a misleading indication of the queue callers experience. So, be sure to view abandonment in light of other measures, and in consideration of callers' varying circumstances.

5. Cost Per Call. There are various ways to calculate cost per call. But the basic formula is to divide total costs by total calls for a given period of time. The potential benefit in following cost per call is to identify the variables that are driving it upwards or downwards, so you understand important tradeoffs.

A climbing cost per call can be a good sign, depending on the variables driving it up. For example, better coordination with other departments may help reduce the number of times a customer has to contact your center. As a result, the fixed costs (in the numerator) get spread over fewer calls (in the denominator), driving cost per call up. But total costs will go down over time because eliminating waste and rework will drive down the variable costs. Similarly, cost per call usually goes down during the busy times of the year and up during the slower times of year.

6. Errors and Rework. Errors and rework refer to the extra time and effort it takes to fix mistakes. A variation on errors and rework is a measure of the percent of calls not completed on the first attempt, which many call centers are striving to minimize.

Errors and rework can be measured in a number of ways. The database may allow you to track repeat calls, unresolved issues and errors in data entry. Monitoring or side-by-side coaching should detect and track specific problems that are occurring during call handling. Call coding in the ACD, where reps use codes to track specific types of calls and issues, can also help trace problems. Transferred calls, escalated calls, customer complaints and correspondence (both to and from customers) can provide additional sources of information.

7. Forecasted Call Load Versus Actual. Underestimating calling demand will mask and defeat all other efforts to provide good service, and over-estimating demand results in waste. As discussed in Chapter 5, good forecasting is the result of constantly tracking results and making improvements to the forecasting process.

8. Scheduled Staff to Actual. This measure is independent of whether you actually have the staff necessary to achieve your targeted service level. How well do the staff you have adhere to schedule? If this is a problem, why?

9. Adherence To Schedule. Adherence factor is a measure of the time an individual is on the phone, available to take calls. It generally consists of all plugged-in time, including talk time, wrap-up, waiting to receive calls, and necessary outgoing calls. As discussed in Chapter 8, when adherence factor improves, service level goes up and occupancy goes down. We'll discuss this measurement more in Chapter 12.

10. Average Handling Time. As discussed in Chapter 5, average handling includes both average talk time and average after-call work. An erratic average handling time often points to the need for more training, especially on how to use the after-call work mode.

High-Level Outputs Versus Process Improvements

There are three important things to keep in mind about these high-level indicators. First, as with any measure, you must ensure that they are as accurate, complete and as unbiased as possible.

Second, these reports should be interpreted in light of how they relate to each other. By themselves, any can lead to erroneous conclusions, but together they paint a fairly complete, high-level picture of call center performance.

Third, tracking high-level measurements won't inherently improve them.

> Tracking high-level measurements won't inherently improve them. To make improvements, you have to work on the factors that cause these outputs to be where they are.

To make improvements, you have to work on the factors that cause these outputs to be where they are. In other words, you have to work at a deeper level, the root causes.

Opportunities for Improvement

Without the appropriate tools, identifying the root causes of quality problems in a call center is a significant challenge. Consider a recurring problem, such as providing incomplete information to callers. Maybe the cause is insufficient information in the database. Or a need for more training. Or maybe a lack of coordination with marketing. Or careless-ness. Or agent stress from a chronically high occupancy rate. Or a combination of any of these factors, coupled with 1001 other things.

If the problem is to be fixed, you need to know *what* to fix. Then, you can take the necessary corrective actions. The tools the quality movement has produced over the years are necessary to understand processes and locate the root causes of problems. If you've had any quality training, you are probably well-versed in their use. Our purpose here is to discuss how they can be applied in the inbound environment.

Flowchart

A flowchart is a map of a process and is used to analyze and standardize procedures, identify root causes of problems and plan new processes. Flowcharts are also excellent communication tools, and can help you visualize and understand the flow of a process.

One of the most useful applications for a flowchart is to analyze the specific types of transactions you handle. When most of us think of a "call," we think of a rather simple, singular event. Not so! Even a simple transaction consists of many steps. To really understand a transaction, especially the more complex variety, it is necessary to chart what happens, step by step.

If you haven't charted your transactions by type, give this task to a few of your agents. In fact, put them in a conference room for a couple of hours. Give them a stack of index cards and have them write each step in a typical transaction on individual cards, then lay the cards out in order on a large table. In a relatively short period of time, they should be able to tell you where there are procedure inconsistencies, database deficien-cies and bottle-necks in the process. Notes on a wall or PC-based flow

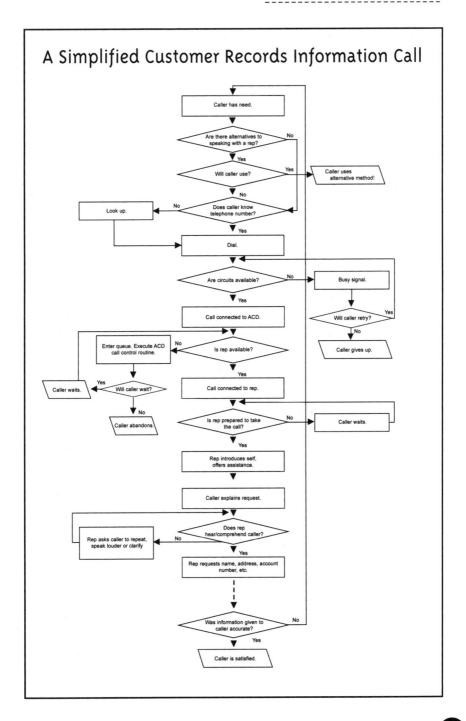

A Simplified Customer Records Information Call

charting software work well, too. You will eventually want to invest more than a couple of hours in this activity, but this will get you started.

Sometimes a sweeping analysis of all the activities required to process incoming transactions is in order. With top management support and direction, representatives from the call center, billing and credit, fulfillment, marketing, information systems and other departments can map out inter-departmental and inter-organizational processes to identify areas that need overhaul.

Example Applications:

- Transactions, step by step
- The planning and management process
- VRU and ACD programming
- Key procedures

Cause-and-Effect Diagram

The cause-and-effect diagram, alternatively called a fishbone diagram after its shape, was first developed by Dr. Kaoru Ishikawa of the University of Tokyo, in the 1940s, and has since become recognized and used worldwide. The example illustrates the relationships between causes and a specific effect you want to study. Preparing a cause-and-effect diagram is an education in itself. Everyone who participates will gain new understanding of the process.

The traditional cause categories used in these diagrams are often referred to as the 4Ms: manpower, machines, methods and materials. A variation on these categories, people, technology, methods and materials/services, works better for call centers. However, these labels are only suggestions, and you can use any that help your group creatively focus on and think through the problem. Possible causes leading to the effect are drawn as branches off the main category. The final step is to prioritize the causes and work on the most prevalent problems first.

There is no one right way to make a cause-and-effect diagram. A good diagram is one that fits the purpose, and the shape the chart takes will depend on the group (see example).

A "production process classification" diagram is a variation on the traditional cause-and-effect diagram, and the cause categories follow the production process. In the transfer rate example, production categories would include: caller develops the need to call, caller dials and directs,

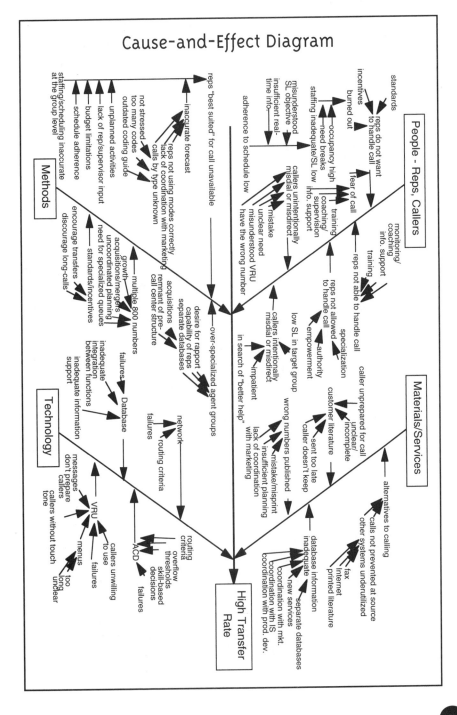

Cause-and-Effect Diagram

call is routed, call is answered, need is identified by rep, and so on.

Example Applications:

- Long calls
- Repeat calls
- Poor adherence to schedule
- Inaccurate forecast

Scatter Diagram

A scatter diagram assesses the strength of the relationship between two variables and is used to test and document possible cause-and-effect. The scatter diagram of average handling time, in Chapter 5 is an example.

If there is positive correlation between the two variables, dots will appear as an upward slope. If there is a negative correlation, the dots will appear as a downward slope. The closer the pattern of dots is to a straight line, the stronger the correlation is between the two variables.

Example Applications:

- Average handling time versus experience level
- Average handling time versus revenue generated
- Service level versus error rate
- Experience level versus quality scores

Pareto Chart

Vilfredo Pareto (1848-1923) was an Italian economist whose theories have had widespread impact. One of the better known results of his work

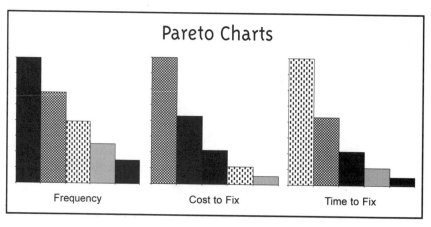

is the Pareto chart, which is a bar chart that ranks the events you are analyzing in order of importance or frequency. For errors by type, a common application, you can create complementary Pareto charts: cost to fix and time to fix. The Pareto principle dictates that you should work first on the things that will yield the biggest improvements.

Example Applications:

- •Errors by type
- •Transactions by type
- •Transactions by customer demographics (e.g., age, region of country and how long they've been customers)
- •Responses to customer surveys

Control Chart

One of the reasons that quality problems in the call center are challenging and often confusing is because they are a part of a complex process, and any process has variation from the ideal. For example, the first chart is a simple view of group performance.

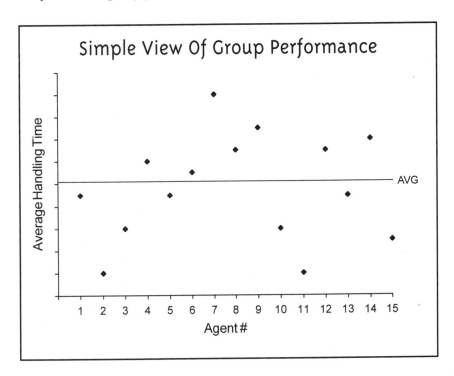

A control chart is a tool that provides information on variation and is based on specific statistical calculations. There are two major types of variation: special causes and common causes. Special causes create erratic, unpredictable variation. For example, an agent with degenerative hearing loss, unusual calls from unexpected publicity or a computer terminal with intermittent problems are special causes. Common causes are the rhythmic, normal variations in the system.

A control chart enables you to bring a process under statistical control by eliminating the chaos of special causes. You can then work on the common causes by improving the system and thus, the whole process. Special causes show up as points outside of the upper control or lower control limits, or as points with unnatural patterns within the limits.

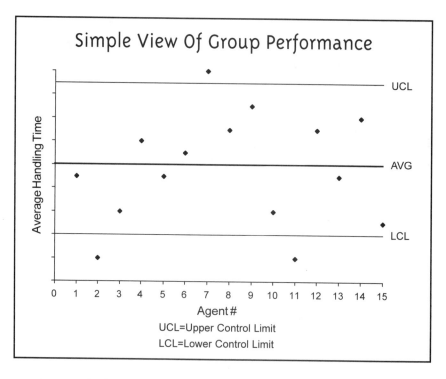

A control chart cannot reveal *what* the problems are. Instead, it reveals *where and when* special causes occur. Once special causes are eliminated, improving the system itself will have far more impact than focusing on individual causes. Improvements to the system will move the entire process in the right direction.

In short, control charts can:

- Control and reduce variation
- Prevent you from chasing the wrong problem
- Give early warning of changes in the process
- Improve predictability
- Improve planning

There are dozens of books and seminars on this subject. The best book we've found to describe the mechanics of producing and using control charts is *AT&T Statistical Quality Control Handbook* (Western Electric Company, Inc.). This classic was written in 1956 for internal use, and is easy to use and understand. For a more philosophical discussion of quality control and insight into the colorful life of W. Edwards Deming, read his pivotal work, *Out of the Crisis* (Massachusetts Institute of Technology, Center for Advanced Engineering Study).

Example Applications:

- Average handling time
- Percent adherence
- Percent defective calls (from monitoring)
- Requests for supervisory assistance (transfers)

Benchmarking

While many of these tools focus on improvements from within, the idea behind benchmarking is that break-through ideas often come from the outside. Benchmarking is the process measuring your products, services and procedures against other organizations.

Before we discuss the specifics, keep some cautions in mind. If you long for an easy-reference chart of performance standards by industry for things like service level, quality, abandonment, busy signals, caller satisfaction levels, and the like, you're not alone - many do. Unfortunately, no such chart exists. If someone produces one, use it at your own risk, because it's likely to be full of meaningless generalities.

Organizations are different enough, even within a given industry, that universally accepted standards are usually not defensible. Things like labor rates, caller demographics, caller tolerances, trunk and network configurations, hours of operation and the mix of part- and full-time

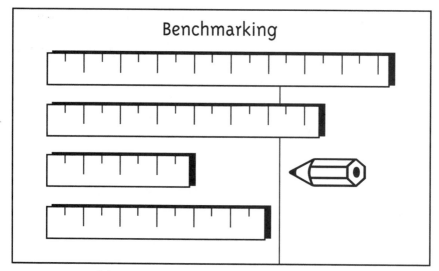

Benchmarking

agents vary widely.

Further, organizations often interpret performance measures differently. For example, three different customer service centers may all have service level objectives of 80 percent answer in 20 seconds. However, one might measure service level as a daily average, another as a monthly average, while another, the number of half-hours per day that met the objective within a specified range.

Several things to note about standards and benchmarks include:

• There is often no officially sanctioned or even carefully considered consensus on what a standard for comparison of call centers would be.

• Most benchmarking studies currently come from informal groups of companies, associations and government organizations, which collaborate and share information. These studies incorporate varying sample sizes and methodologies.

• What is most important is knowing how the results were achieved, not just what the results are.

These cautions in mind, a disciplined, focused benchmarking effort can produce the information necessary to make significant improvements in areas such as forecasting, handling time, service level and customer satisfaction. Bert Cyr, who participated in the Telecommunications Industry Benchmarking Consortium and who spearheaded a major benchmarking project for Canada-based TELUS, recommends that benchmarking begins with careful planning of what to include in the study. He says, "Topics should surround business issues critical to success, include the key functions or processes, and the actual data measures for the chosen processes."

> As best practices become generally accepted, they can no longer be considered "best practices."

Cyr outlines the following general approach:

• Phase 1 - Define processes and collect performance data. This involves getting agreements on processes to be compared and measurements to be used.

• Phase 2 - Analyze collected data and identify best practices. This involves normalizing the raw data for differences, such as currencies, hours of operations, etc., and then identifying the best performers from each category.

• Phase 3 - Analyze best companies. This involves preparing specific recommendations in three general categories: process resources, process efficiency and customer satisfaction.

• Phase 4 - Apply findings. This involves developing a plan to implement improvements.

Benchmarking, like other aspects of quality improvement, should be an ongoing effort. As everyone gets better, what were once cutting edge practices become the norm. As best practices become generally accepted, they can no longer be considered "best practices." The solution, according to Cyr: "Keep benchmarking."

Tools are Just Tools

With any of the tools, there is a danger of getting caught up in the tool and not moving on to problem resolution. Ensure that the tools do not become an end in themselves. Once you identify problems to tackle, you will need to assign clear responsibilities, provide necessary resources and track progress. Results are what matter!

Skills and Knowledge

Are some call centers modern makeovers of industrial-era factories? "How many calls did you take today?" "What's your average handling time?"

> Ensure that the tools do not become an end in themselves.

"My screen is flashing red, which indicates you are more than five minutes late getting back from break."

To the degree that is the case, the age of call center as a factory is slipping away. Most "look it up and say it" agent jobs have been, or will be, automated. The calls agents are handling in the post-automation world are more involved, and require high skill levels and analytical abilities. Your agents are the most important source of incoming call center success.

At the same time, customers will increasingly be smarter, better informed and better equipped (see Chapter 13). The transactions that need live assistance will require reps to know what they're doing - and have the tools to do it with.

The trend is clear. Call centers are paying higher salaries, hiring people with more education and giving them more responsibility. Does this sound contradictory to the idea that the process is where the leverage is? It's not. We need people with the smarts, training and skills to understand the processes they are a part of, and contribute to improvements. People will make the difference in the new generation of call centers.

Addressing Turnover

The typical industry turnover rates of 15 to 30 percent are unacceptable in today's environment. It often takes people 18 months to two years to really become proficient, but that's about when many call centers lose them. Turnover costs in many ways - higher recruiting and training costs; a lower average experience level leading to higher handling times, more transferred calls and lower service levels; the need for more coaching and supervision; and, the impact on everyone's morale when key people leave.

Consequently, leading call centers are working on the root causes of turnover (see box). Many of the problems are byproducts of a poor planning process, so they are working on resource issues. They are also broadening the responsibilities reps have, and finding ways to share management power with them.

We are also noticing a shift in perspective on internal turnover (people leaving the call center for other opportunities in the organization). Conventional wisdom says, it's a good thing. Indeed, the time people spend on the front lines with customers gives them a healthy perspective they carry into other departments. But there has got to be a balance. Losing people too soon can cost the call center - and the organization - dearly.

Common Causes of Turnover

1. Pace of effort required
2. Sense of powerlessness or lack of control
3. Frustration of not being allowed to do a good job
4. Repetition
5. Daily physical confinement (tied to their desk)
6. Over-regimentation
7. The feeling of being spied on
8. The feeling of not being appreciated by others in the organization
9. Handling complaints and problems all day
10. Odd work hours
11. Pay
12. Better opportunities elsewhere

Consequently, a growing number of call center managers are working to expand the time agents spend in the call center before moving elsewhere, (e.g. they are working with others in the organization to encourage agents to stay three or more years, as opposed to one to two years). They are also creating an environment that other employees want to move into, and tempering the perspective that the call center is simply a place people gain experience before moving elsewhere.

Avoiding the Skills Gap

Some call centers will be increasingly overwhelmed by the demands placed on them. Even now, some are struggling with what has been referred to as a "skills gap" - the gap that exists between the skills needed and those that exist. Their pay structures and career paths - or lack thereof - are reminiscent of the days when call centers were filled with entry level positions.

The call centers that will be successful are preparing now. They are cultivating the skills of their people, investing heavily in training and building legitimate, attractive career paths. They are providing what futurist Don Tapscott calls "the leadership necessary for transformation."

Points to Remember

• Quality is built around customer expectations. Since customer expectations are constantly evolving, the definition of quality must also evolve.

• Quality and service level work together. Over the long term, good quality improves service level by reducing waste and rework. And a good service level provides an environment in which high quality can be achieved.

• The process is where the leverage is. There is little use exhorting reps to improve quality, without making improvements to the "system of causes," or process.

• Use the tools to find and fix root causes. Five quality tools - flowchart, cause-and-effect diagram, scatter diagram, Pareto chart and control chart - are especially useful for identifying the root causes of quality problems in a call center.

• Your agents are the most important source of incoming call center success, now and in the future.

[Chapter 12:

→Assessing Performance in a New Era

*It's a self-fulfilling prophecy - if a leader really believes that people
can do more, they'll begin to expect more from themselves.*

-Robert Townsend in *Reinventing Leadership*

The subject of measuring individual agent performance has always
been hotly debated among call center managers. Since performance
measurements are usually tied to expectations and standards, issues
about fairness, what reps can and can't control, why people have different
capabilities and drives, and the processes they are working within always
seem to enter these discussions. Few subjects elicit such strong and
varied opinions. As a result, there are numerous sets of performance
measurements and standards in place, even among call centers with
similar functions.

However, as the call center industry continues to develop, and as call
centers handle increasingly complex transactions, "calls per hour" as an
individual productivity measure is fading, while qualitative measures
continue to gain acceptance. In this chapter, we'll look at the issues
behind several distinct trends, and discuss how focused qualitative
measures, when coupled with an objective measure of adherence to
schedule, can replace less workable standards.

Calls Per Hour Is Fading

Traditionally, calls per hour has been an almost universal productivity measurement in incoming call centers. In fact, many call center managers have viewed calls per hour as virtually synonymous with productivity. While there have always been concerns about sacrificing quality for quantity, calls per hour has, nonetheless, been the preferred benchmark for establishing productivity standards, comparing performance among reps and groups, and assessing the impact of changes and improvements to the call center.

But as a measure of performance, calls per hour is (and always has been) problematic, for several reasons. First, as is often pointed out, when calls per hour is over-emphasized, quality can suffer. Reps may even trick the system to increase their call count, in order to achieve a standard or incentive.

Second, many of the variables that impact calls per hour are out of reps' control. These include call arrival rate, call types, callers' knowledge, callers' communication abilities, the accuracy of the forecast and schedule and the adherence to schedule of others in the agent group.

Further, several mathematical realities are also at work that are not within reps' control. As discussed in Chapter 8, small groups are less efficient (have lower occupancy) than larger groups, at a given service level. Since the number of calls is changing throughout the day, so are the calls per hour averages for a group or individuals within a group.

Some call center managers convert raw calls per hour into true calls per hour, an adjusted measurement that is more fair and meaningful. For example, occupancy, which is not within the control of an individual, can be neutralized by dividing calls handled by percent occupancy. Using the numbers in the table, 5.6 average calls per rep divided by 65 percent

Calls in 1/2 Hour	Service Level	Reps Required	Occupancy	Avg. Calls Per Rep
50	80/20	9	65%	5.6
100	80/20	15	78%	6.7
500	80/20	65	90%	7.7
1000	80/20	124	94%	8.1
Assumption: Calls last an average 3.5 minutes.				

occupancy (first row) is 8.6 normalized calls, as is 6.7 calls divided by 78 percent, 7.7 calls divided by 90 percent, and 8.1 calls divided by 94 percent. Other managers

> As a measure of performance, calls per hour is (and always has been) problematic.

go a step further, and develop statistical control charts to determine whether the process is in control, what it's producing, and which reps, if any, are outside of statistical control.

However, even with these efforts to ensure fairness, calls per hour begins to lose meaning as computer-telephony integration (CTI), skill-based routing, Web integration capabilities and other technologies proliferate, resulting in increasingly sophisticated and varied types of transactions.

Quick Quiz on Rep Control Over Average Calls Per Day

Check boxes next to items over which telephone reps have real control.

- ❏ Adherence to schedule (their own)
- ❏ Number of staff scheduled to answer calls
- ❏ Average talk time (their own)
- ❏ Number of calls coming in
- ❏ Distribution of long calls and short calls
- ❏ Distribution of easy calls and difficult calls

?

For many managers who have depended on calls per hour as the basis for performance measurement, this has left a vacuum: How can you measure productivity in an increasingly varied and complex environment? For a growing number of call centers, the answer is a combination of adherence to schedule and focused qualitative measures.

Adherence and Qualitative Measures Gaining Acceptance

Adherence to schedule is a measurement of how much time during the agents' shift they are taking calls or available to take calls. For example, if adherence to schedule is expected to be 90 percent, each rep should be available to handle calls .90 x 60 minutes, or 54 minutes on average, per scheduled hour.

Adherence consists of time spent in talk time, after-call work, waiting for calls to arrive, and placing necessary outgoing calls. Lunch, breaks, training, etc. are not counted as time assigned to handle calls, and are not factored into the measurement. (Be sure to differentiate the terms adherence to schedule and agent occupancy. They are two different things. In fact, when adherence to schedule goes up, service level will go up, which drives occupancy down. See Chapter 8.)

Adherence can also incorporate the issue of timing - when was a person available to take calls? This is sometimes called "schedule compliance." The idea is to ensure that agents are plugged not only for the amount of time required, but *when* required.

Adherence to schedule should be established at levels that are reasonable and reflect the many things that legitimately keep reps from the phones. It should also be flexible (e.g., adjustable downward) when the workload is light.

A primary advantage of adherence factor is that it is a reasonably objective measurement. Reps cannot control how many calls are coming in, how grouchy or nice callers are, the types of calls they will handle, how accurate resource planning is, and so on. But they *can* be in the right places at the right times.

Next, enter the issue of quality. In most call centers, qualitative criteria continue to become more refined and specific. An important and developing aspect of quality is that reps take the necessary time to handle transactions correctly. This, of course, means not rushing calls. But it also means not spending time on calls over and above what is required to satisfy callers and handle transactions completely and correctly. (Remember the three quality issues from Chapter 11? Quality is identifying, then meeting customer expectations, *using the fewest possible resources.*)

If qualitative measurements are refined enough to ensure that reps are spending the appropriate amount of time handling calls, then adherence and qualitative measurements make a powerful pair. They can effectively replace calls per hour, average call handling time and other measures of output.

> Adherence and qualitative measurements make a powerful pair. They can effectively replace calls per hour, average call handling time and other measures of output.

By focusing on adherence and quality, other measures, such as average handling time, number of calls taken, percent of time spent in talk time and percent of time spent in after-call work, will take care of themselves. Case in point: if you want to increase the number of calls agents are taking, that will take you right back to A) their availability to take calls and B) how they handle the calls that come their way. The number of calls they take will be a byproduct of those two factors. Similarly, if you want to impact average handling time, you will need to go back to the way agents are handling transactions and the process they are working within.

When quality and adherence to schedule objectives replace other performance standards that are outputs, agents' focus is on the things they can directly control. Instead of worrying about *this* number looking good and *that* number lagging, they can focus on doing their job. (Besides, there are plenty of ways reps can trick the system, just as there are numerous ways managers can massage call center reports to say anything they want!)

Assuming adherence and quality objectives are implemented fairly and appropriately, reps will feel they are being assessed on the two things

Ways Reps Can Trick The System

- Reps call each other.
- Hit available, click off the call.
- Let "phantom calls" look like they are handled.
- Remain available, then hit unavailable to go to back of queue.
- Don't disconnect after caller gone.
- Put caller on hold without saying "hello".
- Instead of completing a transfer, remain silently on line.
- Park call on somebody else's extension.
- Tell caller system is down when it isn't.
- Using log-on code for a group with lower productivity.
- "Hello, hello...I can't hear you. Please call back."
- When lots of calls waiting, hit available twice to get credit for two calls.

they can do something about: being in the right place at the right times and handling transactions that come their way, with quality. (Notice the parallels between individual objectives and the definition of call center management!)

Many managers still believe that tracking production outputs, such as calls per hour or average handling time, is necessary. But the trend is clear: Well-defined qualitative measurements, coupled with measures of adherence to schedule, are supplanting standards that are mere after-the-fact outputs.

Of course, focusing on adherence and quality is not feasible in environments where these measurements are vague and indeterminate. They must be implemented fairly, and with foresight and care.

Using Adherence Measurements

The main idea of adherence to schedule is to ensure that reps are in the right places at the right times, doing the right things. In principle, it's a fair standard. But it must be implemented judiciously, or it can backfire in a BIG way.

Terminology

Many call center managers define adherence to schedule differently, and the terms used can vary. Adherence to schedule is a general term that can refer to either (or both) of the following:

> Reps at long last feel they are being assessed on the two things they can control: being in the right place at the right times and handling transactions that come their way, with quality.

1. The amount of time in the course of a shift that agents were available to take calls. Alternative terms include "availability" and "plugged in time."

2. When agents were available, during their shift. Alternative terms include "schedule compliance" or just "adherence." (We use the term adherence interchangeably with adherence to schedule - in other words, we use it in the general sense.)

Virtually all call centers that have adherence to schedule objectives track the amount of time agents are available, and a smaller (but growing) number of call centers also incorporate the issue of timing. Further, there's some latitude for using different variables or activities that qualify as adherent.

Average adherence should be determined individually and for each agent group. Sometimes individuals need specific coaching or training that is not necessary for the whole group. And, tracking adherence as an average for the group reveals how well management is doing in creating an environment in which appropriate adherence objectives can be achieved.

Be sure to include after call work as a part of adherence, along with talk time and the time agents spend waiting for calls to arrive. After call work, when defined appropriately, is a legitimate part of handling time (see Chapter 5). Putting a ceiling on it can be detrimental to quality. If you feel it is too high, you should investigate what is causing it to be where it is, and make appropriate process improvements or adjustments to training.

Getting Good Results

Real-time schedule adherence monitoring capabilities are available in a growing number of workforce management systems. With this capability, the software collects real-time information from the ACD, compares it to schedules and reports variations. Exception reports are based on user-defined thresholds. For example, if an agent is supposed to be back from break at 10:15, and you set a five minute grace period, your screen will highlight that person's name at 10:20 if they aren't back in their seat, ready to handle calls.

Some managers view real-time monitoring systems as *the answer* to the adherence issue. And workforce management vendors sometimes push them hard. But we believe that perspective can be incompatible with the circumstances of today's call center. The inbound environment is increasingly characterized by empowered agents with high levels of skills and training. Monitoring their comings and goings can be reminiscent of strict industrial-era standards.

We are not suggesting that you shouldn't use adherence monitoring technology. But it is best utilized as a tool to provide information at the team level, meaning the people that make up a supervisory group. That's where adjustments are best made.

The alternative is to have strict mandates and tracking at a level above supervisory teams, and have your supervisors spend valuable time filling out "exception reports." As call center consultant Kathleen Peterson puts it, "Do you want reports or do you want results?"

So, how *do* you get good adherence to schedule? We believe there are a number of important prerequisites:

1. Train each person on how much impact they have on the queue, and therefore, how important adherence to schedule is (see Chapter 8).

2. Establish concrete service level and response time objectives that everybody knows and understands (Chapter 3).

3. Educate agents on the essential steps involved in resource planning, so they understand how schedules are produced.

4. Develop appropriate priorities for the wide range of tasks your agents handle.

5. Provide real-time information to agents and back it up with training on how to interpret the information, and what the corresponding actions

should be.

6. Track and manage schedule adherence at the supervisory-group (team) level, as conditions dictate.

7. Track schedule adherence for the entire group for planning purposes and to assess how well management has created a process that enables appropriate schedule adherence.

In sum, adherence to schedule is an important objective. But setting strict standards and watching every move individuals make is generally not the best way to get good results.

Measuring Quality

Most call centers use some form of call evaluation process, typically monitoring (silent, with a beep tone, side by side, or record and review), to evaluate qualitative aspects of call handling, and to identify training and coaching needs. But there's ongoing controversy surrounding the subject of monitoring. (Understandably, many managers don't like the term, either, and prefer alternatives such as coaching or quality assurance.)

Here's Incoming Calls Management Institute's take on the subject (and we suspect, the view of most call center managers):

• Monitoring is not inherently good or evil.

• Whether monitoring results are beneficial or not depend on how and why it is conducted.

• Intentional and unintentional abuses of monitoring do occur, and everyone in the call center management profession should condemn and work to prevent them.

• Managers should have the right to review how well reps are doing the work they are expected to perform.

Rating Systems

Monitoring results can be numerically evaluated in a variety of ways. Basically, the methods can be categorized into one of three groups: 1) scores based on pass or fail, 2) scores based on weighted values for each item, 3) scores based on the proportion or number correct or incorrect.

Pass/fail is a relatively cut and dry approach, assuming the criteria are not overly subjective. If reps score above a set threshold, they pass. If not, they fail. Passing would be equivalent to "good enough." Some pass/fail advocates take a hard line, and declare that if an agent fails on just one item, the entire call must be rated defective. Others look at the overall result, and take a much more lenient approach.

Alternatives To Silent Monitoring

Here are some of the alternatives that call centers are using to supplement (or replace) silent monitoring:

• Reps provide their names to callers at the beginning of a call. This makes them feel more accountable.

• After the call, reps ask callers if they would like to leave a recorded message about their experience, to be reviewed later by the "customer service department."

• Managers walk the floor and listen in on calls. This only gives one side of the conversation, but does provide a feel for what is happening.

• Managers sit down and plug in with reps, to catch them "doing something right."

• Reps simulate calls and roll-play situations in training.

• Incentives are provided at the team level, so that each rep is accountable for others in the group.

• "Mystery shoppers," outside firms, call in and pose as customers. They then provide a report on their experiences.

• New hires or reps who are struggling are seated next to top performers. ■

Proponents of the second method, scores based on weighted values for each item, believe the pass/fail method is inappropriate because it doesn't take into account how different items impact quality. For example, getting correct information from the customer might be much more important than using his or her name several times during the call. With weighted values, management can produce reports that track quality levels, which go beyond just tracking defective calls.

With the third scoring method, the number of items correct or incorrect is expressed as a proportion of the total number of quality criteria. Incorrect items are called defects. Those who argue against this method say that it doesn't recognize the degree of contribution each item makes to quality. But proponents point out that it's much better than an overall pass/fail system, and more objective than a method that assigns values to each criteria.

There is room for opinion, and we've seen all three methods work well - or poorly. But based on our findings, we generally recommend that score results be based on the proportion of defects. The pass/fail method doesn't provide enough information about calls and trends to guide you in making improvements at the individual and process levels. And methods that assign a value to each item are, all too often, overly subjective.

Leveraging the Effort

As qualitative measures become increasingly important, it is essential to get good results from your monitoring efforts. The following are some important steps you can take.

Check the system. Does your monitoring program reflect, in a consistent and unbiased way, what is really going on in the call center? To find out, conduct a simple experiment.

> ### Getting Good Results From Monitoring
>
> - Check the system
> - Refine qualitative criteria
> - Take a good sample
> - Fix problems at the group level
> - Stack monitoring results against other key measures
> - Put reps in your shoes

Have those who do the evaluations independently score five recorded calls. (Or, if you are restricted from recording actual calls, record some role-played calls.)

Then, compare the results. If the scores are significantly different, take the system back to the shop for a tune-up or overhaul. Until you do, you'll be getting mixed results and wasting time and effort. Or worse, you'll be alienating reps who don't trust the results and who aren't getting the recognition and help they need.

Refine qualitative criteria. In some call centers, reps get coaching only when there is a serious problem. Further, neither reps nor supervisors can identify specific, agreed-upon components of a quality call - they just "sort of know" when a call goes as it should. Because most reps produce reasonably good calls most of the time, few get positive reinforcement on things that are specifically going well or additional guidance on things that can use some work.

One way to identify more specific and useful monitoring criteria is to create a flowchart of the major types of calls you are taking. The chart will identify aspects of the call handling process that need improvement (see Chapter 11).

You will also need to update your monitoring criteria, as your call center changes and develops. Monitoring forms can get outdated rather quickly.

Take a good sample. Since monitoring is a sample and not a 100 percent check of every call, it is important to get a representative sampling that accurately reflects activity. Monitoring takes time and often only gets done when things aren't so busy, e.g., when service level is decent and there aren't a zillion calls stacked up in queue.

Of course, the call center atmosphere and the way calls are handled can take on a different tone when service level is low, occupancy is high and the pressure is on. That's when you *really* need a good sample, so be sure to include samples from busy periods.

Another requirement to get a good sample is to monitor everyone, including the most experienced reps. This is necessary to determine where the group's performance level is centered. New hires and some experienced reps may need extra monitoring and coaching, but set an objective for the minimum number of times you monitor everybody. Many call centers monitor around five calls per rep, per month, although this figure can vary widely.

Automated monitoring systems from Teknekron, IBS and others can help. These systems record calls automatically, eliminating the need for real-time agent monitoring. The times, agents and number of calls recorded are all definable. The recordings can then be later reviewed during a non-peak time (see Chapter 13).

Recommended Monitoring Practices
From Incoming Calls Management Institute

• Inform job candidates if monitoring takes place.

• Determine whether or not to tell reps when they are being monitored, in accordance with each individual rep's preference or by appropriate law.

• Advise reps which lines can be monitored and where to find unmonitored lines for personal calls.

• Monitoring equipment should only monitor what is said on the line, not what is said by the rep between calls at his/her workstation.

• Permit only qualified personnel to monitor for quality or to evaluate the results of monitoring.

• Clearly inform reps about the purpose of monitoring, how it is conducted and how the results are used. Post the organization's written monitoring policies for all employees to see.

• Do not publicly post monitoring results by name or other data which could identify an individual.

• Do not single out individual reps for unsatisfactory performance detected by monitoring, when the unsatisfactory performance is common to the group.

• Use standardized and consistently applied evaluation forms and monitoring techniques.

• Use objective criteria in evaluation forms and techniques.

• Monitor all reps periodically to determine where the performance level of the group is centered. This level is management's responsibility. New hires, reps whose performance indicates a need for more training and coaching, and reps who request it should be monitored more frequently.

• Give feedback promptly.

• Permit only personnel with a legitimate business need to monitor calls for orientation purposes. Examples are: new call center personnel who will be involved with call handling, consultants working on call center improvements, and visitors approved by management who are studying the call center's operations. ∎

Fix problems at the group level. Monitoring tends to be inherently focused on individuals: "Joe, you're doing a great job. You were helpful, you identified the caller's need correctly. Just a couple of things to work on..." However, this method may be inefficient and erratic, as it fixes problems that may be common to the whole group - one rep at a time. Can you afford to provide every rep with a personal trainer?

An infinitely more powerful way to leverage the monitoring process is to have a mechanism for getting the scores back to someone who can analyze results for the entire group. Problems common to many reps can then be addressed at the group level through training, restructuring the database to provide better information support, identifying better probing techniques or other process improvements.

Begin analyzing group scores by ranking the most common errors in order of frequency. This will identify training and improvement priorities.

You may also benefit from creating a statistical control chart of the group's scores and plotting each person's performance on the chart. Reps outside the control limits will need individual attention. But if they are within the limits, it's a problem common to the group that requires a solution at the group level (see Chapter 11).

Stack monitoring results against other key measures. Another way to leverage your quality improvement efforts is to compare monitoring results to other key call center measures. Start with monitoring scores versus:

- customer satisfaction surveys
- service level by day
- average handling time
- experience level

Is there a correlation? In what way? Some call center managers have discovered that when service level drops significantly, quality scores begin to fall. Others have noticed that scores improve during reps' initial months with the call center, then begin to plateau. You will gain new insights by investigating these correlations.

Put reps in your shoes. Without exception, call centers that have the most effective monitoring programs are those which involve reps in the process. Some call centers use peer monitoring. Others use reverse monitoring, where reps monitor supervisors or team leaders. Others have reps monitor and score their own recorded calls. Many call centers incorporate monitoring in their training programs, and have groups of reps independently score recorded calls and discuss results.

Putting reps in your shoes taps into two phenomena. First, the better the reps understand and buy into the quality criteria, the easier it will be for them to excel. Second, reps will become their own in-process inspectors, correcting problems before they happen. Agents buy into the monitoring process to the degree that it helps them identify areas that need improvement, and recognizes and rewards them for the things that are going well. And, as the quality movement has stated so clearly, those closest to the work understand it best.

Points to Remember

• Calls per hour as a productivity measurement is problematic. Too many variables are outside of agents' control.

• Adherence to schedule and qualitative measurements can effectively replace other measurements that are merely after-the-fact outputs.

• Adherence to schedule must be implemented appropriately, or it can backfire.

• Qualitative measurements have become more focused, as they've become more important in today's environment.

• For best results, involve agents in establishing and maintaining the monitoring process.

Part Five:

Leadership in the Digital Age

New management techniques, coupled with new capabilities in call center technologies, are changing call centers dramatically. Forward-thinking call center managers recognize the opportunities - and challenges - that these new technologies and methodologies bring. They are moving forward with foresight and planning, and creating cultures in which change is welcomed.

Chapter 13: New Technologies, New Possibilities

Chapter 14: Characteristics of the Best Managed Call Centers

[Chapter 13:

New Technologies, New Possibilities

We think we invent technology, but technology also invents us.

-Richard Farson, in *Management of the Absurd*

New management techniques coupled with new capabilities in call center technologies are changing call centers dramatically. A notable example in recent years has been the shift from bull-pen style call factories to multi-skilled team building and agent empowerment. Other examples include innovative uses of computer-telephone integration (CTI), multimedia applications, geographically dispersed virtual call centers, and the progression towards customized treatment of individual calls.

The opportunities for better serving customers, empowering agents and increasing efficiency are immense. The challenge for call center professionals is to identify the technologies that, if implemented and managed appropriately, will further the principles and mission of the organization.

But new technologies are not passive, and they often present new management challenges. To get good results, they must be implemented with foresight and good planning.

CTI - A New World Of Opportunities

Although CTI has been around in various forms for several decades, it has moved to center stage in the past few years. The basis of CTI is to integrate computers and telephones so they can work together seamlessly and intelligently.

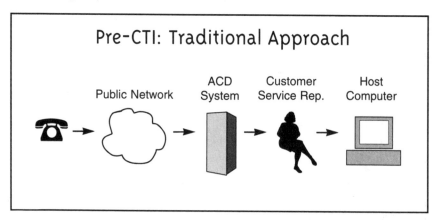

Until recently, CTI has been cost-effective only for large call centers. Most early implementations required custom developed codes, and the data links between components were expensive. Further, hardware and software on both the ACD and the computers often had to be upgraded.

But a number of converging trends are fueling CTI's development, making it feasible for even the smallest call centers. First, many call centers are migrating information systems to PC-based client/server architecture, which doesn't require costly and complex host mainframe programming. (Further, there are a growing number of ACDs that are PC-based. Keith Dawson, editor of *Call Center Magazine*, predicts the day when "we'll be able to walk into Staples or Egghead and buy a shrink-wrapped call processing application.")

Second, new widely accepted standards (e.g., TAPI and TSAPI) that govern how computer equipment can communicate with telephone systems have emerged. These standards make it possible for developers to write applications that can run on a wide range of platforms, which has sparked intense development from existing manufacturers and new venture capital-backed software companies.

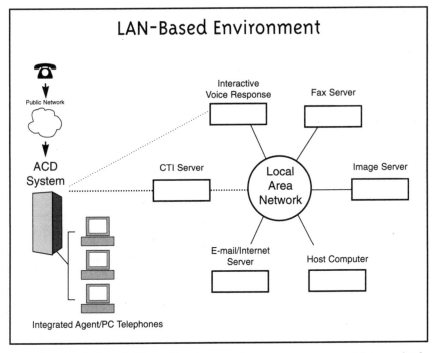

Third, off-the-shelf applications and programming tool kits, which are now available from manufacturers and third-party vendors, are reducing the need to create custom code. And middleware, software that mediates between many different kinds of hardware and software on a network, is further simplifying development. Finally, costs are dropping, as CTI becomes more widespread and development costs are spread over more installations.

CTI Applications

Like any new technology, CTI has been a learning experience, with commensurate research and development costs. But early installations are being leveraged into better, more cost-effective approaches.

Some of CTI's applications for inbound call centers include:

- Synchronized voice and data delivery
- Simultaneous voice and data transfer
- Voice and data conferencing
- Automatic information retrieval for callers
- Segmenting and prioritizing callers

- Caller-specific messaging and routing
- Enhanced performance reporting
- Online training tools
- Enhanced marketing research
- Automated switching between inbound and outbound (call blending)
- Desktop-based productivity tools

You will hear varying cost estimates from consultants and suppliers, ranging from "$50,000 to $5 million per project" or "$200 to $3,000 per agent position." But the fact is, you won't know what the costs are until you explore the alternatives in the context of your present systems, and your present and future objectives.

The future of CTI looks bright. New, creative uses will proliferate, and end-users will increasingly design applications themselves. Reports that give deeper meaning to what callers do and experience will develop

Benefits of Systems Integration
• Improve and expand services
• Increase agent productivity
• Increase revenue
• Lower operating costs
• Enhance customer perception
• Develop a strategic advantage

further. Customer databases will become more and more involved in handling calls. And increasingly, having both a computer terminal and a telephone on a desk will seem like a relic of the good ol' days, as the functions from each are built into one unit.

Changing Job Roles

A significant challenge CTI presents is in managing changing job roles. For example, a major result of CTI is the elimination of most "look it up, then say it" agent jobs. As discussed in Chapters 11 and 12, the agent jobs that are emerging in the post-automation call center world are those that add value through problem identification and problem resolution. Agents will require high skill levels and analytical abilities.

It will be increasingly important for call center managers to cultivate and broaden the skills of agents and supervisors, and for organizations to provide attractive career paths for them. Similarly, the role of call center managers is in transition, as they coordinate a broader range of activities and technologies.

Intelligently Routing Calls

"Dynamic reconfiguration," a term coined by Rolm ACD designers in the late 1970s, was the capability whereby the ACD automatically changed system thresholds based on real-time circumstances. It was a precursor to today's intelligent routing capabilities, which go far beyond these pioneering efforts.

For example, ACD software with "if-then" programming ability has made it possible for system managers to design flexible and sophisticated call handling routines: "If the queue is backed up beyond eight callers in group A, then..." You can specify routing, priority, announcements and information-access alternatives for each call, based on specific criteria.

Further, since callers often have different needs and expectations, agents with a mix of aptitudes and skills are often required. With skill-based routing, you can route individual calls to the agents best-suited to handle them (see Chapter 6).

Applied well, these capabilities can deliver quicker, more effective service for callers, and efficiencies for the call center. As discussed in Chapters 6 and 8, if these capabilities are implemented without good planning, the contingencies can outstrip the call center's ability to understand and manage them, creating inefficiencies and poor service.

The Phenomenal Impact of Voice Processing

The growth of voice processing technology and its impact on call centers has been nothing less than phenomenal. When coupled with computer databases and ACDs, voice response units (VRUs) allow callers to interact with databases and the ACD via speech recognition or, more commonly, touchtone (touchtone is a registered trademark of AT&T). VRU technology is also an important component in CTI and skill-based routing applications, because it can capture information that identifies the caller or the reason for the call.

For callers, voice processing systems are becoming a way of life, along the lines of banks' automated teller machines. And call centers continue to open up new information to callers - flight arrival and departure, account balances, stock prices and schedules, to name a few common examples.

Utilities can program their systems to automatically play an outage

Hello. You have reached the Acme Company. To contact a customer service representative, press "one" on your touch tone phone. If you're calling from a rotary phone, you're so helplessly behind the times, we wouldn't <u>want</u> you for a customer, so you can stay on hold until you rot.

Cartoon by Mort Gerberg © 1997

announcement after getting four or five calls from the same neighborhood. And some call centers are automating surveys by transferring callers into a VRU that guides them through a series of questions and allows them to respond using their keypad (i.e., press 1 for yes, 2 for no).

Speech recognition, which can detect and respond to specific words, phrases or sentences, is already fairly common in some environments, such as the financial industry. It has the potential to increase effectiveness over touchtone alone, because some callers either don't have or don't want to use touchtone.

Further, the proliferation of wireless telephone services has created a growing segment of callers who are mobile and, therefore, have difficulty using touchtone during calls. (Just try to find those buttons on your mobile phone without putting everyone else on the expressway in danger!) Speech recognition can also eliminate the need for long, rigid menus.

Voice processing applications have created an interesting shift in caller attitudes. Despite the justifiable concern of many call center managers that some callers do not like automation, a growing segment of callers actually prefer it. Voice processing systems have created callers who frequently use automated systems and have loyalties to and expectations of them.

The problem created is not an easy one. The call center must efficiently accommodate both callers who prefer live agents, and those who choose automation.

Spanning Time Zones and Geography

Distributed call centers are not new, but the underlying technologies are markedly improving. For example, the ACD networks of yesteryear, which inter-flowed calls over tie-lines based on simple programmable thresholds, could all too easily send calls from the frying pan into the fire. With if-then programming language and real-time intelligence, today's ACDs and networks can make much better distribution decisions.

Advanced Network Alternatives

The network services offered by inter-exchange carriers have become increasingly intelligent. For example, they allow you to route calls based on a variety of criteria, such as originating area code or prefix, dialed number identification service (DNIS), time of day, day of week and other parameters that you control.

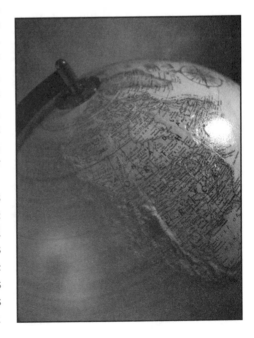

Call allocation services allow users to program the network to send defined percentages of calls to various sites. However, in some large networks, this still means making numerous adjustments throughout the day.

Consequently, many ACDs now feature look-ahead inter-flow, whereby the ACD analyzes traffic conditions and agent availability in each location, then sends calls to the agents with the right skill sets, wherever they may be.

The parameters for inter-flow decisions are programmable, and can include criteria such as available agents, time of day, and calls in primary and secondary queues. Generally, ACDs are interconnected via dedicated integrated services digital network (ISDN) trunks, which are designed to handle the constant back and forth signaling between the systems.

Many ACDs also provide satellite office capability with full ACD functionality. A dedicated connection (T1 or ISDN) links the ACD and the subsystem at the remote site. The remote site is fully integrated with the primary ACD for routing, queuing and reporting purposes.

In another development, GeoTel, a Boston-area company, provides technology that allows ACDs from multiple vendors to communicate real-time with the network. Based on this information, the network routes calls to the call centers and agents best suited to handle them, given real-time conditions.

Teloquent, another company in Boston, provides systems that put a new spin on the conventional definition of ACDs. Their technology includes software that runs on a controller PC and enables users to build a distributed ACD, based on public ISDN services. The switching is done at an ISDN central office, eliminating the need for premises-based switching equipment. A virtual packet circuit between each agent's terminal and the controller is established for call control and reports. Agents use telephones connected to their PCs through ISDN cards.

Robert Gable, author of *Toll-Free Services, A Complete Guide to Design, Implementation and Management*, predicts that these developments are just the beginning of a trend towards increasing ACD-like functionality in the network. As he puts it, "The natural evolution of [toll-free] services will be to provide full ACD functionality at the network level...all present geographic restrictions will be erased and the subscriber will realize a true distributed call center environment."

Telecommuting Capabilities

Telecommuting has had an interesting history in call centers. A handful of organizations have had telecommuting programs in their call centers for years, but in the early '90s, the subject became a hot topic in call center circles. The potential benefits were compelling: tap into a larger workforce, attract and retain employees who need flexible hours, handle peak periods efficiently, have backup when incapacitating weather strikes, save money and space, and comply with governmental restrictions on commuting.

Consequently, dozens, perhaps hundreds, of organizations initiated telecommuting programs in their call centers, many diving in head first. Some were successful and are still going strong. Others ran into high costs, inadequate technologies and challenging new management issues. As a result, many of these early efforts were scaled back or tabled.

What a difference a handful of years has made! As the '90s come to a close, interest in telecommuting is again high, but this time the success stories continue to mount. Recent successes can be attributed to better planning before launch, more disciplined pilot studies, lower costs (e.g., for ISDN services), and improved technologies.

There are a variety of technical approaches that have recently emerged to make telecommuting more feasible. For example, the major ACD vendors and third party suppliers now offer solutions that allow remote agents to log into the primary ACD, through either existing phone lines or ISDN services. Further, distributed ACDs inherently provide telecommuting capabilities. With these solutions, off-site agents appear to the ACD just like any other agent for call distribution, monitoring and reporting purposes.

The data side of telecommuting can still be a challenge in environments that require high bandwidth. But faster modems, compression capabilities and ISDN lines are providing workable alternatives. And there are an increasing number of trials that utilize fiber and cable TV services, which have ample bandwidth to handle current and future needs. As is often the case with technology, features and speed will progress and costs will decline.

Managing Distributed Environments

The advantages of virtual call centers are significant and can include improved service, the elimination of the eggs in one basket syndrome, reduction of commute times for agents, placement of call centers where agents with the right skills are and the ability to take advantage of time zones. The management challenges are those inherent to managing multiple sites, and leading people distributed across time and geography.

We will review this further in Chapter 14.

Better Informed Reps, Managers and Callers

Technology that provides call center information to managers, agents and callers is evolving in various ways. Examples include:

• The ability to send real-time information to agents' telephone sets, a capability of many ACDs. Or alternatively, the ability to send performance statistics to workstations in easy-to-decipher graphs and numbers, such as with Teknekron's Orkistra! or AT&T's CallMaster PC products. These approaches augment traditional wall-mounted reader-boards.

• Real-time adherence monitoring software, which shows the discrepancies between actual and planned schedules, and thresholds on real-time monitors (see discussion in Chapter 12).

• Remote access to call center information. ACDs are increasingly equipped with LAN interfaces that allow anyone on the corporate LAN (permitted to do so) to have access to real-time ACD reports. Further, some ACD and software providers enable remote telephone access, whereby managers can call into the system and hear real-time call center reports and projections, and agents can check work schedules or report in sick.

• Automated monitoring, such as with Teknekron's AutoQuality! system. This technology records calls automatically, eliminating the need for real-time agent monitoring. The times, agents and number of calls recorded are all definable. The recordings can then be later reviewed during a non-peak time. Since the recordings are digital, it's easy to find and review specific calls. Also, supervisors can insert voice annotations into the original recordings for training purposes.

• Screen monitoring, which gives supervisors the ability to view an agent's screen content while listening to the conversation. If used in conjunction with voice, or silent monitoring available through the ACD, the supervisor gets the whole story on how agents are handling the call.

• Expected wait time announcements to callers, available through a growing number of ACDs. The system looks at real-time data, calculates the expected wait, and relays that information to callers via intelligent system announcements (see Chapter 2). This can be coupled with options for the caller, such as to remain holding, leave a message for later callback, or use VRU-based services.

These capabilities create new management issues. For example, monitoring capabilities can be great sources of stress for agents. Or they can be used to identify improvement opportunities and coach agents to higher levels of performance.

Similarly, technology that gives managers outside the call center access to call center information may bring unwanted attention. Or it may be a boon to the interest level and support the call center receives.

Enabling Tools, New Efficiencies

A plethora of new tools are enabling call centers to improve service and are freeing reps from tedious work of days gone by. For example:

• Applications can be accessed via icon-based GUI (pronounced "gooey") windows, allowing for simultaneous tasks to be accomplished.

• Document scanning and on-screen retrieval can boost the number of calls you handle on the first attempt dramatically.

• Auto greetings allow agents to pre-record their introductions. Then, when calls come in, their greetings go out in digital clarity, while they are collecting their thoughts and otherwise catching their breath. It may not sound like much, but agents who use it love it. And it starts every call off with the right greeting and a chipper voice.

• While other technologies are getting most of the adoration, facsimile technologies have quietly and significantly improved many call centers. Faxes can be presorted or generated dynamically. Further, callers can obtain information by using automated fax-back or fax on demand applications. And giving agents the ability to fax documents directly from their terminal during talk time, can be an impressive time-saver. A wide range of voice processing and PC-based fax-server platforms provide these capabilities at a moderate cost.

• Call blending technology enables agents who are handling inbound calls to be switched to outbound when the call volume drops to a programmable level. The system monitors the rate of inbound traffic and agent availability, and launches outbound campaigns as circumstances permit (see Chapter 7).

• In a twist on conventional call distribution, Teledata Solutions, Inc. has developed Call-Link, which resides in a call control window on the agent's PC screen. Using a mouse, agents can point to a call to answer next from a list of eligible calls in queue, as shown on the screen. This enables them to literally select the most important call based on real-time conditions. When coupled with CTI, agents can review the caller's records before deciding which call to answer.

> "A plate of silver and one of zinc are taken into the mouth, the one above, the other below the tongue. They are then placed in contact with the wire, and words issuing from the mouth are conveyed by the wire."
>
> - 1854 English newspaper, describing how the yet-to-be invented telephone might work.

Mono-Media is Going, Going...

Just as some call centers are beginning to grapple with things like voice response technology, distributed call centers and CTI, new developments are significantly changing call centers. For example, there's a huge effort to develop and refine services on the World Wide Web.

In a short time, the Web has become a major force in customer service. We live in an era in which online services have become so important that the big players run expensive competitive ads during televised Super Bowl and NBA playoffs.

A case in point, discount brokerage Charles Schwab provides a popular Web site for online trading. When a recent installation of new software caused the site to shut down intermittently for a few hours, the ordeal made national news. Spokesperson Tom Taggart had to remind disgruntled customers and the press that they could have switched to that old standby, the telephone.

But we haven't seen anything yet. While there has been plenty of hype surrounding the information superhighway, a high-speed broadband network that connects the home to the outside world is going to happen. Consider the possibilities. Think about these ingredients, and ponder ways they can be combined:

- Telephone
- Fiber optics
- Television
- Computer
- Wireless
- Interactive
- Digital
- Virtual-reality
- Software
- Multimedia
- Cellular
- Pagers
- Networks
- Entertainment

In coming months and years, these components will be sliced, diced and mixed in numerous, yet-to-be-imagined ways.

Seven Key Trends

What do we make of all this? What should we prepare for? Seven important trends have emerged from these developments. They are not predictions. They have already been set in motion and are changing the call center landscape significantly - and rapidly.

1. Consumers are demanding choices. As Gordon MacPherson put it, "A new breed of technology-sophisticated consumers is demanding a choice of how they will be served. They often know what the choices could be, and they will become increasingly critical if you do not offer the choices they think you should offer." It's up to you to open up and develop the alternatives.

2. Callers are increasingly being treated as individuals. In their well-received book, *The One To One Future*, authors Don Peppers and Martha Rogers popularized the term "mass customization." Their view is that interactive technologies allow us to collaborate and interact with each customer individually, but on a mass, efficient scale.

CTI capabilities that allow the database to become an active part of processing calls is a notable call center example. Skill-based routing is another.

3. Transactions requiring live assistance continue to increase. Automated alternatives continue to make up a greater and greater percentage of total customer contacts. And that means call volumes are dropping, right? Not in most cases! In most call centers, the number of live answer calls continues to grow, even as they represent a smaller portion of the transaction pie, because transactions of all types are increasing that rapidly.

New technologies don't simply automate existing transactions. They create new services. And new services create additional interactions. In their book, *Canadian Telecom In Transition*, Ian and Lis Angus cite "society's insatiable and ever-expanding appetite for telecommunications" as one of the driving forces in the telecommunications industry today. The public's use of call centers is a prime example (see Chapter 9). The message in this: prepare for growth.

Seven Key Trends
1. Consumers are demanding choices
2. Callers are increasingly treated as individuals
3. Transactions requiring live assistance continue to increase
4. Agents require high levels of skill
5. Live answer is being rationed
6. Call centers are increasingly distributed
7. Multimedia will prevail

4. Agents require high levels of skill. Will technologies such as the Web and VRU services eventually eliminate the need for reps? Almost certainly not. (In fact, in many cases, new Web services are actually creating calls, the result of expanded services.) But they will leave your call center with transactions that are increasingly complex.

5. Live answer is being rationed. Given the growth in the industry, forward-thinking call centers are doing everything possible to automate as many types of transactions as possible, within the realm of caller acceptance and expectations. In other words, they are rationing live answer. They are insuring that their highly-trained, highly-paid reps are handling transactions that really require the human touch.

6. Call centers are increasingly distributed. Telecommuting, networked call centers and satellite call centers have proliferated rapidly in recent years. The industry is reaching the point where virtually any place with up-to-spec communications technology and a skilled and flexible labor force is a candidate for regional, national or international-oriented call centers. Once again, it's skills and know-how that will matter. Outsourcing and partnering will flourish. And you may find yourself collaborating with other organizations in creative ways (see Chapter 7). The call center as *a place* will fade.

7. Multimedia will prevail. Multimedia appeals to the way we are wired up. We communicate best when our senses work together. And that's a driving force in the popularity and proliferation of multimedia services. Once callers get a taste of multimedia, they won't want to go back.

And whiz-bang multimedia technology won't be on customers' minds. They don't give a hoot how it works. They just want it to be reliable, intuitive and accessible. For example, as they're utilizing your web site and decide they want further help, they want a knowledgeable rep a click away. And if they end up in a queue - queues will still happen - they'll want to know how long the wait will be and what their immediate alternatives are.

If there are any two messages in these developments that stand out above all others, it is these: 1) With so many choices, keep your eyes on what matters. The purpose of any new technology should be to support the governing principles and mission of

> ## Three Roles for Technology
>
> 1. When no service would be available otherwise, provide automated assistance.
>
> 2. Provide automated assistance to increase the productivity of reps.
>
> 3. Completely offload transactions that can be automated.

your organization. 2) Inaction is the worst action you can take. The time to plan your call center's migration into the next era is now.

Points to Remember

• Advanced call center technologies are creating enormous opportunities for better serving customers, empowering agents and increasing efficiency in the call center.

• These technologies are not passive, and they are changing caller behavior, causing significant reallocations of resources, creating political shifts in call centers and changing the responsibilities of agents and managers.

• Consequently, new capabilities must be implemented with foresight and care, and must support the organization's mission.

• The key trends that have been set in motion provide a framework for understanding the changes taking place and preparing your call center for tomorrow's environment.

[Chapter 14:

Characteristics of the
Best Managed Call Centers

*You don't know what you don't know until you know it....the right
solution is a continuous search for the right solution.*

- Dr. Ichak Adizes

I n some call centers, you can feel the energy as soon as you walk in
the door. It takes many forms: pride of workmanship, a feeling of
community, good planning and coordination. Everybody knows
what the mission is and everybody is pulling in the same direction. The
call center "clicks."

What do the best call centers have in common? There are plenty of
benchmarking studies that address the subject - sort of. They reveal
various results - e.g., customer satisfaction and retention, service levels,
planning accuracy, organizational structure, costs and revenues, employee
satisfaction and turnover. The problem is, they rarely relay the *how*
behind the results.

Consequently, there are lots of opinions on the subject. And that's
what the issues summarized here represent - our opinion. These are the
12 characteristics we see over and over in what we believe to be the
world's best managed call centers, those that consistently outperform
others in their respective industries.

I. They Have a Supporting Culture

Culture, the inveterate principles or values of an organization, tends to guide behavior. Culture can either support and further, or, as some have learned the hard way, ruin the best laid plans for organizational change.

Characteristics of the Best Managed Call Centers

1. They have a supporting culture.
2. They know that their people are the key to success.
3. They focus quality around customer expectations.
4. They view the incoming call center as a total process.
5. They have an established, collaborative planning process.
6. They have an effective mix of people and technology.
7. They have a practical balance between specialization and pooling.
8. They leverage the key statistics.
9. They get the budget and support they need.
10. They effectively hurdle distance, time and politics.
11. They are willing to experiment.
12. They see the possibilities.

There's no guaranteed formula for creating a supporting culture. But managers in well-run call centers agree that shaping the culture of the organization is a primary leadership responsibility. They do not believe that culture should be left to fate. As a result, they spend an inordinate amount of time understanding their organization and the people who are part of it.

A primary ingredient in a high-performance culture is effective communication. Communication creates meaning and direction for people. Organizations of all types depend on the existence of what leadership scholar Warren Bennis calls "shared meanings and interpretations of reality," which facilitate coordinated action.

An Annual Celebration at UPS

In 1994, United Parcel Service (Mahwah, NJ) kicked off what has now become an annual employee recognition tradition. Each fall, UPS honors internal help desk reps by hosting a

> breakfast meeting off-site as an employee recognition "grand finale." According to Darlene Van Der Zyde, help desk manager at UPS, "We designate one day a year to get the whole team together off the phones to recognize them for a job well done. We have recognition programs throughout the year, but this event is the biggest."
>
> Management presents awards at the event, but the reps do more than simply accept accolades. They also take part in organizing the celebration and coming up with themes and skits. "This is their day to shine," says Van Der Zyde. "They love having the visibility in front of senior management."
>
> The impact on morale has been impressive. "They get pumped-up for it every year," says Van Der Zyde. "It's a real team-building event." ■

Management consultant Richard Farson warns that "many programs in management training today are moving us in the wrong direction because they fail to appreciate the complexity and paradoxical nature of human organizations. Thinking loses out to how-to-do-it formulas and techniques, if not slogans and homilies, as the principle management guides."

Judging by their actions, the most effective call center managers seem to agree with Farson. They seem to be comfortably resigned to the fact that, as Farson puts it, "We can never quite master our relationships with each other." Consequently, they are okay with the realization that they will often be spending more of their time on "people issues" than on anything else.

2. They Know that Their People are the Key to Success

The most important implication of the trends discussed in Chapters 11-13 is clear: Your people will make or break you. They are your key to success.

Call centers with an eye on the future are cultivating the skills of their people, today. They are investing heavily in training and are building legitimate, attractive career paths. As recognized consultant Don Tapscott writes, "There is no sustainable competitive advantage today other than organizational learning."

Remember that you hire a "total person," not simply a rep, supervisor or manager. When you begin to look at people with their inherent talents and abilities - not just as job categories with specific duties - this kind of ongoing investment makes a lot of sense.

Leading call centers are also working hard to develop both formal and informal communication channels in their organizations. Keeping people well informed helps them prepare for and accept change. "Today's business world is and has been about change," notes industry consultant Kathleen Peterson. "The concept of change becomes personal and its meaning and level of acceptance are based clearly on how the change is communicated and what people believe it to mean."

3. They Focus Quality Around Customer Expectations

The best managed call centers have an incessant focus on evolving customer needs and expectations. They are continually redefining quality around those expectations (Chapter 11). They know that what worked yesterday will not necessarily work tomorrow.

An Astounding Challenge

CLEAR Communications (New Zealand), a telecommunications services provider with call centers in Auckland and Christchurch, has lately been grappling with the issue of ever-increasing customer expectations. Since the company's inception in 1990, shortly after New Zealand deregulated its telecommunications market, CLEAR has garnered around 20 percent market share. Much of the growth can be attributed to top-notch service and favorable word-of-mouth advertising. "We strive to do more than just meet our customers' expectations," says Roz White, CLEAR's Customer Services Manager in Auckland. "We want to 'astound' them."

Surveys have indicated that CLEAR customers have been impressed with the company's service. But CLEAR is discovering first-hand a basic reality of customer psychology. When you improve your service, customers rather quickly progress through four stages:

1) They appreciate it.
2) They get used to it.
3) They expect it.
4) They demand it.

And the competition doesn't sit still either! So how do you stay ahead of expectations? That was one of the questions CLEAR posed to a group of their managers and supervisors participating in a series of workshops, in early 1997.

The results of their discussion? At the top of the list, remember that it is critical to continually assess customer expectations, because they are always evolving. You also need to leverage the feedback you are getting into service innovations and improvements. " We value every contact with our customers, and use the 5,000 opportunities we have each day to provide all areas of our business with real-time customer feedback," says White.

White's group also concluded that, over time, even modest improvements add up. "We are keen to make the quantum leaps...and to ensure we are seen as a world-class call centre," she says. "But these are fewer and further apart. Incremental improvements or fine tuning (toning), ensures that we are continually moving forward, and therefore staying one step ahead of our customers' expectations." ∎

4. They View The Incoming Call Center as a Total Process

Call centers that consistently get the best results view the call center as a total process. That has been a major theme in this book, and it takes many forms:

• Understand how the call center supports the organization's direction.

• Ensure that everyone in the call center and those with key supporting roles outside the call center have a basic understanding of how call centers operate (have them read Chapters 8 and 9!).

• Develop an effective, collaborative planning and management process.

• Take the initiative in coordinating with other departments.

• Integrate the call center's activities effectively with other departments within the organization.

• Recognize the process to be where most quality problems occur, and constantly work to improve it.

• Be prepared to respond to changing conditions.

The days of the call center as an island unto itself - "That's the call center over there, and they handle sales and customer service" - is fast fading. The reality is that the call center is an important part of a much bigger process.

5. They Have an Established, Collaborative Planning Process

Effective planning was the primary theme in Chapters 3-9. A major objective of good planning is to "get the right number of people in the right places at the right time."

But systematic planning accomplishes more than that. It also contributes to effective communication. It creates a body of information that wouldn't otherwise be available. ("Here's our call load pattern and, therefore, why the schedules are structured as they are.") "It is the catalyst for people to think about the future and see their contributions in the context of the big picture," says call center consultant Laurie Solomon.

Perhaps most important, systematic planning necessitates communication about values on issues such as resource allocations, budgeting and workload priorities. In sum, it forces the kind of communication that an active call center desperately requires.

6. They Have an Effective Mix of People and Technology

In the emerging call center environment, personal contact with callers will need to be rationed. There is simply too much caller demand to have your people handling routine calls or tasks that technology can readily handle. But it is detrimental to force callers to use machines when a person is necessary or when they prefer live answer.

Leading call centers continue to work on finding the right mix of people and technology. We like how telecommunications consultant Ann

Smith put it: "Technology can get you where you're going fast, so you better be headed in the right direction. And the right direction means recognizing where technology fits and the importance people will always have in the process."

As discussed in Chapter 13, new technologies are not passive, and they are changing caller expectations, causing reallocations of resources, creating power shifts in call centers, and changing the responsibilities of agents and managers. The challenge for call center professionals is to sort through the many choices and identify the technologies that can further the mission of the organization. Then, implement them with the necessary foresight and planning.

7. They Have a Practical Balance Between Specialization And Pooling

In one sense, pooling resources is at the heart of the incoming call center industry. It is a primary function of ACDs and networks. But new capabilities in intelligent ACDs and advanced network services give call centers the means to slice and dice the incoming call load anyway they choose.

Consequently, as discussed in Chapter 8, the pooling principle is not an all-or-nothing proposition. There is a continuum between specialization and pooling.

Call centers will increasingly handle each call according to its individual needs and characteristics. The impetus in call center planning will remain on cross training and broadening the skills of reps, as feasible. But there will be overlap and contingencies, and the rigidly defined answer groups of the past will diminish.

The trick is to find the right balance between specialization and pooling. Leading call centers don't "wing it." Instead, they:

• Flowchart their system and network programming to identify weaknesses in routing logic.

• Avoid unnecessary complexity in agent group structure.

• Expand responsibilities for reps, as possible.

• Hire multi-lingual agents, when possible.

• Improve information systems and training so agents are equipped to handle a broad range of transactions.

• Get as close to the pooled end of the spectrum as circumstances allow.

8. They Leverage the Key Statistics

As discussed in Chapter 11, high-level indicators of call center performance include:

- Average call value (for revenue-producing call centers)
- Customer satisfaction
- Service level
- Percent abandoned
- Cost per call
- Errors and rework
- Forecasted call load versus actual
- Scheduled staff to actual
- Adherence to schedule
- Average handling time

The call centers that get the best results have three things in common, relative to these statistics. First, they ensure that the measurements are as accurate, complete and as unbiased as possible. They are aware of how easily statistics can be misinterpreted. Second, they view the reports in light of how they relate to each other. They know that a single report, outside the context of the others, can lead to erroneous conclusions. Third, they know that simply tracking high-level measurements won't inherently improve results. Instead, they work on the factors - the root causes - that cause these outputs to be where they are.

9. They Get the Budget and Support They Need

It's crazy. Far too many call centers are operating under the auspices of, "Okay, here are the resources we're willing to give you, and here's what we want you to achieve..." That is the proverbial cart before the donkey.

Consider an analogy. Airlines couldn't possibly operate a flight without a tangible connection between the results they want to achieve and the supporting resources they need. They start with an objective - fly 300 people from Washington to London. The objective is not a wishful goal. Instead, it is a specific pre-determined outcome supported by carefully calculated resources.

Similarly, the best call centers first decide on the objectives they want to achieve. They then allocate the resources necessary to support those objectives, through careful calculations and planning (Chapters 3-9).

10. They Effectively Hurdle Distance, Time and Politics

Today, fiber optic cables crisscross the globe, and satellites provide virtually ubiquitous world-wide telecommunications service. Computer and telecommunications technologies have spawned organizations that span geography and time.

Trends in the call center industry are indicative of these developments. For example, distributed call centers, where two or more centers share the call load, can span a region, a country or the globe. Telecommuting programs continue to steadily proliferate. And cross-functional teams, with responsibilities for everything from forecasting the workload to improving quality, have become common.

While new technologies have provided enormous new capabilities, they haven't eliminated the natural barriers that exist between people who work in distributed environments, including:

• People who work in different places and/or at different times tend to have trouble seeing themselves as an integral part of a larger, unified team.

• The informal opportunities that people have for getting to know each other in traditional settings, such as in the hallways and break room, may be rare.

• A large amount of information is exchanged outside the formal context of memos and meetings. As a result, information is often unevenly distributed among the group.

Call center managers increasingly have the responsibility of getting results from people that work in different locations, don't report directly to them, or don't work at the same time. Managers in the best managed call centers recognize that the success of their operations depends on how well they master the art of managing and leading in a distributed environment.

Jaclyn Kostner, author of the well-received book, *Virtual Leadership,* concludes that, "The key way to build high performance across distance is to build trust." Unfortuntely, there is no fool-proof, specific formula for achieving trust. It cannot be bought or mandated. In that sense, it's like leadership - hard to define and defies a specific recipe for those who want to create it.

There are, however, tangible, conscientious steps call center managers are taking to create environments where trust is likely to flourish:

• Create a clear vision for the call center.

• Create opportunities for the people in the distributed environment to get to know each other. (We know of one call center director who had managers in distributed sites record short answers to questions about themselves, e.g., what's your dream vacation? How did you end up in the call center? She then combined the responses and sent the compiled tape to the team. Another manager set up a World Wide Web page profiling the members of a multi-site team, then gave everyone a short quiz on the interests and backgrounds of the other members.)

• Look for ways to keep everyone involved. Often, some amount of expediency must be traded for the sake of fostering a collaborative environment.

• Take steps to ensure that everyone gets key information at the same time.

• Spend a disproportionate amount of time tending to the needs and relationships of the more "distant" members of the group. (Distant may mean the members who work the night shift, or those who are in a site thousands of miles away.)

• Look for ways to scrap, or at least, minimize the impact of unnecessary hierarchies and cumbersome bureaucracies, which tend to wreak havoc on distributed teams.

II. They are Willing to Experiment

The most successful call centers continually review and reassess how they do things, and the results they are achieving. What can be improved? What should be scrapped? What assumptions no longer make sense? What can be done differently? Can an outsider do it better or more efficiently?

They would agree with the advice of management consultant Dr.

Ichak Adizes, who reminds us, "You don't know what you don't know until you know it....the right solution is a continuous search for the right solution."

12. They See the Possibilities

These identical two-year old twins are wearing T-shirts which say, "If I'm Sad, Call 1-800 Grandma." If that's truly an indication of how the public perceives inbound call centers, then that's a significant compliment to all of us!

Faith and Charity Peeler, Pasadena, Maryland. Age 2 (1995). Used with permission.

After all, Grandma forecasts the workload well because she's always there when needed. Talk about skill-based routing - she's just the person for the job! She empathizes, she doesn't rush, and she rarely makes mistakes. She's trained, experienced, and empowered to solve the problem, whatever it may be. With Grandma, customer satisfaction is high!

The call center industry has come a long way in recent years. Customer expectations are high. And, for good reason. For the most part, incoming call centers have learned how to deliver. Collectively, they have invested billions in equipment, networks, and software. They have spent untold hours training and equipping people. They have learned the nuances of forecasting, staffing, and the behavior of queues. They continue to improve processes and find new and better ways to get things done. And, they have identified evolving customer needs, and are constantly changing to meet those needs.

What's next? Where are we going from here? Our hunch is, some call center managers view the future with apprehension. They fear the impact and uncertainties new technologies will bring. They are concerned about ever-heightening competition. They contemplate the increasingly diverse transactions their call center will handle. They wonder how they're going to keep up in an environment that is on fast-forward.

There's no doubt about it, there will be changes and challenges ahead. None of us can afford to stand still for long. We suppose that is the case for just about everyone in this crazy digital world.

But remember, the very things that are bringing uncertainties are also bringing opportunities. More than ever, organizations need incoming call center professionals who can help them sort through the changes and make the transition into the next era.

The opportunities are immense. What a great time to be involved with incoming call centers!

Appendix

Sample Job Description for Incoming Call Center Managers
Recommended by Incoming Calls Management Institute

I.   Job Title
       A. Incoming Call Center Manager

II.   Principal Accountabilities
       A. Meet organization's sales/customer service objectives
       B. Assure all callers receive service which is prompt, friendly, courteous, accurate and helpful
       C. Provide customer feedback to others in organization

III.   Standards for Measuring Success
       A. Meet service level and response time objectives provisioned in budget
       B. Meet customer satisfaction survey objectives
       C. Meet cost-per-call standards
       D. Meet quality objectives

IV.   Reports to
       A. Vice President, Customer Service or Sales

V.   Dimensions
       A. Dollar amount of annual budget
       B. Number of persons supervised
             1. Exempt
             2. Non-exempt
       C. Annual workload
       D. Size of ACD and network

VI.   Duties
       A. Conduct caller requirement studies
       B. Conduct caller satisfaction studies
       C. Forecast workload
       D. Prepare work schedules
       E. Prepare budget
       F. Prepare disaster contingency plans
       G. Configure call center systems
       H. Prepare customer feedback reports
       I. Develop agents
             1. Monitor performance
             2. Identify training requirements
             3. Provide training

4. Conduct performance appraisals
5. Provide ongoing coaching
6. Develop and guide empowered teams

J. Maintain agent morale
K. Make continuous work process improvements
1. Identify steps in work processes
2. Identify improvement opportunities
3. Test improvement opportunities
4. Fully implement improvements with best results
5. Continually monitor performance in key areas

L. Take Safety Precautions for
1. Stress-related illnesses
2. Computer-related illnesses
3. Noise-related illnesses
4. Preventing accidents

VII. Tools Used
A. Automatic call distributor
B. Interactive voice response
C. Computer-telephony integration
D. World Wide Web
E. E-mail
F. Video
G. Facsimile
H. Imaging
I. Workforce management system
J. Database programs
K. Specialized customer service/sales software programs

VIII. Education, Experience and Training Required
A. Education
1. Bachelor's Degree or demonstrated ability to think critically, organize thoughts, write and speak properly

B. Desirable Experience
1. Customer contact work
2. Supervision
3. Teaching
4. Personal computer
5. Call center technology
6. Budgeting

        7. Industry experience

  C. Training

        1. Quality improvement techniques

        2. Queuing theory

        3. Call center planning framework

        4. Customer behavior

        5. Budgeting

        6. Leadership

        7. Call center technologies

        8. Performance appraisal and coaching

        9. Time management

        10. Organization's products and services

        11. Organization's industry

        12. Teaching methods

IX.   Coordinates with

  A. Information Systems (IS)

  B. Telecommunications

  C. Human Resources

  D. Marketing and Corporate Communications

  E. Production/Manufacturing

  F. Suppliers/Outsourcers

  G. Upper Management

Notes

Chapter 1

Call Center Definition, source: Incoming Calls Management Institute, *Essential Skills and Knowledge for Effective Incoming Call Center Management* seminar, 1990-1997.

Planning steps, source: Incoming Calls Management Institute, *Essential Skills and Knowledge for Effective Incoming Call Center Management* seminar, 1990-1997.

Charles Handy quote, source: Rowan, Gibson, Ed., *Rethinking the Future*, Nicholas Brealey Publishing, 1997, page 32.

Michael Porter quote, source: Rowan, Gibson, Ed., *Rethinking the Future*, Nicholas Brealey Publishing, 1997, page 51.

Chapter 2

Three driving forces (calls bunch up, visible and invisible queue, and seven factors of caller tolerance), source: Incoming Calls Management Institute, *Essential Skills and Knowledge for Effective Incoming Call Center Management* seminar, 1990-1997.

Three types of traffic arrival, source: J. Jewett, J. Shrago, J. Gilliland, B. Yomtov, *Traffic Engineering Tables: The Complete Practical Encyclopedia*, Telephony Publishing Corporation, 1980.

Word Perfect reference, source: *Service Level Newsletter*, July 1994.

British Airways case study, source: *Service Level Newsletter*, April 1996.

Chapter 3

Service level charts, source: Incoming Calls Management Institute, 1990-1997.

Cheryl Odee Helm quote, source: "In the Center with Cheryl Odee Helm," *Service Level Newsletter*, November 1996.

Incremental Revenue (Value) Analysis, source: Incoming Calls Management Institute, 1990-1997.

Martin Prunty quote, source: Interview with Martin Prunty, July 11, 1997.

Response time sample, source: Sampling by the authors of several dozen call centers, between May and June 1997.

Chapter 4

Henry Dortmans quote, source: Interview with Henry Dortmans, July 1, 1997.

Notes

AT&T, Duke Power, Eddie Bauer references, source: Authors' notes from proceedings at *1995 World Conference on Incoming Call Center Management*, August 1995, Orlando, FL.

Chapter 5

Daniel B. Nickell quotes, sources: 1) Nickell, Daniel B., *Forecasting On Your Microcomputer*, Tab Books, 1988. 2) Interview with Daniel B. Nickell, October 28, 1996.

Breaking down a forecast, source: Incoming Calls Management Institute, *Essential Skills and Knowledge for Effective Call Center Management* seminar, 1990-1997.

Worksheets (Sales, Direct Marketing, Customer Service), source: MacPherson, Gordon F., Jr., "Forecasting Calls," *Service Level Newsletter*, June 1990.

Makridakis, Syros and Steven C. Wheelright, Ed., *The Handbook of Forecasting: A Manager's Guide*, John Wiley & Sons, 1987.

Forecasting Study, source: Incoming Calls Management Institute, 1992.

Chapter 6

W. Edwards Deming quote, source: Deming, W. Edwards, *Out of the Crisis*, Massachusetts Institute of Technology, 1986.

Mike Hills reference, source: Interview with Mike Hills, July 15, 1997.

Erlang C software program reference, source: Incoming Calls Management Institute, copyright 1986.

Skill-based routing case, source: Prunty, Martin A., *The Road Ahead to the Next Generation Call Center* seminar, Telecom Group, Inc. and Incoming Calls Management Institute, 1996.

Todd Tanner quote, source: Interview with Todd Tanner, July 15, 1997.

Maggie Klenke quote, source: Klenke, Maggie, conference proceedings, *1996 World Conference on Incoming Call Center Management*, August 27-29, 1996, Phoenix, AZ.

Traffic Engineering Tables and Formulas, source: Jewett, J., J. Shrago, J. Gilliland, B. Yomtov, *Traffic Engineering Tables: The Complete Practical Encyclopedia*, Telephony Publishing Corporation, 1980.

Chapter 7

Rostered staff factor (shrink factor) illustrations, source: Incoming Calls Management Institute, *Essential Skills and Knowledge for Effective Call Center Management* seminar, 1990-1997.

Vanguard swat team reference, source: Authors' notes from Conference proceedings, *1995 World Conference on Incoming Call Center Management*, August 1995, Orlando, FL.

Met Life Call Centers reference, source: Authors' notes from Conference proceedings, *1995 World Conference on Incoming Call Center Management*, August 1995.

WearGuard and Cross Country Motor Club case study, source: Mayben, Julia, "WearGuard Corp, Cross Country Motor Club Sharing Staff to Manage Peak Seasons," *Service Level Newsletter*, October 1996.

Telecommuting programs, source: Authors' notes from conference proceedings, *Telecommute 1996*, October 1996, Phoenix, AZ.

Service level graphs, source: Incoming Calls Management Institute, *Essential Skills and Knowledge for Effective Call Center Management* seminar, 1990-1997.

Chapter 8

Immutable laws, graphs, tables and examples, source: Incoming Calls Management Institute, *Essential Skills and Knowledge for Effective Call Center Management* seminar, 1990-1997.

Chapter 9

Ten things senior managers should understand, some points adapted from the booklet: MacPherson, Jr. Gordon F., "What Senior Managers Need to Know About Incoming Call Centers," *Service Level Newsletter*, 1988.

Reporting to senior management, source: Cleveland, Brad, "Q&A", *Service Level Newsletter*, May and June 1993.

Stephanie Winston quote, source: Winston, Stephanie, *The Organized Executive*, Warner Books, 1983.

Winston Churchill quote, source: Tripp, Rhoda Thomas, Editor, *The International Thesaurus*, Perennial Library, 1970.

W. Edwards Deming quote, source: Deming, W. Edwards, *Out of the Crisis*, Massachusetts Institute of Technology, 1986.

Notes

Liberfone case study, source: Interview via e-mail with Wouter Tiems, June 26, 1997.

Laurie Solomon quote, source: Interview with Laurie Solomon, June 30, 1997.

Chapter 10

"Due to our inability to staff..."(cartoon), source: Kathleen Peterson.

Real-time management graphs and examples: Incoming Calls Management Institute, *Essential Skills and Knowledge for Effective Call Center Management* seminar, 1990-1997, and *"The Best of Service Level Newsletter - Volume 1," Service Level Newsletter*, 1990.

Chapter 11

What is a quality call?, and costs when quality is lacking, sources: Incoming Calls Management Institute, *Essential Skills and Knowledge for Effective Call Center Management* seminar, 1990-1997, and *"The Best of Service Level Newsletter - Volume 1," Service Level Newsletter*, 1990.

AT&T Statistical Quality Control Handbook, Western Electric Company, Inc., 1956.

W. Edwards Deming quote, source: Deming, W. Edwards, *Out of the Crisis*, Massachusetts Institute of Technology, 1986.

Flowchart, source: MacPherson, Gordon, F. Jr., "A Deeper Look: Flowcharting a Simple Call," *The Best of Service Level Newsletter - Volume 4, Service Level Newsletter*, 1997, page 358.

Cause and effect diagram, source: Cleveland, Brad, "The Cause and Effect Diagram, a Useful Tool for Sorting Out Quality Problems" *The Best of Service Level Newsletter - Volume 4, Service Level Newsletter*, 1997, page 399.

Bert Cyr quote, source: "In The Center with Bert Cyr," *Service Level Newsletter*, December, 1993.

Don Tapscott quote, source: Tapscott, Don, proceedings from *Call Centre Canada* conference, April 1-3, 1996, Toronto, ON.

Chapter 12

Kathleen Peterson quote, source: Interview with Kathleen Peterson, June 26, 1997.

Alternatives to silent monitoring, source: MacPherson, Gordon F., Jr., "Lets Open Our Minds on Silent Monitoring," *Best of Service Level Newsletter - Volume 1, Service Level Newsletter*, 1990, page 4.

Recommended monitoring practices, source: Incoming Calls Management Institute, 1993.

Chapter 13

Keith Dawson reference, source: Dawson, Keith, *The Call Center Handbook*, Flatiron Publishing, Inc., 1996, page 33.

Robert Gable reference, source: Gable, Robert, *Toll-Free Services, A Complete Guide to Design, Implementation and Management*, Artech House, 1995, page 137.

"Plate of silver·" reference, source: Brooks, John, *Telephone, The First Hundred Years*, Harper and Row, 1975, page 36.

"Schwab's Site on Web Shut for Part of Day," *Wall Street Journal*, June 12, 1997, page B5.

Gordon F. MacPherson, Jr. quote, source: MacPherson, Gordon F., Jr., "The New Forces of Change," *Best of Service Level Newsletter - Volume 4, Service Level Newsletter*, 1997, page 460.

Don Peppers and Martha Rogers quote, source: Peppers, Don and Martha Rogers, *The One to One Future*, Doubleday, 1996.

Ian and Lis Angus reference, source: Angus, Ian and Lis Angus, *Canadian Telecom in Transition*, Telemanagement Press, 1995, page 17.

Chapter 14

Warren Bennis reference, source: Bennis, Warren and Robert Townsend, *Reinventing Leadership*, William Morrow and Company, Inc., 1995.

Darlene Van Der Zyde quote, source: Interview with Darlene Van Der Zyde, May 19, 1997.

Richard Farson quote, source: Farson, Richard, *Management of the Absurd*, Simon and Schuster, 1996, page 36.

Don Tapscott quote, source: Tapscott, Don, The Digital Economy, McGraw-Hill, 1986.

Kathleen Peterson quote, source: Peterson, Kathleen, *Powerful Leadership and Communication Skills for Call Center Mangers*, Incoming Calls Management Institute and Powerhouse Training Consultants, Inc., 1997.

CLEAR Communications case study, source: Interview with Roz White via e-mail, July 21, 1997.

Notes

Laurie Solomon quote, source: Interview with Laurie Solomon, June 30, 1997.

Ann Smith quote, source: Interview with Ann Smith, July 26, 1997.

Jaclyn Kostner quote, source: Kostner, Jaclyn, *Virtual Leadership*, Warner Books, 1996.

Dr. Ichak Adizes quote, source: Dr. Ichak, as quoted in *Manage*, January 1993, page 14.

Glossary

Acronyms

ACD	Automatic Call Distributor
ACS	Automatic Call Sequencer
ACW	After-Call Work
AHT	Average Handling Time
AHT	Average Holding Time on Trunks
ANI	Automatic Number Identification
ARU	Audio Response Unit
ASA	Average Speed of Answer
ATA	Average Time to Abandonment
ATB	All Trunks Busy
BRI	Basic Rate Interface
CCR	Customer Controlled Routing
CCS	Centum Call Seconds
CD-ROM	Compact Disc Read Only Memory
CED	Caller Entered Digits
CIO	Chief Information Officer
CLI	Calling Line Identity
CO	Central Office
CPE	Customer Premises Equipment
DN	Dialed Number
DNIS	Dialed Number Identification Service
FX	Foreign Exchange Line
GOS	Grade of Service
IS	Information Systems
ISDN	Integrated Services Digital Network
IT	Information Technology
IVR	Interactive Voice Response
IXC	Inter Exchange Carrier
LAN	Local Area Network
LEC	Local Exchange Carrier
LED	Light Emitting Diode
MAC	Moves, Adds and Changes
NCC	Network Control Center
NPA	Numbering Plan Area
OCR	Optical Character Recognition
PABX	Private Automatic Branch Exchange
PBX	Private Branch Exchange
PRI	Primary Rate Interface
PSN	Public Switched Network

Glossary

PUC	Public Utility Commission
RAN	Recorded Announcement Route
RFI	Request for Information
RFP	Request for Proposal
RSF	Rostered Staff Factor
TAPI	Telephony Applications Programming Interface
TCP/IP	Transmission Control Protocol/Internet Protocol
TSAPI	Telephony Services Application Programming Interface
TSF	Telephone Service Factor
TSR	Telephone Sales or Service Representative
UCD	Uniform Call Distributor
VRU	Voice Response Unit
WAN	Wide Area Network
WATS	Wide Area Telecommunications Service
WWW	World Wide Web

Definitions

Abandoned Call. Also called a Lost Call. The caller hangs up before reaching an agent.

Activity Codes. See Wrap-Up Codes.

Adherence To Schedule. A general term that refers to how well agents adhere to their schedules. Can include both A) how much time they were available to take calls during their shifts, including the time spent handling calls and the time spent waiting for calls to arrive (also called Availability), and B) when they were available to take calls (also called Compliance or Adherence). See Real-Time Adherence Software and Occupancy.

After-Call Work (ACW). Also called Wrap-up and Post Call Processing (PCP). Work that is necessitated by and immediately follows an inbound transaction. Often includes entering data, filling out forms and making outbound calls necessary to complete the transaction. The agent is unavailable to receive another inbound call while in this mode.

Agent. The person who handles incoming or outgoing calls. Also referred to as customer service representative (CSR), telephone sales or service representative (TSR), rep, associate, consultant, engineer, operator, technician, account executive, team member, customer service professional, staff member, attendant and specialist. Did we miss any?

Agents. See Average Number of Agents.

Agent Group. Also called Split, Gate, Queue or Skills Group. A collection of agents that share a common set of skills, such as being able to handle customer complaints.

Agent Out Call. An outbound call placed by an agent.

Agent Status. The mode an agent is in (Talk Time, After-Call Work, Unavailable, etc.).

All Trunks Busy (ATB). When all trunks are busy in a specified trunk group. Generally, reports indicate how many times all trunks were busy, and how much total time all trunks were busy. What they don't reveal is how many callers got busy signals when all trunks were busy.

Analog. Telephone transmission or switching that is not digital. Signals are analogous to the original signal.

Announcement. A recorded verbal message played to callers.

Answer Supervision. The signal sent by the ACD or other device to the local or long distance carrier to accept a call. That's when billing for either the caller or the call center will begin, if long distance charges apply.

Answered Call. When referring to an agent group, a call counted as answered when it reaches an agent.

Application Based Routing and Reporting. The ACD capability to route and track transactions by type of call, or application (e.g., sales, service, etc.), versus the traditional method of routing and tracking by trunk group and agent group.

Architecture. The basic design of a system. Determines how the components work together, system capacity, upgradeability, and the ability to integrate with other systems.

Audiotex. A voice processing capability that enables callers to automatically access pre-recorded announcements. See Voice Processing.

Auto Available. An ACD feature whereby the ACD is programmed to automatically put agents into Available after they finish Talk Time and disconnect calls. If they need to go into After-Call Work, they have to manually put themselves there. See Auto Wrap-up.

Auto Greeting. Agent's pre-recorded greeting that plays automatically when a call arrives.

Auto Wrap-up. An ACD feature whereby the ACD is programmed to automatically put agents into After-Call Work after they finish Talk Time and disconnect calls. When they have completed any After-Call Work required, they put themselves back into Available. See Auto Available.

Automated Attendant. A voice processing capability that automates the attendant function. The system prompts callers to respond to choices (e.g., press one for this, two for that.") and then coordinates with the ACD to send callers to specific destinations. This function can reside in an on-site system or in the network.

Automatic Call Distributor (ACD). The specialized telephone system used in incoming call centers. It is a programmable device that automatically answers

Glossary

calls, queues calls, distributes calls to agents, plays delay announcements to callers and provides real-time and historical reports on these activities. May be a stand-alone system, or ACD capability built into a CO, network or PBX.

Automatic Call Sequencer (ACS). A simple system that is less sophisticated than an ACD, but provides some ACD-like functionality.

Automatic Number Identification (ANI). A telephone network feature that passes the number of the phone the caller is using to the call center, real-time. ANI may arrive over the D channel of an ISDN PRI circuit (out of band signaling), or before the first ring on a single line (inband signaling). ANI is delivered from long distance companies. Caller ID is the local phone company version of ANI, and is delivered inband. ANI is a North American term, and Calling Line Identification (CLI) is an alternative term used elsewhere.

Auxiliary Work State. An agent work state that is typically not associated with handling telephone calls. When agents are in an auxiliary mode, they will not receive inbound calls.

Availability. See Adherence to Schedule.

Available State. Agents who are signed on to the ACD and waiting for calls to arrive.

Available Time. The total time that an agent or agent group waited for calls to arrive, for a given time period.

Average Delay. See Average Speed of Answer.

Average Delay of Delayed Calls. The average delay of calls that are delayed. It is the total Delay for all calls divided by the number of calls that had to wait in queue. See Average Speed of Answer.

Average Handle Time (AHT). The sum of Average Talk Time and Average After-Call Work for a specified time period.

Average Holding Time on Trunks (AHT). The average time inbound transactions occupy the trunks. It is: (Talk Time + Delay Time)/Calls Received. AHT is also an acronym for Average Handling Time, which has a different meaning.

Average Number of Agents. The average number of agents logged into a group for a specified time period.

Average Speed of Answer (ASA). Also called Average Delay. The average delay of all calls. It is total Delay divided by total number of calls. See Average Delay of Delayed Calls.

Average Time to Abandonment. The average time that callers wait in queue before abandoning. The calculation considers only the calls that abandon.

Base Staff. Also called Seated Agents. The minimum number of agents required to achieve service level and response time objectives for given period of time. Seated agent calculations assume that agents will be "in their seats" for the entire period of time. Therefore, schedules need to add in extra people to accommodate breaks, absenteeism and other factors that will keep agents from the phones. See Rostered Staff Factor.

Basic Rate Interface (BRI). One of two basic levels of ISDN service. A BRI line provides two bearer channels for voice and data and one channel for signaling (commonly expressed as 2B+D). See Primary Rate Interface (PRI) and Integrated Services Digital Network.

Beep Tone. An audible notification that a call has arrived (also called Zip Tone). Beep tone can also refer to the audible notification that a call is being monitored.

Benchmark. Historically, a term referred to as a standardized task to test the capabilities of devices against each other. In quality terms, benchmarking is comparing products, services and processes with those of other organizations, to identify new ideas and improvement opportunities.

Best in Class. A benchmarking term to identify organizations that outperform all others in a specified category.

Blockage. Callers blocked from entering a queue. See Blocked Call.

Blocked Call. A call that cannot be connected immediately because A) no circuit is available at the time the call arrives, or B) the ACD is programmed to block calls from entering the queue when the queue backs up beyond a defined threshold.

Busy Hour. A telephone traffic engineering term, referring to the hour of time in which a trunk group carries the most traffic during the day. The average busy hour reflects the average over a period of days, such as two weeks. Busy Hour has little use for incoming call centers, which require more specific resource calculation methodologies.

Call. Also called Transaction and Customer Contact. A term referring to telephone calls, video calls, Web calls and other types of contacts.

Call Blending. Combining traditionally separate inbound and outbound agent groups into one group of agents responsible for handling both inbound and outbound contacts. A system that is capable of call blending automatically puts agents who are making outbound calls into the inbound mode and vice versa, as necessitated by the incoming call load.

Call By Call Routing. The process of routing each call to the optimum destination according to real-time conditions. See Percent Allocation and Network Inter-flow.

Call Center. An umbrella term that generally refers to reservations centers, help desks, information lines or customer service centers, regardless of how they are organized or what types of transactions they handle. The term is being challenged by many, because calls are just one type of transaction and the word center doesn't accurately depict the many multi-site environments.

Call Control Variables. The set of criteria the ACD uses to process calls. Examples include routing criteria, overflow parameters, recorded announcements and timing thresholds.

Call Detail Recording. Data on each call, captured and stored by the ACD. Can include trunk used, time in queue, call duration, agent who handled the call, number dialed (for outgoing), and other information.

Call Forcing. An ACD feature that automatically delivers calls to agents who are available and ready to take calls. They hear a notification that the call has arrived (e.g. a beep tone), but do not have to press a button to answer the call.

Call Load. Also referred to as Work Load. Call Load is the product of (Average Talk Time + Average After-Call Work) x call volume, for a given period.

Caller ID. See ANI.

Caller-Entered Digits (CED). Digits callers enter using their telephone keypads. The ACD, VRU, or network can prompt for CEDs.

Calling Line Identity (CLI). See Automatic Number Identification.

Calls In Queue. A real-time report that refers to the number of calls received by the ACD system but not yet connected to an agent.

Carrier. A company that provides telecommunications circuits. Carriers include both local telephone companies and long distance providers.

Cause-and-Effect Diagram. A tool to assist in root cause identification, developed by Dr. Kaoru Ishikawa.

CD-ROM. Compact Disc Read Only Memory. These discs hold as much as 660 megabytes of memory.

Central Office (CO). Can refer to either a telephone company switching center or the type of telephone switch used in a telephone company switching center. The local central office receives calls from within the local area and either routes them locally or passes them to an inter-exchange carrier (IXC). On the receiving end, the local central office receives calls that originated in other areas, from the IXC.

Centum Call Seconds (CCS). 100 call seconds, a unit of telephone traffic measurement. The first C is the Roman numeral for 100. 1 hour = 1 Erlang = 60 minutes = 36 CCS.

Chief Information Officer (CIO). A typical title for the highest ranking executive responsible for an organization's information systems.

Circuit. A transmission path between two points in a network.

Client/Server Architecture. A network of computers that share capabilities and devices.

Collateral Duties. Non-phone tasks (e.g., data entry) that are flexible, and can be scheduled for periods when call load is slow.

Common Causes. Causes of variation that are inherent to a process over time. They cause the rhythmic, common variations in the system of causes, and they affect every outcome of the process and everyone working in the process. See Special Causes.

Compliance. See Adherence to Schedule.

Computer Simulation. A computer technique to predict the outcome of various events in the future, given many variables. When there are many variables, simulation is often the only way to reasonably predict the outcome.

Computer Telephony Integration (CTI). The software, hardware and programming necessary to integrate computers and telephones so they can work together seamlessly and intelligently.

Conditional Routing. The capability of the ACD to route calls based on current conditions. It is based on "if-then" programming statements. For example, "if the number of calls in agent group 1 exceeds 10 and there are at least 2 available agents in group two, then route the calls to group two."

Continuous Improvement. The ongoing improvement of processes.

Control Chart. A control chart sifts out (identifies) two types of variation in a process, common causes and special causes. See Common Causes and Special Causes.

Controlled Busies. The capability of the ACD to generate busy signals when the queue backs up beyond a programmable threshold.

Cost Center. An accounting term that refers to a department or function in the organization that does not generate profit. See Profit Center.

Cost of Delay. The money you pay to queue callers, assuming you have toll-free service.

Cost Per Call. Total costs (fixed and variable) divided by total calls for a given period of time.

Customer Contact. See Call.

Database Call Handling. A CTI application, whereby the ACD works in sync with the database computer to process calls, based on information in the database. For example, a caller inputs digits into a voice processing system, the database retrieves information on that customer and then issues instructions to the ACD on how to handle the call (e.g., where to route the call, what priority the call should be given in queue, the announcements to play, etc.).

Day of Week Routing. A network service that routes calls to alternate locations, based on the day of week. There are also options for day of year and time of day routing.

Delay Announcements. Recorded announcements that encourage callers to wait for an agent to become available, remind them to have their account number ready, and provide information on access alternatives. In some systems, delay announcements are provided through recorded announcement routes (RANs).

Delay. Also called Queue Time. The time a caller spends in queue, waiting for an agent to become available. Average Delay is the same thing as Average Speed of Answer. Also see Average Delay of Delayed Calls.

Delayed Call. A call which cannot be answered immediately and is placed in queue.

Dialed Number (DN). The number that the caller dialed to initiate the call.

Dialed Number Identification Service (DNIS). A string of digits that the telephone network passes to the ACD, VRU or other devise, to indicate which number the caller dialed. The ACD can then process and report on that type of call according to user-defined criteria. One trunk group can have many DNIS numbers.

Digital. The use of a binary code - 1s and 0s - to represent information.

Direct Call Processing. See Talk Time.

Dual-Tone Multifrequency (DTMF). A signaling system that sends pairs of audio frequencies to represent digits on a telephone keypad. It is often used interchangeably with the term Touchtone (an AT&T trademark).

Dynamic Answer. An ACD feature that automatically reconfigures the number of rings before the system answers calls, based on real-time queue information. Since costs don't begin until the ACD answers calls, this feature can save callers or the call center money when long distance charges apply.

Electronic Mail (E-mail). Electronic text mail.

Envelope Strategy. A strategy whereby enough agents are scheduled for the day or week to handle both the inbound call load and other types of work. Priorities are based on the inbound call load. When call load is heavy, all agents handle calls, but when it is light, some agents are reassigned to work that is not as time-sensitive.

Erlang. One hour of telephone traffic in an hour of time. For example, if circuits carry 120 minutes of traffic in an hour, that's two Erlangs.

Erlang, A.K. A Danish engineer who worked for the Copenhagen Telephone Company in the early 1900s and developed Erlang B, Erlang C and other telephone traffic engineering formulas.

Erlang B. A formula developed by A.K. Erlang, widely used to determine the number of trunks required to handle a known calling load during a one hour period. The formula assumes that if callers get busy signals, they go away forever, never to retry ("lost calls cleared"). Since some callers retry, Erlang B can underestimate trunks required. However, Erlang B is generally accurate in situations with few busy signals.

Erlang C. Calculates predicted waiting times (delay) based on three things: the number of servers (reps); the number of people waiting to be served (callers); and the average amount of time it takes to serve each person. It can also predict the resources required to keep waiting times within targeted limits. Erlang C assumes no lost calls or busy signals, so it has a tendency to overestimate staff required.

Error Rate. Either the number of defective transactions or the number of defective steps in a transaction.

Escalation Plan. A plan that specifies actions to be taken when the queue begins to build beyond acceptable levels.

Exchange Line. See Trunk.

Executive Summary. A brief summary of the key points of a more detailed report or study.

Facsimile (FAX). Technology that scans a document, encodes it, transmits it over a telecommunications circuit, and reproduces it in original form at the receiving end.

Fast Clear Down. A caller who hangs up immediately when they hear a delay announcement.

Fax on Demand. A system that enables callers to request documents, using their telephone keypads. The selected documents are delivered to the fax numbers they specify.

Flowchart. A step by step diagram of a process.

Flushing Out the Queue. Changing system thresholds so that calls waiting for an agent group are redirected to another group with a shorter queue or available agents.

Full-Time Equivalent (FTE). A term used in scheduling and budgeting, whereby the number of scheduled hours is divided by the hours in a full work week. The hours of several part time agents may add up to one FTE.

Gate. See Agent Group.

Gateway. A server dedicated to providing access to a network.

Grade of Service. The probability that a call will not be connected to a system because all trunks are busy. Grade of service is often expressed as "p.01" meaning 1% of calls will be "blocked." Sometimes, grade of service is used interchangeably with service level, but the two terms have different meanings. See Service Level.

Handled Calls. The number of calls received and handled by agents or peripheral equipment. Handled calls does not include calls that abandon or receive busy signals.

Handling Time. The time an agent spends in Talk Time and After-Call Work, handling a transaction. Handling Time can also refer to the time it takes for a machine to process a transaction.

Help Desk. A term that generally refers to a call center set up to handle queries about product installation, usage or problems. The term is most often used in the context of computer software and hardware support centers.

Historical Reports. Reports that track call center and agent performance over a period of time. Historical reports are generated by ACDs, third party ACD software packages, and peripherals such as VRUs and Call Detail Recording Systems. The amount of history that a system can store varies by system.

Holding Time. See Average Holding Time on Trunks.

Home Agent. See Telecommuting

Imaging. A process whereby documents are scanned into a system and stored electronically.

Immutable Law. A law of nature that is fundamental, and not changeable (e.g., the law of gravity). In an inbound call center, the fact that occupancy goes up when service level goes down, is an immutable law.

Incoming Call Center Management. The art of having the right number of

Glossary

skilled people and supporting resources in place at the right times to handle an accurately forecasted workload, at service level and with quality.

Incremental Revenue (Value) Analysis. A methodology that estimates the value (cost and revenue) of adding or subtracting an agent.

Index Factor. In forecasting, a proportion used as a multiplier to adjust another number.

Integrated Services Digital Network (ISDN). A set of international standards for telephone transmission. ISDN provides an end-to-end digital network, out-of-band signaling, and greater bandwidth than older telephone services. The two standard levels of ISDN are Basic Rate Interface (BRI) and Primary Rate Interface (PRI). See Basic Rate Interface and Primary Rate Interface.

Inter Exchange Carrier (IXC). A long-distance telephone company.

Interactive Voice Response (IVR). See Voice Response Unit.

Interflow. See Overflow.

Internal Help Desk. A group that supports other internal agent groups, e.g. for complex or escalated calls.

Internal Response Time. The time it takes an agent group that supports other internal groups (e.g., for complex or escalated tasks) to respond to transactions that do not have to be handled when they arrive (e.g., correspondence or e-mail). See Response Time and Service Level.

Internet "Call Me" Transaction. A transaction that allows a user to request a callback from the call center, while exploring a Web page. Requires interconnection of the ACD system and the Internet by means of an Internet Gateway.

Internet "Call Through" Transaction. The ability for callers to click a button on a Web site and be directly connected to an agent while viewing the site. Standards and technologies that provide this capability are in development.

Internet Phone. Technology that enables users of the Internet's World Wide Web to place voice telephone calls through the Internet, thus by-passing the long distance network.

Intraflow. See Overflow.

Invisible Queue. When callers do not know how long the queue is or how fast it is moving. See Visible Queue.

Judgmental Forecasting. Goes beyond purely statistical techniques and encompasses what people believe is going to happen. It is in the realm of intuition, interdepartmental committees, market research and executive opinion.

Law of Diminishing Returns. The declining marginal improvements in service level that can be attributed to each additional agent, as successive agents are added.

Load Balancing. Balancing traffic between two or more destinations.

Local Area Network (LAN). The connection of multiple computers within a building, so that they can share information, applications and peripherals. See Wide Area Network.

Local Exchange Carrier (LEC). Telephone companies responsible for providing local connections and services.

Logged On. A state in which agents have signed on to a system (made their presence known), but may or may not be ready to receive calls.

Long Call. For staffing calculations and traffic engineering purposes, calls that approach or exceed thirty minutes.

Longest Available Agent. A method of distributing calls to the agent who has been sitting idle the longest. With a queue, Longest Available Agent becomes "Next Available Agent."

Longest Delay (Oldest Call). The longest time a caller has waited in queue, before abandoning or reaching an agent.

Look Ahead Queuing. The ability for a system or network to examine a secondary queue and evaluate the conditions, before overflowing calls from the primary queue.

Look Back Queuing. The ability for a system or network to look back to the primary queue after the call has been overflowed to a secondary queue, and evaluate the conditions. If the congestion clears, the call can be sent back to the initial queue.

Lost Call. See Abandoned Call.

Middleware. Software that mediates between different types of hardware and software on a network, so that they can function together.

Modem. A contraction of the terms Modulator/Demodulator. A Modem converts analog signals to digital and vice versa.

Monitoring. Also called Position Monitoring or Service Observing. The process of listening to agents' telephone calls for the purpose of maintaining quality. Monitoring can be: A) silent, where agents don't know when they are being monitored, B) side by side, where the person monitoring sits next to the agent and observes calls or C) record and review, where calls are recorded and then later played back and assessed.

Multilingual Agents. Agents that are fluent in more than one language.

Multimedia. Combining multiple forms of media in the communication of information. (E.g, a traditional phone call is "monomedia," and a video call is "multimedia.")

Murphy's Law. If anything can go wrong, it will. Not a good perspective to live by, but worth considering when designing agent groups, routing configurations and disaster recovery plans.

Network Control Center. Also called Traffic Control Center. In a networked call center environment, where people and equipment monitor real-time conditions across sites, change routing thresholds as necessary, and coordinate events that will impact base staffing levels.

Network Inter-flow. A technology used in multi-site call center environments to create a more efficient distribution of calls between sites. Through integration of sites using network circuits (such as T1 circuits) and ACD software, calls routed to one site may be queued simultaneously for agent groups in remote sites. See Call by Call Routing and Percent Allocation.

Next Available Agent. A call distribution method that sends calls to the next agent who becomes available. The method seeks to maintain an equal load across skill groups or services. When there is no queue, Next Available Agent reverts to Longest Available Agent.

Noise Canceling Headset. Headsets equipped with technology that reduces background noise.

Non ACD In Calls. Inbound calls which are directed to an agent's extension, rather than to a general group. These may be personal calls or calls from customers who dial the agents' extension numbers.

Occupancy. Also referred to as agent utilization. The percentage of time agents handle calls versus wait for calls to arrive. For a half-hour, the calculation is: (call volume x average handling time in seconds) / (number of agents x 1800 seconds). See Adherence to Schedule.

Off The Shelf. Hardware or software programs that are commercially available and ready for use "as is."

Offered Calls. All of the attempts callers make to reach the call center. There are three possibilities for offered calls: 1) they can get busy signals, 2) they can be answered by the system, but hang up before reaching a rep, 3) they can be answered by a rep. Offered call reports in ACDs usually refer only to the calls that the system receives.

Off-Peak. Periods of time other than the call center's busiest periods. Also a term to describe periods of time when long distance carriers provide lower rates.

Open Ticket. A customer contact (transaction) that has not yet been completed or resolved (closed).

Outsourcing. Contracting some or all call center services to an outside company.

Overflow. Calls that flow from one group or site to another. More specifically, Intraflow happens when calls flow between agent groups and Interflow is when calls flow out of the ACD to another site.

Overlay. See Rostered Staff Factor.

Pareto Chart. A bar chart that arranges events in order of frequency. Named after 19th century economist Vilfredo Pareto.

PBX/ACD. A PBX that is equipped with ACD functionality.

Peaked Call Arrival. A surge of traffic beyond random variation. It is a spike within a short period of time.

Percent Allocation. A call routing strategy sometimes used in multi-site call center environments. Calls received in the network are allocated across sites based on user-defined percentages. See Call by Call Routing and Network Interflow.

Percent Utilization. See Occupancy.

Poisson. A formula sometimes used for calculating trunks. Assumes that if callers get busy signals, they keep trying until they successfully get through. Since some callers won't keep retrying, Poisson can overestimate trunks required. See Erlang B and Retrial Tables.

Pooling Principle. The Pooling Principle states: Any movement in the direction of consolidation of resources will result in improved traffic-carrying efficiency. Conversely, any movement away from consolidation of resources will result in reduced traffic-carrying efficiency.

Position Monitoring. See Monitoring.

Post Call Processing. See After-Call Work.

Predictive Dialing. A system that automatically places outbound calls and delivers answered calls to agents. When the dialer detects busy signals, answering machines or ring no answer, it puts the number back in queue.

Primary Rate Interface (PRI). One of two levels of ISDN service. In North America, PRI typically provides 23 bearer channels for voice and data and one channel for signaling information (commonly expressed as 23B+D). In Europe, PRI typically provides 30 bearer lines (30B+D). See Basic Rate Interface and Integrated Services Digital Network.

Private Automatic Branch Exchange (PABX). See Private Branch Exchange.

Private Branch Exchange (PBX). A telephone system located at a customer's site that handles incoming and outgoing calls. ACD software can provide PBXs with ACD functionality. Also called private automatic branch exchange (PABX).

Private Network. A network made up of circuits for the exclusive use of an organization or group of affiliated organizations. Can be regional, national or international in scope and are common in large organizations.

Process. A system of causes.

Profit Center. An accounting term that refers to a department or function in the organization that does not generate profit. See Cost Center.

Public Switched Network (PSN). The public telephone network which provides the capability of interconnecting any home or office with any other.

Quantitative Forecasting. Using statistical techniques to forecast future events. The major categories of quantitative forecasting include Time Series and Explanatory approaches. Time Series techniques use past trends to forecast future events. Explanatory techniques attempt to reveal linkages between two or more variables. See Judgmental Forecasting.

Queue. Holds callers until an agent becomes available. Queue can also refer to a line or list of items in a system waiting to be processed (e.g., e-mail messages).

Queue Display. See Readerboard.

Queue Time. See Delay.

Random Call Arrival. The normal, random variation in how incoming calls arrive. See Peaked Call Arrival.

Glossary

Readerboards. Also called displayboards or wall displays. A visual display, usually mounted on the wall or ceiling, that provides real-time and historical information on queue conditions, agent status and call center performance.

Real-Time Adherence Software. Software that tracks how closely agents conform to their schedules. See Adherence to Schedule.

Real-Time Data. Information on current conditions. Some "real-time" information is real-time in the strictest sense (e.g., calls in queue and current longest wait). Some real-time reports require some history (e.g. the last x calls or x minutes) in order to make a calculation (e.g. service level and average speed of answer). See Screen Refresh.

Real-Time Management. Making adjustments to staffing and thresholds in the systems and network, in response to current queue conditions.

Received Calls. A call detected and seized by a trunk. Received calls will either abandon or be answered by an agent.

Record and Review Monitoring. See Monitoring.

Recorded Announcement Route (RAN). See Delay Announcement.

Reengineering. A term popularized by management consultant Michael Hammer, which refers to radically redesigning processes to improve efficiency and service.

Response Time. The time it takes the call center to respond to transactions that do not have to be handled when they arrive (e.g., correspondence or e-mail). See Service Level.

Retrial Tables. Sometimes used to calculate trunks and other system resources required. They assume that some callers will make additional attempts to reach the call center if they get busy signals. See Erlang B and Poisson.

Retrial. A caller who "retries" when they get a busy signal.

Rostered Staff Factor (RSF). Alternatively called an Overlay, Shrink Factor or Shrinkage. RSF is a numerical factor that leads to the minimum staff needed on schedule over and above base staff required to achieve your service level and response time objectives. It is calculated after base staffing is determined and before schedules are organized, and accounts for things like breaks, absenteeism and ongoing training.

Round Robin Distribution. A method of distributing calls to agents according to a predetermined list. See Next Available Agent and Longest Waiting Agent.

Scatter Diagram. A chart that graphically depicts the relationship between two variables.

Schedule Compliance. See Adherence to Schedule.

Scheduling Exception. When an agent is involved in an activity outside of the normal, planned schedule.

Screen Monitoring. A system capability that enables a supervisor or manager to remotely monitor the activity on agents' computer terminals.

Screen Pop. A CTI capability. Callers' records are automatically retrieved (based on ANI or digits entered into the VRU) and delivered to agents, along with the calls.

Screen Refresh. The rate at which real-time information is updated on a display (e.g. every 5 to 15 seconds). Note, screen refresh does not correlate with the time-frame used for real-time calculations. See Real-Time Data.

Seated Agents. See Base Staff.

Service Bureau. A company that handles inbound or outbound calls for another organization.

Service Level Agreement. Performance objectives reached by consensus between the user and the provider of a service, or between an outsourcer and an organization. A service level agreement specifies a variety of performance standards that may or may not include "service level." See Service Level.

Service Level. Also called Telephone Service Factor, or TSF. The percentage of incoming calls that are answered within a specified threshold: "X% of calls answered in Y seconds." See Response Time.

Service Observing. See Monitoring.

Shrink Factor. See Rostered Staff Factor.

Silent Monitoring. See Monitoring.

Skill Group. See Agent Group.

Skill-Based Routing. An ACD capability that matches a caller's specific needs with an agent that has the skills to handle that call, on a real-time basis.

Smooth Call Arrival. Calls that arrive evenly across a period of time. Virtually non-existent in incoming environments.

Special Causes. Variation in a process caused by special circumstances. See Common Causes.

Speech Recognition. The capability of a voice processing system to decipher spoken words and phrases.

Split. See Agent Group.

Supervisor Monitor. Computer monitors that enable supervisors to monitor the call handling statistics of their supervisory groups or teams.

Supervisor. The person who has front-line responsibility for a group of agents. Typical ratios are one supervisor to every 10-15 agents. However, help desks can have one supervisor for every 5 people, and some reservations centers have one supervisor for every 30 or 40 agents. Generally, supervisors are equipped with special telephones and computer terminals that enable them to monitor agent activities.

T1 Circuit. A high speed digital circuit used for voice, data or video, with a bandwidth of 1.544 megabits per second. T1 circuits offer the equivalent of twenty-four (24) analog voice trunks.

Talk Time. The time an agent spends with a caller during a transaction. Includes everything from "hello" to "goodbye."

Telecommuting. Using telecommunications to work from home or other locations instead of at the organization's premises.

Telephone Service Factor. See Service Level.

Telephony Applications Programming Interface (TAPI). CTI protocol developed by Microsoft and Intel.

Telephony Services Application Programming Interface (TSAPI). CTI protocol developed by Novell and AT&T.

Threshold. The point at which an action, change or process takes place.

Tie line. A private circuit that connects two ACDs or PBXs across a wide area.

Toll-Free Service. Enables callers to reach a call center out of the local calling area without incurring charges. 800 and 888 service is toll-free. In some countries, there are also other variations of toll-free service. For example, with 0345 or 0645 services in the United Kingdom, callers are charged local rates and the call center pays for the long distance charges.

Touchtone. A trademark of AT&T. See Dual-Tone Multifrequency.

Traffic Control Center. See Network Control Center

Transaction. See Call.

Transmission Control Protocol/Internet Protocol (TCP/IP). The protocols that govern the exchange of sequential data. TCP/IP was designed by the U.S. Department of Defense to link dissimilar computers across many kinds of networks. It has since become a common standard for commercial equipment and applications.

True Calls Per Hour. Actual calls an individual or group handled divided by Occupancy for that period of time. See Occupancy.

Trunk. Also called a Line, Exchange Line or Circuit. A telephone circuit linking two switching systems.

Trunk Group. A collection of trunks associated with a single peripheral and usually used for a common purpose.

Trunk Load. The load that trunks carry. Includes both Delay and Talk Time.

Trunks Idle. The number of trunks in a trunk group that are non-busy.

Trunks in Service. The number of trunks in the trunk group that are functional.

Unavailable Work State. An agent work state used to identify a mode not associated with handling telephone calls.

Uniform Call Distributor (UCD). A simple system that distributes calls to a group of agents and provides some reports. A UCD is not as sophisticated as an ACD.

Universal Agent. Refers to either A) An agent who can handle all types of incoming calls or B) An agent who can handle both inbound and outbound calls.

Virtual Call Center. A distributed call center that acts as a single site for call handling and reporting purposes.

Visible Queue. When callers know how long the queue that they just entered is, and how fast it is moving (e.g., they hear a system announcement that relays the expected wait time). See Invisible Queue.

Voice Processing. A blanket term that refers to any combination of voice processing technologies, including Voice Mail, Automated Attendant, Audiotex, Voice Response Unit (VRU) and Faxback.

Voice Response Unit (VRU). Also called Interactive Voice Response Unit (IVR) or Audio Response Unit (ARU). A VRU responds to caller entered digits or speech recognition in much the same way that a conventional computer responds to keystrokes or clicks of a mouse. When the VRU is integrated with database computers, callers can interact with databases to check current information (e.g., account balances) and complete transactions (e.g. make transfers between accounts). See Voice Processing.

Wide Area Network (WAN). The connection of multiple computers across a wide area, normally using digital data circuits.

Workforce Management Software. Software systems that, depending on available modules, forecast call load, calculate staff requirements, organize schedules and track real-time performance of individuals and groups.

Workload. Often used interchangeably with Call Load. Work load can also refer to non-call activities.

World-Wide Web (WWW). The capability that enables users to access information on the internet in a graphical environment.

Wrap-Up Codes. Codes agents enter into the ACD to identify the types of calls they are handling. The ACD can then generate reports on call types, by handling time, time of day, etc.

Wrap-up. See After-Call Work.

Zip Tone. See Beep Tone.

Index

Abandoned calls, 20-22, 27-28, 30-31, 33-35, 38, 56-57, 87, 108, 133, 141, 149, 165, 172, 174-175, 186, 242
Absenteeism, 6, 109, 112, 159, 185
ACD, calculating service level, 30-31
ACD, controlled busies, 57
ACD, intelligent, 139, 170, 223, 241
ACD, modes, 55, 69, 76
ACD, networks, 99, 225-226
ACD, PC-based, 220
ACD, reporting, 34, 45, 49-52, 57-58, 148-149, 152, 155, 164-166, 208, 228
ACD, routing, 139, 142
ACD, skill-based routing, 94-98
ACD, visible queue, 18
Adherence monitoring technology, 208
Adherence to schedule, 133, 161, 185, 187, 192, 201-209, 215, 242
Adizes, Dr. Ichak, 235, 244-245
After-call work, 6, 55-56, 58, 67-69, 76-77, 80-81, 83, 90, 92, 111, 125, 130, 162-163, 167-168, 183, 187, 204-205, 207
Agent status, 164-165, 167
All trunks busy, 57
American Express, 116
Angus, Ian and Lis, 232
AT&T, 195, 223, 228
AT&T Universal Card Services, 48
Auto greetings, 229
Auto-available, 162
Auto-wrap, 162
Automated monitoring systems, 212
AutoQuality!, 228
Availability, 90, 99, 164, 205, 207, 226
Average call value, 35-36, 185, 242
Average group productivity, 83, 137-138
Average handling time, 55, 67-70, 75, 83, 100, 102, 146, 164, 187, 192, 195, 198, 205-206, 214, 242
Average speed of answer, 27-29, 91-93, 131-132, 134-135, 140-141, 150-151, 165, 172, 174-175, 245
Average time to abandonment, 165, 172-175
Bard Technologies, 88
Base Staff, 6, 23, 53, 79-106, 107-113, 120, 131, 147, 163
Beep-tone, 162
Benchmark, 35, 195-197, 202, 235
Benchmarking, 35, 195-197, 235
Bennis, Warren, 236

Blockage, 29, 38, 149
Boeing, 88
Bogel, John C., 115
Breaking down a forecast, 61-63
British Airways, 21
Budgeting, 7, 23, 37, 43, 134, 153-158, 240, 242
Budgets, 7, 54, 76, 82, 105, 113, 129, 144, 147, 153-158
Busy signals, 18, 20-21, 56-57, 75, 86-87, 89, 103-104, 142, 149, 168, 171, 174-176, 182, 189, 195
Calculate Costs, 155-156
Call allocation, 99, 225
Call blending, 120, 229
Call center, defined, 7
Call Center Magazine, 220
Call center process, 181, 184-185
Call forcing, 162
Call load, 6, 30, 53-59, 61, 63, 65-67, 69, 71-73, 75-77, 80-81, 83, 97-99, 103, 105, 115, 119-120, 124, 130-131, 133, 141, 146, 150, 152, 155, 157, 159, 161-163, 187, 240-243
Call types, 69, 96, 152, 202
Caller behavior, 10, 18-22, 165, 234
Caller tolerance, 11-12, 18-22, 34-35, 37-38, 57, 81, 97, 195
Calls per hour, 132, 201-203, 205-206, 215
Cause-and-effect diagram, 190-191, 200
Charles Schwab, 230
Churchill, Winston, 149
CLEAR Communications, 238
Client/server architecture, 220
Coaching, 186, 198, 207, 209, 212-213
Collateral work, 115
Collecting data, 6, 44-52
Common causes, 194
Computer simulation, 6, 13, 28, 85, 87-89, 93-99, 106
Computer telephony integration, 9, 49, 203, 219-223, 230-231
Concentrated shifts, 115-116
Control chart, 193-195, 200, 203, 214
Controlled busy signals, 149, 168, 171
Conventional shifts, 114
Corel, 17
Cost of delay, 142-143
Cost per call, 186, 242
Costs when quality is lacking, 182-183

Index

Cross Country Motor Club, 117-118
Customer expectations, 8, 180-181, 200, 204, 236, 238-239, 245
Customer satisfaction, 148, 157, 181, 183-185, 196-197, 214, 235, 242, 245
Customer survey, 35, 37, 149, 181, 193
Cyr, Bert, 196-197
Dawson, Keith, 220
Defective calls, 184, 195, 210
Delay, 16, 27, 31, 33, 39, 56, 79-81, 84-85, 90, 92, 103, 105, 141-143, 164, 168-169, 171-175, 184-185
Delay announcements, 16, 81, 171-174
Delrina, 17
Deming, W. Edwards, 82, 155, 179, 195
Dialed number identification service, 225
Direct marketing campaigns, 66
Disneyland, 15, 102
Display thresholds, 166
Distributed call centers, 99, 219, 225-227, 230, 243
DLYDLY, 91-92
DNIS, 225
Dortmans, Henry, 47
Driving forces, 11-22
Duke Power, 48
Dynamic reconfiguration, 223
E-mail, 6, 9, 26, 41-43, 46-47, 67, 93, 107, 109, 121, 149, 221
Eddie Bauer, 48
Envelope strategy, 120-121
Erlang, A.K., 4, 85-86
Erlang B, 93, 103-104
Erlang C, 4, 6, 28, 84-91, 93-95, 97, 99-102, 105-106, 132-133
Error rate, 39, 192
Errors and rework, 183-184, 186, 242
Escalation plan, 160, 165, 167, 171, 176
Excellence, 179
Executive summary, 153
Experience level, 70, 192, 198, 214
Explanatory forecasting, 71
Farson, Richard, 219, 237
Fast clear-down, 171-172
Fax, 6, 9, 19, 26, 41-42, 46, 67, 96, 107, 121, 221, 229
Fax on demand, 229
Fax-back, 229
First delay announcement, 16, 171-172
Flowchart, 48, 52, 140, 188, 200, 212, 241

Flushing out the queue, 170
Forecast, 4-8, 10, 13, 20, 23, 26, 35, 38, 42, 46-48, 50-51, 53-77, 79-80, 83, 88-89, 94, 98-99, 101, 103, 107-108, 110, 112, 115, 119, 123, 125, 131, 133, 143, 148, 155, 159, 163, 167, 181, 185- 187, 192, 196, 202, 242-243, 245-246
Forecasting problems, 74
Gable, Robert, 226
GeoTel, 226
Grade of service, 26, 104
Handy, Charles, 8
Harrington, Dea, 117-118
Helm, Cheryl Odee, 31
Help desk, 7, 16, 25, 41, 51, 100, 113, 206-207
Hewlett-Packard, 118
Hills, Mike, 86, 89
Hills B formula, 86, 89
Historical data, 50, 54-56, 58, 63, 67, 72, 75, 89, 157
Holiday week index factors, 64
Holiday weeks, 60, 63
Human Relations, 179
IBS, 212
If-then programming, 225
Immutable laws, 129-130, 143
In-process inspectors, 215
Incoming call center management, defined, 4
Incoming Calls Management Institute, 4, 74, 79, 90-91, 209, 213
Incremental revenue analysis, 35-36
Index factors, 62-64
Intelligent network, 139
Internal part-timers, 115
Intra-day forecast, 55, 63-65, 167
Intra-week forecasting, 65
Invisible queue, 15-18
ISDN, 226-227
Ishikawa, Dr. Kaoru, 190
JC Penney, 116
Judgmental forecasting, 71-74
Key performance indicators, 185
Klenke, Maggie, 100
Knowledge requirements, 10
Kostner, Jaclyn, 243
Lands' End, 15
Law of diminishing returns, 133-134, 161
Liberfone, 156-157
Line chart, 122, 153

L.L. Bean, 15
Local area network, 49, 221, 228
Long calls, 100
Longest current wait, 164-165
LWOP, 116
MacPherson, Gordon F. Jr.,11, 231
Management by Objectives, 179
Management by Walking Around, 179
Messages for callback, 168
Met Life, 116
Microsoft, 17, 118, 138
Middleware, 221
Monitoring, recommended practices, 213
Monitoring, record and review, 209
Monitoring, rating systems, 209-211
Monitoring, silent monitoring, 209-215, 228
Multimedia, 7, 18, 25, 219, 231-233
Mystery shoppers, 210
Network inter-flow, 87, 99
Nickell, Daniel B., 53
Number of calls in queue, 92, 164-165
Occupancy, 87, 92-93, 101-102, 129-133,
    136-138, 141, 146-147, 156, 184, 187-
    188, 202-204, 212
Offered calls, 56, 75, 77
One Minute Managing, 179
Overflow, 37, 89, 139, 167-170, 175, 185
P(0), 91-92
Pareto chart, 70, 152, 192-193, 200
Pareto principle, 152, 193
Pareto, Vilfredo, 192
Part-time staff, 115
Peaked call arrival, 11, 14-15, 22, 54, 58, 100-
    101, 113, 146
Peppers, Don, 231
Perception of the queue, 11, 37
Peterson, Kathleen, 208, 238
Piepenbrink, Barbara, 117-118
Pipkins, 86
Planning steps, 5-7, 42, 75, 77, 107-108, 121,
    154
Plugged in time, 207
Poisson, 90, 103
Pooling principle, 138-140, 241
Porter, Michael, 9
Professional Skills, 9
Prunty, Martin, 41
Q1, 91-92
Q2, 91-92, 166
Qualitative measures, 201, 203-204, 211

Quality, 4-6, 31-33, 53-54, 82, 118, 136, 148,
    155, 160, 168, 177, 179-185, 187-189,
    191-193, 195, 197, 199-200, 202, 204-
    207, 209-215, 228, 236, 238, 240, 243
Quantitative forecasting, 71, 77
Queue, 11-13, 15-22, 28, 31-33, 37-38, 49,
    57, 69, 85-87, 92, 94, 99, 103, 125,
    130, 134-135, 137, 140-142, 146, 148-
    149, 160-168, 170-172, 174-175, 186,
    189, 206, 208, 212, 223, 226, 230, 233,
    246
Queue displays, 160, 166
Queue jockeys, 17-18
Queue statistics, 161
QVC, 14
Random call arrival, 10, 12-13, 15, 28, 37, 58,
    84, 87, 130, 159, 163-164
Rating systems, 209
Readerboard, 12, 135, 161, 228
Real-time management, 13, 15, 50, 101, 159-
    161, 163, 167, 171, 176
Reengineering, 179
Reporting call center activity, 148-153
Resource planning, 3, 5-8, 26, 42, 98, 163,
    176, 204, 208
Response time, 26-27, 40-43, 49, 51, 79, 94,
    108-109, 136, 154, 163, 167, 181, 185-
    186, 208
Retrial tables, 103
Rockwell, 18, 88
Rogers, Martha, 231
Rolm, 223
Root causes, 75, 180, 188, 198, 200, 242
Rostered staff factor, 5-7, 26, 36, 46, 54, 80,
    107, 109-110, 125, 155
Sales forecast, 65-66
Scatter diagram, 192, 200
Schedule adherence, 108, 125, 208-209
Schedule compliance, 204, 207
Schedules, 5-7, 26, 33, 38, 46, 50-51, 53-55,
    76, 80, 94, 106-113, 115, 119-121, 125,
    131, 133, 147, 155, 159, 163, 181, 185,
    208, 223, 228, 240
Scheduling, 4, 7, 10-11, 23, 42-43, 48, 50-51,
    54, 72, 74, 88, 101, 107-109, 111, 113-
    121, 123-125, 138, 144, 148
Scientific Management, 179
Screen monitoring, 228
Screen refresh, 164
Second delay announcement, 172-173

Index

Secondary groups, 168
Senior management, 30, 34, 39-40, 118, 127, 145-147, 149, 151, 153-158, 237
Service bureau, 14, 118
Service level, 3-8, 19-23, 25-35, 37-43, 46, 53-54, 79-81, 83-84, 86-87, 89-93, 97, 100-103, 105, 108-110, 115, 118, 121-125, 127, 129-134, 136-139, 141-143, 146-152, 154-155, 159-161, 163-167, 169, 171-173, 175, 177, 179-187, 189, 191-193, 195-200, 202, 204, 208, 212, 214, 235, 242
Service level, calculating, 30-31
Service level, choosing, 5, 33-39
Service level graphs, 39, 121-125
Shrinkage, 5-6, 26, 46, 54, 80, 107, 109-113, 120, 125, 155
Silent monitoring, alternatives, 210
Situational Leadership, 179
Skill-based routing, 6, 87, 89, 94-99, 139-140, 203, 223, 232, 245
Skills gap, 199
Smith, Ann, 240-241
Smooth traffic, 14
Solomon,Laurie, 158, 240
Sources of data, 45
Special causes, 194
Specialization, 139-140, 236, 241
Speech recognition, 223-224
Stacked bar chart, 151
Staff-to-trunk ratio, 81-82
Staffing, 4, 6, 10-11, 13, 15, 22-23, 28, 42-43, 48, 50, 53-55, 74, 76, 79, 81-82, 84-87, 89-90, 93-94, 96, 98-101, 105-109, 113-115, 117-118, 125, 129, 131, 133-134, 141, 143, 146-148, 159, 176, 183, 185, 246
Staggered shifts, 114
Sub-optimizing, 82
Summary ACD reports, 148
Supervisor monitors, 161
Swat team, 115, 168, 171
System announcements, 168-169, 171-174, 228
System of causes, 184, 200
Systems Modeling Corporation, 88
Taggart, Tom, 230
Talk time, 6, 36, 55-56, 58, 67-69, 76-77, 80, 83, 90-93, 97, 103, 111, 130-131, 135, 142, 162-163, 168, 183-185, 187, 203-205, 207, 229
Tanner, Todd, 98
TAPI, 220
Tapscott, Don, 200, 237
TCS, 88, 100
Teknekron, 212, 228
Telecommunications budget, 147
Telecommunications Industry Benchmarking Consortium, 196
Telecommuting, 7, 116-117, 226-227, 233, 243
Teledata Solutions, Inc., 230
Teloquent, 226
TELUS, 196
Theory Z, 179
Tiems, Wouter, 156-157
Time series forecasting, 71, 77
TKLD, 91, 93
Toll-free service, 19, 141-142, 146, 226
Total Quality Management, 179
Transactions by type, 152, 188, 193
True calls per hour, 202
Trunk costs, 34
Trunk load, 28, 80-81, 103-105, 131, 134-135, 141
Trunking, 6, 43, 53, 79, 81, 86, 97, 105, 147, 157, 185
Trunks, 5-6, 22-23, 26-27, 29, 35, 38, 46, 54, 57, 76, 79-83, 85, 87, 89, 91, 93, 95, 97, 99, 101-105, 108, 110, 141, 155, 175, 181, 184-185, 226
TSAPI, 220
TSRs, 91
Turnover, 32, 87, 146, 156, 198-199, 235
United Airlines, 138
United Parcel Service, 236-237
USAA, 138
Van Der Zyde, Darlene, 237
Vanguard, 115
Video calls, 6-9, 18, 25-26, 93, 149
Virtual call center, 99, 219, 225, 227, 230, 243
Visible queue, 15-18, 22
Voice mail, 26, 42, 121, 170
Voice processing, 70, 149, 223-225, 229
VRU, 18-19, 45, 47, 80, 96, 104-105, 107, 136-137, 149, 157, 185, 190, 223-224, 229, 232
WearGuard, 117-118
White, Roz, 238-239

Wilson, David, 21
Winston, Stephanie, 149
Word Perfect, 17
Workforce management systems, 50, 58, 88, 208
World Wide Web, 6-7, 9, 19, 25, 41, 46-47, 70, 93, 136-137, 153, 186, 203, 230, 232-233, 244
Wrong ways to calculate staff, 83

How to Reach the Authors

We would love to hear from you! How could this book be improved? Has it been helpful? No comments are off limits! You can reach us at:

Incoming Calls Management Institute
P.O. Box 6177
Annapolis, MD 21401

Phone: 410-267-0700
Fax: 410-267-0962
Email: icmi@incoming.com
http://www.incoming.com

About Incoming Calls Management Institute

Incoming Calls Management Institute (ICMI), based in Annapolis, Maryland, is dedicated to meeting the unique educational needs of incoming call center managers. Founded in 1986, ICMI is a leading think-tank and provider of educational events for incoming call center managers worldwide. ICMI regularly presents call center management training courses throughout North America, Europe and the Pacific Rim. Call Center Press, a division of ICMI, publishes high quality educational books and training materials for incoming call center managers.

For more information, contact:

Incoming Calls Management Institute
P.O. Box 6177
Annapolis, Maryland
21401
USA

Phone: 410-267-0700
Fax: 410-267-0962
Email: icmi@incoming.com
http://www.incoming.com

Order Form

Yes. I would like to order:

Quantity	Item	Price
	Call Center Management On Fast Forward Book - $34.95 each	
	11-20 Copies (10% off) - $31.45 each	
	21-50 Copies (20% off) - $27.95 each	
	50+ Copies (30% off) - $24.45 each	
	CD-ROM Tools for Incoming Call Center Managers* - $49.00 each	
	Shipping & Handling @ $3.00 per item	
	Tax (5% MD only)	
	Total in U.S. Dollars	

*CD-ROM includes software with the Erlang C and Erlang B formulas to calculate staff, occupancy, trunk load, service level, average speed of answer and calls in queue, as well as miscellaneous other software tools.

❏ Yes, please send me a free issue of *Service Level Newsletter* and information on other publications and seminars.

Please ship my order and/or information to:

Name _____

Title _____

Company _____

Address _____

City _____ State _____ Postal Code _____

Telephone (   ) _____ Fax (   ) _____

E-Mail _____

Method of Payment (Check one)

_____ Check enclosed (Make payable to ICMI, Inc., U.S. Dollars only)

_____ Invoice me

_____ Charge to: ❏American Express ❏Mastercard ❏Visa

Account No. _____ Expiration Date _____

Name on Card _____

Fax order to: **410-267-0962**
call us at: 800-672-6177 (410-267-0700)
order online at: www.incoming.com
or mail order to: ICMI, Inc.
P.O. Box 6177
Annapolis, MD 21401

Order Form

Yes. I would like to order:

Quantity	Item	Price
	Call Center Management On Fast Forward Book - $34.95 each	
	11-20 Copies (10% off) - $31.45 each	
	21-50 Copies (20% off) - $27.95 each	
	50+ Copies (30% off) - $24.45 each	
	CD-ROM Tools for Incoming Call Center Managers* - $49.00 each	
	Shipping & Handling @ $3.00 per item	
	Tax (5% MD only)	
	Total in U.S. Dollars	

*CD-ROM includes software with the Erlang C and Erlang B formulas to calculate staff, occupancy, trunk load, service level, average speed of answer and calls in queue, as well as miscellaneous other software tools.

❏ Yes, please send me a free issue of *Service Level Newsletter* and information on other publications and seminars.

Please ship my order and/or information to:

Name _____

Title _____

Company _____

Address _____

City _____ State _____ Postal Code _____

Telephone ( ) _____ Fax ( ) _____

E-Mail _____

Method of Payment (Check one)

_____ Check enclosed (Make payable to ICMI, Inc., U.S. Dollars only)

_____ Invoice me

_____ Charge to: ❏American Express ❏Mastercard ❏Visa

Account No. _____ Expiration Date _____

Name on Card _____

Fax order to: **410-267-0962**
call us at: 800-672-6177 (410-267-0700)
order online at: www.incoming.com
or mail order to: ICMI, Inc.
P.O. Box 6177
Annapolis, MD 21401

Order Form

Yes. I would like to order:

Quantity	Item	Price
	Call Center Management On Fast Forward Book - $34.95 each	
	11-20 Copies (10% off) - $31.45 each	
	21-50 Copies (20% off) - $27.95 each	
	50+ Copies (30% off) - $24.45 each	
	CD-ROM Tools for Incoming Call Center Managers* - $49.00 each	
	Shipping & Handling @ $3.00 per item	
	Tax (5% MD only)	
	Total in U.S. Dollars	

*CD-ROM includes software with the Erlang C and Erlang B formulas to calculate staff, occupancy, trunk load, service level, average speed of answer and calls in queue, as well as miscellaneous other software tools.

❏ Yes, please send me a free issue of *Service Level Newsletter* and information on other publications and seminars.

Please ship my order and/or information to:

Name _____

Title _____

Company _____

Address _____

City _____ State _____ Postal Code _____

Telephone (   ) _____ Fax (   ) _____

E-Mail _____

Method of Payment (Check one)

_____ Check enclosed (Make payable to ICMI, Inc., U.S. Dollars only)

_____ Invoice me

_____ Charge to: ❏American Express ❏Mastercard ❏Visa

Account No. _____ Expiration Date _____

Name on Card _____

Fax order to: 410-267-0962
call us at: 800-672-6177 (410-267-0700)
order online at: www.incoming.com
or mail order to: ICMI, Inc.
P.O. Box 6177
Annapolis, MD 21401

Order Form

Yes. I would like to order:

Quantity	Item	Price
	Call Center Management On Fast Forward Book - $34.95 each	
	11-20 Copies (10% off) - $31.45 each	
	21-50 Copies (20% off) - $27.95 each	
	50+ Copies (30% off) - $24.45 each	
	CD-ROM Tools for Incoming Call Center Managers* - $49.00 each	
	Shipping & Handling @ $3.00 per item	
	Tax (5% MD only)	
	Total in U.S. Dollars	

*CD-ROM includes software with the Erlang C and Erlang B formulas to calculate staff, occupancy, trunk load, service level, average speed of answer and calls in queue, as well as miscellaneous other software tools.

❏ Yes, please send me a free issue of *Service Level Newsletter* and information on other publications and seminars.

Please ship my order and/or information to:

Name _____

Title _____

Company _____

Address _____

City _____ State _____ Postal Code _____

Telephone ( ) _____ Fax ( ) _____

E-Mail _____

Method of Payment (Check one)

____ Check enclosed (Make payable to ICMI, Inc., U.S. Dollars only)

____ Invoice me

____ Charge to: ❏American Express ❏Mastercard ❏Visa

Account No. _____ Expiration Date _____

Name on Card _____

Fax order to: **410-267-0962**
call us at: 800-672-6177 (410-267-0700)
order online at: www.incoming.com
or mail order to: ICMI, Inc.
P.O. Box 6177
Annapolis, MD 21401

Order Form

Yes. I would like to order:

Quantity	Item	Price
	Call Center Management On Fast Forward Book - $34.95 each	
	11-20 Copies (10% off) - $31.45 each	
	21-50 Copies (20% off) - $27.95 each	
	50+ Copies (30% off) - $24.45 each	
	CD-ROM Tools for Incoming Call Center Managers* - $49.00 each	
	Shipping & Handling @ $3.00 per item	
	Tax (5% MD only)	
	Total in U.S. Dollars	

*CD-ROM includes software with the Erlang C and Erlang B formulas to calculate staff, occupancy, trunk load, service level, average speed of answer and calls in queue, as well as miscellaneous other software tools.

❑ Yes, please send me a free issue of *Service Level Newsletter* and information on other publications and seminars.

Please ship my order and/or information to:

Name _____

Title _____

Company _____

Address _____

City _____ State _____ Postal Code _____

Telephone (   ) _____ Fax (   ) _____

E-Mail _____

Method of Payment (Check one)

____ Check enclosed (Make payable to ICMI, Inc., U.S. Dollars only)

____ Invoice me

____ Charge to: ❑American Express   ❑Mastercard   ❑Visa

Account No. _____ Expiration Date _____

Name on Card _____

Fax order to: **410-267-0962**
call us at: 800-672-6177 (410-267-0700)
order online at: www.incoming.com
or mail order to: ICMI, Inc.
P.O. Box 6177
Annapolis, MD 21401